Medical Caregiving Narratives of the First World War

For the wound dressers,
past, present, and future

Medical Caregiving Narratives of the First World War

Geographies of Care

Marie Allitt

EDINBURGH
University Press

Edinburgh University Press is one of the leading university presses in the UK. We publish academic books and journals in our selected subject areas across the humanities and social sciences, combining cutting-edge scholarship with high editorial and production values to produce academic works of lasting importance. For more information visit our website: edinburghuniversitypress.com

© Marie Allitt 2023, 2024

Edinburgh University Press Ltd
13 Infirmary Street, Edinburgh, EH1 1LT

First published in hardback by Edinburgh University Press 2023

Typeset in 11/13pt Adobe Sabon by
Cheshire Typesetting Ltd, Cuddington, Cheshire

A CIP record for this book is available from the British Library

ISBN 978 1 4744 8992 8 (hardback)
ISBN 978 1 4744 8993 5 (paperback)
ISBN 978 1 4744 8994 2 (webready PDF)
ISBN 978 1 4744 8995 9 (epub)

The right of Marie Allitt to be identified as the author of this work has been asserted in accordance with the Copyright, Designs and Patents Act 1988, and the Copyright and Related Rights Regulations 2003 (SI No. 2498).

Contents

List of Figures vi
Acknowledgements vii

Introduction 1

1. Corpography: Reconceptualising Somatic Geographies 30
2. Layering: Appropriating Medical Spaces 66
3. Protrusions, Openings, and Depths: A Medical Grotesque 102
4. Countering: Representing Coping Strategies 145
5. Surfaces: Articulating Pain and Trauma 181

Conclusion 218

Bibliography 226
Index 243

Figures

2.1 Magic lantern slide showing Indian soldiers in beds in the Music Room of the Royal Pavilion during its use as a military hospital, 1915. Royal Pavilion & Museums, Brighton & Hove. BY-SA 4.0 Creative Commons   80
2.2 Monochrome photograph showing Indian soldiers in rows of beds inside the Dome during its use as a military hospital, 1915. Royal Pavilion & Museums, Brighton & Hove. BY-SA 4.0 Creative Commons   81
5.1 Pages from Irene Rathbone's diary, showing a playscript. From The Private Papers of Miss B I Rathbone, Documents.557, IWM Collections. Photos by Imperial War Museum   195

Acknowledgements

It can be difficult to pinpoint the exact moment that a project truly began, but I can. My first exposure to the intersections of medicine and literature and medical humanities during my undergraduate degree at the University of Glasgow set me up for my commitment to this field. I will be forever grateful to Gavin Miller, David Shuttleton, and Megan Coyer, who guided me through those early days of what has become my deepest passion, and Olga Taxidou, whose excellent eye strengthened my work during my research master's at the University of Edinburgh.

This book developed out of my PhD thesis. I am grateful to the University of York and Department of English and Related Literature for providing institutional support along the way. I wish to pay particular thanks to the Humanities Research Centre, which is one of the treasures of the University. Thank you for providing an opportunity and space for community, belonging, and the nurturing of numerous lifelong friendships. I would also like to extend my sincere gratitude to my PhD supervisor, Richard Walsh, for his continuous support, motivation, and patience throughout my research. Thank you for encouraging and challenging me to be a better reader, writer, and thinker. I also express my gratitude to my thesis advisors, Trev Broughton and Hugh Haughton, for advice early on in this project, and to Alice Hall, who has been a tremendous supporter during and post-PhD. I want to extend especial thanks to Anne Whitehead, whose intellectual care, exceptional insight, and all-round generous support has continued to help me find my place in medical humanities. I am tremendously grateful for all the friendships, collaborations, and connections I have made while being involved in the Northern Network for Medical Humanities Research.

I would like to extend my thanks to the Historial de la Grande Guerre for my place at the 2018 summer school, which gave me the opportunity to experience the geographies of France and

Belgium and visit many important sites, including the guided tour at DOVO-SEDEE.

Small extracts of this book have previously been published in 'Temporary Hospitals', *The Polyphony*, 2 April 2020, https://thepolyphony.org/2020/04/02/temporary-hospitals/, and '"just a bleeding edge": Sensuous Geographies and the Impact of Space in Medical Accounts of the First World War', *Shining Signs of the Day: Spaces and Senses in Transatlantic Culture*, Madrid: Biblioteca Benjamin Franklin, 2019, pp. 47–55.

Thank you to the anonymous readers of my manuscript and to all at Edinburgh University Press for their care and attention throughout this process, especially Ersev Ersoy and Susannah Butler. I extend my gratitude to Penguin Random House US for permission to use quotes from Mary Borden's *The Forbidden Zone*. All attempts were made to receive permission from Borden's estate for further territory rights. I would also like to thank the Imperial War Museum for the photographs and permission to use images of Irene Rathbone's personal diary, and the book's cover image, 'Ypres, 1915' by Gilbert Rogers. All attempts were made to seek permission from the copyright holders of Irene Rathbone's and Katherine Hodges' private papers held at the Imperial War Museum. I also wish to extend my thanks to the School of Literatures, Languages and Cultures at the University of Edinburgh for research funds to help me cover permissions costs.

Thank you to friends and collaborators who have provided community and care throughout the years on this project and beyond: I hope you know who you are and how important your friendship is. I am tremendously grateful to those who responded to early drafts, shared ideas, and provided endless sources of humour, inspiration, and friendship, at York: Rosy Alexander-Jones, Alex Alonso, Laura Blomvall, Sarah Cawthorne, Amy Creighton, Salina Cuddy, Jennie England, Julia Erdosy, Megan Girdwood, Stephen Grace, Nik Gunn, Fiona Mozley, Karl O'Hanlon, Jack Quin, Simon Quinn, Anna Reynolds, Phillip Roberts, Tim Rowbotham, Andrew Stead, Carla Suthren, and Yu-Hua Yen. To those beyond York, thank you for the various kinds of support along the way and since: Victoria Bates, Erin Bramwell, Francesca Bratton, Clare Hickman, Fiona Johnstone, Beatriz Pichel, Katherine Rawling, Jennifer Wallis, and Rebecca Wynter. I feel very fortunate for the scholars I have met throughout my time in academia so far, and for being surrounded by truly inspiring and brilliant people.

Thank you, Max Gee for our many conversations on films, writing, bodies, and posthumans, the motivational talks helping me to keep perspective, and all your stimulating wisdom. Thank you, Sally Frampton, inspiring co-writer extraordinaire, for making sense of my half-formed ideas, boosting my confidence, and for your kindness and support during really tough times. Thank you, Ashleigh Blackwood for rationalising my irrationality, keeping me grounded in my love of literature and medicine, your ever-perceptive insight, and reminding me of the joy of bouquets of newly sharpened pencils.

Last but not least, I would like to thank my family: my siblings, Martin, Michelle, and Matthew, who continue to inspire me to pursue my dreams and ambitions. Thank you for humouring my imagination all the times you had to play bookshops and restaurants with me. Thank you to my brothers-in-law, Michael and Marc. A very special thank you to my cheeky niece and nephew, Evie and Thomas, whose cuddles can cure many ills, and who always make me laugh and smile. I am immensely grateful to my parents, Kathryn and Richard, whose generous support has helped me financially and emotionally throughout this journey. Thank you for picking me up when I've been knocked down. Thank you for your unrelenting faith in me; for your continued investment in my passion and skill. Thank you for all those years of reading to me before bed; for taking me to beautiful and fascinating places; for filling my life with stories, and encouraging me to keep asking questions. Thank you for giving me the map and the compass, and teaching me how to use them.

Introduction

In the diary of her experiences as an ambulance driver on the Romanian Front, Katherine Hodges highlights the toll of the job, the work, and position she is in:

> One often has to load up one's own ambulance and it's ticklish work, two girls lifting a stretcher with a huge man lying on it up into the ambulance, especially as they often yell as you move them. They are smashed up too, poor devils. One man we took in the other day had half his face gone, his shoulder broken, a very bad abdominal wound, all one leg in pieces, both arms wounded and both feet badly too. He died after two days. It's difficult to realise how all this is affecting one's point of view. At present I am quite incoherent in my mind. I suppose it will adjust itself in time.[1]

This extract pertains to Hodges' experience with the Scottish Women's Hospitals Transport Unit, in late 1916, when she was attached to the First Serbian Unit. Hodges draws our attention to the role of the ambulance driver, which not only involves physical hard work but is also emotionally and psychologically challenging. The ambulance driver, like all medical caregivers in the war context, cannot help but be affected by the sights they witness and the mutilated bodies they touch. While showing us examples of the states of broken and damaged bodies in her care, she tells us she is beginning to see how it is affecting her, maybe even changing her. She alludes to the effect this might be having on everyone, including her fellow caregivers. Yet, there is no language with which to articulate this

---

[1] Katherine Hodges, 'A Driver at the Front', Private Papers of Miss K Hodges, Imperial War Museum Collections, Documents.1974, 24.

distress, and no sense of respite, so she must trust that her mind 'will adjust in time'. That military-medical caregivers might too suffer from war trauma was not seriously considered until many decades later, following the Vietnam War (1954–75).[2]

It is not often that the caregivers communicate their own feelings of suffering, but when they do it is with a poignancy and power which demands that we attend to the medic as someone whose embodied experience is enduring disruption and who is potentially undergoing immense strain. This particular extract from Hodges especially captures the idea of the caregiver, in this instance the ambulance driver, as susceptible to secondary or vicarious suffering, a consequence of witnessing pain and caring for the wounded. The caregiver is inculcated in the perpetuation of pain, while simultaneously an onlooker and empathetic witness. They are also a vulnerable psyche, emotionally and psychologically exposed to the environment and dangers of war, and the potential trauma which comes from confronting endless numbers of mutilated bodies.

This book centralises the writings of the caregivers, engaging with their unique perspective on both military-medical caregiving and a broader insight into the phenomenology of caregiving. Predominantly, these writings were published between 1915 and the early 1930s, but I also engage with some material which emerged later. By exploring the experiences of doctors, nurses, stretcher bearers, orderlies, and ambulance drivers, and crucially the ways they represent those experiences, I explore the complexities that accompany both the experience and the attempt to articulate and communicate it. The intensity of their experiences is manifest in their representations, their hypersensitivity to the literal and figurative qualities of their sensory environment, and the somatic and spatial disorientation that accompanies the crisis situations of care in wartime. This book explores the representation of such caregiving experiences in first-hand life writing, focusing primarily on memoirs, diaries, and semi-novelisations. These specific examples of life writing have more in common with trauma and illness narratives than traditional autobiography. Accordingly, I examine them through the lens of traumatic writing, attentive to the ways in which these texts are similar to narratives of illness and could be considered a kind of pathography.

---

[2] Carol Acton and Jane Potter, *Working in a World of Hurt: Trauma and Resilience in the Narratives of Medical Personnel in Warzones* (Manchester: Manchester University Press, 2015), 5.

In the context of this particular research, the status of the 'medic' or 'caregiver' is far more obscure and fluid than in other situations. Here, I apply the terms medic and caregiver, often interchangeably, to all persons performing and participating in different types of medical caregiving, which includes both professional and volunteer medics, with highly varying degrees of prior experience and training. In the latter chapters, where I am talking explicitly about writing decisions, I refer to them as medic-writers. By classing doctors, nurses, orderlies, ambulance drivers, and stretcher bearers together as medics and caregivers, I intend to open up the question of how we classify medical personnel, and to emphasise that 'caregiving' takes many forms, within and beside medicine.

The issue of secondary or vicarious suffering and trauma is crucial to the reading of these accounts. While treating Vietnam War veteran medics, prominent trauma specialist Charles Figley identified 'secondary or vicarious trauma' in one of his patients as caused 'by the pain and suffering he experienced from treating those in harm's way; by the guilt he felt each time one of his patients died; by being obsessed with reacting quickly enough to save lives'.[3] We can confidently extrapolate that these are experiences, and consequences, shared by medics throughout modern conflict in the twentieth and twenty-first centuries. In their transformational study, *Working in a World of Hurt: Trauma and Resilience in the Narratives of Medical Personnel in Warzones* (2015), Carol Acton and Jane Potter build on Figley's and others' discussions of trauma in order to explore the trauma and resilience of medical personnel in warzones, from the First World War, Second World War, the Vietnam War, and the wars in Iraq (2003–11) and Afghanistan (2001–present). They note that, given developments in psychology and the understanding of medics' trauma, more recent discussions 'would exclude the terms "secondary" and "vicarious" from the definition, noting that constant witnessing and participating in severe injury and death are directly rather than vicariously traumatic'.[4] There continues to be debate over the extent of direct or vicarious suffering experienced by all caregivers, but however much psychological understanding has developed, and continues to develop, the concepts of 'secondary' and 'vicarious' remain significant. Hodges' comment shows us how the medic is affected in consequence of the wounds the soldiers sustain, but we can also understand that there are somatic and sensuous

[3] Ibid.
[4] Ibid.

dimensions of the medical situation that only the medic experiences, and thus that she or he is directly affected by the traumatic environment. The more we learn and understand about mental health, particularly in relation to trauma, the more we appreciate that one experience of psychological turmoil is never the same as another, so we come to rely more and more on individual testimony.

It is difficult to distinguish between concepts of direct and vicarious trauma in precise terms, and this is perhaps a reason for the relative lack of attention to caregivers' experience of trauma. We can be uncomfortable with the idea of the medic's pain when others are so visibly suffering and dying: as Acton and Potter note, 'historically medical personnel have, perhaps, been unwilling to "write" their own suffering in a world where the suffering of the combatant is perceived to be so much greater'.[5] There is a culturally pervasive phenomenon of downplaying personal pain in order to focus on the pain of others. Acton and Potter elaborate that

> In place of the writer's suffering, it is common for medical life-writings, especially those published during the war years, to exalt and thus foreground the courage of Tommy Atkins – the enlisted or conscripted soldier – and officer alike. Their writing presupposes that the wounded combatant is the reason for their existence at the front, and it is he who is central to the narrative.[6]

If indeed their purpose is defined by the presence of the wounded men, we can read through the relationship between medic and patient to how medics deal with what is in front of them. It is rare that medics explicitly declare how much they are struggling, so this recognition requires us to probe further when we see the cracks beginning to show.

The major contribution of this book is its intervention in critical medical humanities discourse.[7] Specifically, this book complements

---

[5] Ibid., 33.
[6] Ibid., 63.
[7] The grounding for my understanding of critical medical humanities, and the frame within which I position my own research, is Anne Whitehead, 'The Medical Humanities: A Literary Perspective, Overview', in *Medicine, Health and the Arts: Approaches to the Medical Humanities*, ed. Victoria Bates, Alan Bleakley, and Sam Goodman (London: Routledge, 2015), 107–27, and Anne Whitehead and Angela Woods, 'Introduction', in *The Edinburgh Companion to the Critical Medical Humanities*, ed. Anne Whitehead and Angela Woods with Sarah Atkinson, Jane Macnaughton, and Jennifer Richards (Edinburgh: Edinburgh University Press, 2016).

ongoing research within the 'second wave' of medical humanities scholarship: I seek to redress the neglect of wartime caregivers, whose stories have often been absent from the discussion. This is not to question the importance of the stories and testimonies that are currently visible but instead to further recognise the importance of firsthand, lived experiences. The significant advances in critical medical humanities, especially in its 'first wave', have successfully shed a light on patient experiences, and given voice to the voiceless patient. The revolutionary work of Rita Charon with the development of narrative medicine has demonstrated the vitality of stories in the communication of health, while the work on pathographies and illness narratives in the 1980s and 1990s by Arthur Frank, Arthur Kleinman, and Anne Hunsaker Hawkins set in motion the impetus to ensure the voice of patient experience is given due authorial weight and exposure. This research has helped put the patient back into the doctor–patient encounter, and continues to do so. The risk, however, is that we lose sight of the person in the role of the doctor (and other caregiving roles), as well as neglecting the fact that the medical encounter must, at its heart, be an interpersonal encounter. In order to understand the human connection within these interactions, we need to examine the people beneath the labels of both 'doctor' and 'patient'. We need to reorientate the doctor–patient encounter as an encounter between the person-witnessing-pain and the person-in-pain. Additionally, this provides an opportunity to remove the *doctor*–patient encounter from the top of the hierarchy and open up the conversation to other caregivers, both within and outside traditional medical structures.

The priority to reconsider the perspective of the person in the caregiving role particularly comes to the fore in Chapter 3, where my consideration of the medics' representations of wounds and wound care aims to dispel the reductive image of the medic as authoritarian and absolute. The trajectory of Chapter 3 reveals the complex tensions felt by the medic, who must simultaneously alleviate and perpetuate pain and suffering. The medic repeatedly experiences ethical dilemmas, which compound their own sense of struggle and suffering. I explore medics' representations of wounds in order to uncover how they situate themselves in relation to such injuries and symptoms; but it is significant that as the discussion develops in this chapter (and throughout the latter chapters), not only are the issues surrounding care relevant to the war context but they provide wider insight into medical caregiving roles in all settings and contexts. I study the medics' point of view – the voices, the experiences, and the representations of those experiences – in order to learn more about the medical encounter, and about encounters within medical spaces. Sensitivity to the institutional context remains important, especially in cases where we have to consider not only the medical institutional power structures but also the military. The military and medical institutional contexts are key precisely because they determine the literal medical spaces in which the caregivers work, and the ability to move across spaces. These contexts also determine who and how these caregivers can engage in caregiving, and through whose access and authority.

The First World War provides a vital lens through which to explore the landscape of caregiving. This is a landscape which might be considered outside of traditional medical infrastructure; where the medical provision often relied on the temporary, the arbitrary, as well as the charitable and voluntary. The unprecedented scale of war, in global reach as well as biopower, meant that medical provision was at times insubstantial. This was a moment of crisis, with ill-preparation for the reality of war. This context gives us an opportunity to recalibrate our notions of caregiving, which should never be assessed uncritically or unreflectively. The war context also illuminates, by looking to extreme circumstances, the welfare of the caregivers, whose health is so often neglected. In modern medical discourse, practitioners in hands-on roles are described as being on the frontline – a battle metaphor inherited in problematic ways. As Chapter 1 illustrates, even by 1914 the very idea of a battlefield or frontline was already a misnomer, with the nature of modern warfare changing its spatial face. When Susan Sontag identified the damage of battle metaphors to describe illness and disease, she simultaneously highlighted the problems of bringing martial discourse into the wider medical sphere. That the metaphor has not only persisted but been instilled so uncritically into current medicine serves to muddy clinical waters, perpetuating 'a quasi-militaristic culture fond of hierarchy'.[8] More troubling still is how the perpetuation of the 'frontline' discourse insists on the rhetoric of heroism, sacrifice, and sometimes futility, which risks further marginalisation of caregivers' health, welfare, and safety.[9] Arguably, an opportunity to explore a military context of caregiving might help the wider disentanglement of medicine's martial metaphors.

---

[8] Alan Bleakley, 'Force and Presence in the World of Medicine', *Healthcare* 5, no. 58 (2017): doi:10.3390/healthcare5030058.

[9] Derek Macallan, 'COVID-19: Why It's Time to Drop the Term "Frontline"', *Commentary*, Royal College of Physicians, March 2021, 16. More discussion on contemporary healthcare and the crisis of COVID in the Conclusion.

This book also contributes to existing scholarship on First World War medical narratives, and advances it. My literary readings and analysis offer an intervention in the historiographic discourse on these sources: the interdisciplinary nature of the project involves engagement with cultural and social history, but my literary-critical mode of attention to the narratives and the issues that arise gives greater weight to the voices of the caregivers themselves as writers. The work of Acton and Potter, *Working in a World of Hurt*, paves the way in this respect, synthesising a multidisciplinary approach to the testimonies of medical personnel. Close attention to the voices of those involved assists in the effort to reconcile military historiography with personal stories and the lived experience of war. Whereas historiography does not allow much opportunity to unpick dimensions of the personally experiential, a literary approach centres on personal representation and the complexities of representation itself. Thus, my approach is able to interrogate the representations of experiences as framed within personal memoir.

It is not my intention to diagnose or pathologise either the writers of these texts or their written accounts. I do not presume to understand the trauma that may or may not be present in these experiences or writings. I take it as a given that these caregivers are susceptible to trauma, not only from their close proximity to pain and suffering but owing to the fact that, like combatants, they too are often exposed to dangers of injury, infection, and death. I do not impose a label of trauma, and indeed avoid the conflation and anachronism of 'shell shock' and posttraumatic stress disorder, although others may read these texts with this in mind. Instead, I address the idea of the psychological or affective terrain through the imagery presented, and suggest how these writers may be commenting on the experience of trauma, as they experienced it in the moment of caregiving and later, in the moment of writing. Often, these terms do not map to our knowledge of trauma or its terminology, so I do not put words in the writers' mouths. The issue of direct and vicarious trauma returns, but it is impossible, and unethical, to attempt definitive diagnosis. My engagement with the question of trauma and traumatic writing particularly comes through in Chapters 4 and 5, where I explore representations of coping mechanisms and fractural expression, respectively.

As Acton and Potter rightly note, 'the experience of medical personnel is strikingly absent'[10] from conventional discussions of war

---

[10] Acton and Potter, *Working*, 1.

experience. Despite the prominence of popular and academic scholarship on the First World War, very little attention has been given to the lived experience of the military-medical caregivers. There has been very little discussion about the psychological consequences of warfare on medical personnel, notably in the context of the First World War: Acton and Potter's work marks a crucial milestone in such scholarship. However, it is not that non-combatants have been entirely absent from discussions of traumatic effects – there were articles in *The Lancet* in 1916 and 1918 considering 'war shock' in civilians, and even cows – yet medical personnel have been largely eclipsed in discussions of trauma.[11] It was not until after the Vietnam War that medical personnel were recognised as also vulnerable to the trauma of war, and the often long-term suffering it inspires, with recognition of a post-Vietnam syndrome, which later became known as posttraumatic stress disorder.[12] The writings of nurses and other medical personnel have tended to be addressed separately, in discussions of medical roles more concerned with, for example, the feminist and gender dimensions of female war writing. In fact, such priorities typify existing scholarship in the field of First World War medicine, along with its associated literary-critical contributions. In this book, I intentionally address this division, by placing each of these types of caregivers alongside one another.

This book is, in part, inspired by Santanu Das's *Touch and Intimacy in First World War Literature* (2005), which developed a focus on haptic geographies in relation to combatant writing, and offered some preliminary exploration of nurses' accounts. Das focuses on touch and war experience in order to draw 'attention to its physicality, to the material conditions which produced the literature'.[13] While most of Das's scholarship here is focused on combatant writings with the focus on proximities, intimacies, and environment, his focus on nurses' writings, however, is less about the spatial and more about emphasising how much their writing has been overlooked. Rather than explore the distinct geography of caregiving experiences, Das offers in-depth discussions and psychoanalytic approaches to the presentation and representation of

---

[11] 'War Shock in the Civilian', *The Lancet* 187, no. 4827 (4 March 1916): 522; 'Shell Shock in Cows', *The Lancet* 191, no. 4927 (2 February 1918): 187–8; Santanu Das, *Touch and Intimacy in First World War Literature* (2005; Cambridge: Cambridge University Press, 2008), 195.
[12] Acton and Potter, *Working*, 4.
[13] Das, *Touch*, 6.

trauma. This preliminary focus on the writings of medical personnel as well as the application of the spatial, sensory, and geographical marks a significant point of departure. My approach builds on this scholarship, but it actively advances the 'phenomenological geography'[14] that Das posits in the first part of his book on to caregivers' writings.

Spatial Medical Humanities

The 'second wave' of critical medical humanities is provoking deep consideration for the role of space, architectures, and environment when it comes to health, medicine, and caregiving. This approach enables us to reconfigure and reconceptualise the 'primal scene'[15] of critical medical humanities, by exploring the significance of the objects in the room, the emotions in the room, and the room itself. The environments in which medical caregiving take place are so often overshadowed by the communicative and tactile imperatives of the consultation, examination, or procedure. But, what might a reminder of such spaces bring to the discussion of the clinical encounter and further instances of caregiving? For practitioners, medical spaces and spaces of medicine are not only workplaces but also sites of potential intense emotion and experience, where medical personnel navigate conflicts between medicine and caregiving, empathy and self-care, life and death, harm and healing. In order to read these spaces, with an eye to the physical, multisensory, psychological, and affective, this book offers conceptual and theoretical frameworks with which to explore the different geographies of care.

Recent years have seen increased attention to health architectures, ethnographies of healthcare design, histories of hospitals, and emphases on therapeutic and healing environments. Attendance to the spatial in medical life writing is, however, still in its early stages. In order to understand the immediate experiences of healthcare and medical space, I turn to Havi Carel's *Phenomenology of Illness* (2016) to both understand bodily experiences and explore a phenomenology of caregiving. This is caregiving in its most active sense: touching and handling broken bodies, whether hauled into the ambulance or turned uncomfortably in their beds, in environments filled with cries and screams of suffering. Although Carel's work is

---

[14] Ibid., 73.
[15] Whitehead and Woods, 'Introduction', 2–3.

unambiguously centred on the illness experience, there is certainly overlap and useful frameworks through which to explore the experiences of caregiving. Specifically, this work enables a sustained spatial focus on such experiences; 'Viewing illness as transforming one's being-in-the-world, including one's relationship to the environment, social and temporal structures, and one's identity, has helped capture the pervasive nature of illness.'[16] I argue that such a framework may apply to these caregivers' accounts, and allow us to gain further insight into both the lived experience of providing hands-on care as well as being vulnerable bodies, potentially undergoing mental distress. I tread this path with caution, not wishing to supplant the distinctive experience of illness with the medic's experience. I adapt this framework to the caregivers' bodies, not to suggest that they experience what the ill, or even their patients, experience but instead to bring the body of the caregiver back into the conversation. This approach proffers a phenomenological experience of caregiving, with emphasis on the embodied, multisensory experience of care and of the spaces in which these encounters take place. This is especially evident in Chapter 1, where I interrogate the embodiment of caregiving, which is immersed in military spaces that overlap with or transition into medical spaces. This work centralises space and spatial experience, and champions a subset of critical medical humanities that is especially attuned to the spatial.

In this book, 'geographies' becomes a vital term for approaching the different experiences of space, architectures, and environments, because it incorporates a nexus of movement, mapping, and being. I consider not only physical spaces but different kinds of conceptual geographies: somatic; sensuous; figurative; affective; representational; and relational. As we begin to see a more considered focus on the environment and environmental factors in stories of illness, we must also be alert to the experience of space by caregivers: bring the background into the foreground. I am particularly influenced by Paul Rodaway's *Sensuous Geographies: Body, Sense and Place* (1994), which introduces a framework of haptic, auditory, olfactory, and visual geographies, enabling us to access multisensory experience. It is from Rodaway's work that I espouse the use of 'geographies', which also allows me to both engage with the sensory dimensions as well as orientate myself with how the multisensory is informed by, and in turn informs, the spatial experience.

---

[16] Havi Carel, *Phenomenology of Illness* (Oxford: Oxford University Press, 2016), 37.

In commenting on the unique perspective of First World War nurses, Das highlights the importance of 'the voice of one who is inside the moment',[17] speaking to the need for first-hand experiences and the voices of lived experience. The spatial aspect of this comment, '*inside* the moment', strikes to a core factor here, which is that such experiences are only visible by being within them. Although we might consider caregivers to be onlookers and observers of pain and suffering, they are also 'inside the moment'. This is not to suggest that the caregiver can ever 'know' the pain of their patients; as Carel has explained, 'the ill person is the only one who experiences the illness from within, although others may have an experience of someone else's illness':[18] only the one in pain knows that pain. However, there is a unique point of witnessing which the caregiver, and the caregiver alone, knows – another potential terrain of suffering and trauma for the witness. The closeness between medic and patient, emotionally and physically, demands that we consider their situation in terms of somatic, sensuous, and spatial geographies. This book directly explores the influence of geographies along phenomenological, psychological, and affective lines, as mediated by textual representation.

We need to think critically about the phenomenological, affective, embodied circumstances within and around different clinical encounters, examining the imperceptible dimensions of, for example, the field hospital, the operating theatre, or the consultation room, and the variegated emotional landscapes of medicine and care. By thinking about different manifestations of space, spatiality, and geographies, we can access the unexplored terrain of relationships between bodies, between bodies and objects, and between bodies and environments. The interdisciplinary and literary-critical focus of this book actively explores and unravels imagery, metaphor, and irony used to depict the lived experience, embodiment, and phenomenological geographies of medical and caregiving spaces.

My focus on spatiality in this book calls for us to pay attention to environments of medicine and care, while also proposing a reconsideration of space in its relation to First World War medical care. Existing conceptions of military spatiality have tended to focus on strategic territorial gains and losses, while archaeological research has begun to explore the geology and ecology of the war landscape. Scholarship is yet to provide specific accounts of the military-medical

[17] Das, *Touch*, 175.
[18] Carel, *Phenomenology of Illness*, 46.

spaces, however, and very little attention has been given to space and medicine in the context of the First World War. My address to spatiality is concerned both with the medical spaces (literally the hospitals, ambulances, operating rooms), and with the spatial experiences of medical personnel, including the role space has within medical encounters, and how the experience of space is represented.

The spatial argument of this book takes as its premise that existing scholarship is tied to a recurrent image of the individual in war as occupying a liminal space. It is my contention, however, that the concept of liminality does not allow for in-depth discussions of the position and status of either the combatant or non-combatant. Certainly, when we think about space and spatiality in the First World War, in both literal and figurative terms, what most immediately comes to mind is the image of 'no man's land'. In fact, in *No Man's Land: Combat and Identity in World War I* (1979), Eric Leed states:

> Astonishing numbers of those who wrote about their experience of war designate No Man's Land as their most lasting and disturbing image. This was a term that captured the essence of an experience of having been sent beyond the outer boundaries of social life, placed between the known and the unknown, the familiar and the uncanny.[19]

No man's land becomes symbolically representative of both a marginalised status and the defining symbol of combat experience. The concept of liminality, derived from the Greek for 'threshold', concerns transitional experiences and states, often involving the literal movement of the body, and personal identification with the environment. In these terms it is fair to say that war experience adheres to Arnold van Gennep's and Victor Turner's anthropological ideas about rites of passage, which 'are divided into rites of separation (preliminal), transition (liminal), and incorporation (post-liminal)'.[20] No man's land, conceived this way, becomes a 'symbolic and spatial area of transition'.[21] But the analogy is often invoked too casually, with too much metaphorical obscurity, raising more questions than answers.

---

[19] Eric J. Leed, *No Man's Land: Combat and Identity in World War I* (Cambridge: Cambridge University Press, 1979), 15.
[20] Subha Mukherji, 'Introduction', in *Thinking on Thresholds: The Poetics of Transitive Spaces* (London and New York: Anthem Press, 2011), xix.
[21] Arnold van Gennep, *The Rites of Passage* (1909; Abingdon: Routledge, 2004), 18.

Liminality is only one part of the spatial story of war, and my sources invite us to redraw the map of military-medical experience.

The discourse surrounding no man's land as liminal is not confined to a purely spatial image, as it necessarily involves temporality. The medical environment is intelligible as a figurative no man's land in this sense, from the perspective of the wounded. In the receipt of medical treatment, the patient is indeed occupying an in-between state: they move from the point of crisis and pain, to healing, or to a bleaker outcome; in the best case, once they have been saved and treated, they are then moved to rehabilitation, and on to their next posting. But the medical environment is not liminal for the medics, who remain in these places, seeing wounded after wounded, with little prospect of an end in sight. For the individual suffering firsthand there must be some kind of transition ahead, but that is not so for the medic: their body is not in crisis in the same way; there is no inevitability that their role will come to an end, or that they themselves will be evacuated home like the soldier. We can accept the general idea that all those involved are temporarily part of an interruption to normal life, and so the four-year period of the war is a temporary experience away from home. Yet, when we look at medics' representations of their experience, although they recognise that the war (and their service) will end someday, and that their surroundings are temporary and improvised, the reality of the situation confines them to the here and now. Consequently, the experience cannot be liminal, or at least not dominantly liminal, but must involve a deeper and more encompassing sense of space.

As an instance of the whole arc of military experience, then, it might be valid to suggest that the medic's experience is liminal; but the sustained physicality of the medical encounter with the wounded triggers a spatial awareness and result which is more than liminality. Liminality may be the spatial concept most readily associated with these extreme and traumatic experiences, but to stop there risks missing significant details concerning the intricacies of the war experience and medical encounter, and the complexities of communicating these experiences. Furthermore, by adopting this analogy, we risk negating or ignoring the agency and identity of the caregiver. No man's land is a convenient spatial image to characterise the medics' experience, but it unwittingly buries a more complex spatial and geographical discourse in the mud. No man's land has become a reflex way of conceptualising war and military-medical space.

Many critics adopt the notion of the liminal implicitly, through metaphor and analogy, without even realising it – and certainly without offering further qualification. Even Das, when he rightly observes that nurses are generally absent from discussions of the effects of trauma, adopts this image in his effort to foreground the medical experience: 'the figure of the nurse is strangely left out: neither a soldier nor a civilian, she is not granted a place even in this medical "no man's land"'.[22] No man's land, as Leed and Das demonstrate, can become an easy shortcut to thinking about the spatial experience of war; and summary discussions too routinely maintain that the medical space is in-between; as Acton and Potter point out, 'Medical personnel have occupied this space between front and home in wars throughout the centuries, whether as camp-followers [. . .], military surgeons, or regimental mates.'[23] If we consider a broader temporal span of modern conflict, in which the nature of battle changes, the 'no man's land' analogy may shift away from its specific associations with trench warfare, but it still retains a sense of the liminal: in the war in Afghanistan troops conceived of medical centres as the 'center of an hourglass',[24] once again combining the spatial and the temporal. Acton and Potter's adoption of the analogy mirrors those who have relegated the spatial to this 'lasting image' of the in-between. While it may be one of the most enduring images of the First World War, liminality is not the only or primary experience of spatiality.

By resorting to the liminal image, we risk restricting the medical environment to the realm of the symbolically marginal, and missing the lived experiences of real people. We risk losing sight of the immersed, somatic, and sensuous dimensions of the medical roles, and neglecting their stories. As a way to set liminality in context as only part of the spatial medical story of the war, I appeal more broadly to spatial theories and to human geography, invoking spatially conceptualised terms in order to reconsider these texts and the experiences they represent. I draw on a fuller range of spatial concepts, such as: Rodaway's haptic and olfactory geographies, Derek Gregory's 'Corpography', Henri Lefebvre's *The Production of Space*, Carel's and Maurice Merleau-Ponty's respective phenomenologies of illness and perception, Michel Foucault's heterotopias, and Gilles Deleuze and Félix Guattari's smooth and striated spaces. Considering the narratives through the lens of these spatial concepts reciprocally compels consideration for the sensory landscapes.

---

[22] Das, *Touch*, 195.
[23] Acton and Potter, *Working*, 2.
[24] Ibid. Acton and Potter echo Michael Winship's description of troops in Afghanistan.

This book is both conceptually informed by a richer array of spatial concepts and structured around them. It encompasses the medic's relation to the medical space; literal and figurative dimensions of medical spaces; spaces of and in the body; psychological and emotional spaces; and textual spaces. In order to access the multiple geographies of the war landscape and the environment of medical caregiving, and to elaborate on the complex notions of space involved, the structure of the book follows a trajectory from literal movement within space towards more figurative conceptions of space and spatial experience.

First World War Medical Experiences

In the latter part of the nineteenth century, closer attention had been given to medical provisions in the British military. The Crimean War (1853–6) is credited with prompting rapid improvements in sanitary conditions, reducing death from disease. From then on, military medicine grew in importance for the British government and in public consciousness. The First World War marked a key moment in military medicine, as well as medical developments more generally, with momentous improvements in advanced wound care, and increased recourse to, for example, tetanus vaccination, blood transfusions, and X-rays. However, it takes time to perfect the 'medical machine',[25] and changes were introduced responsively, rather than pre-emptively. The First World War medical landscape was characterised by responsive action, especially given the transitions between two kinds of warfare, across three distinct phases of military action over the four years. Medical provision, like military tactics, had to adapt across the different phases of the war: from the initial war of movement, the conflict hardened, by the winter of 1914, into the static trench warfare with which we are culturally most familiar, until it reverted to a war of movement with the 'Spring Offensive' of 1918. Ironically, the static trench warfare, with very little movement for years, enabled the development of a more effective and efficient medical system:[26] Casualty Clearing Stations were able to acquire better provisions and equipment, without the risk of its falling into

---

[25] Mark Harrison, *The Medical War: British Military Medicine in the First World War* (Oxford: Oxford University Press, 2010), 17.
[26] Fiona Reid, *Medicine in First World War Europe: Soldiers, Medics, Pacifists* (London and New York: Bloomsbury, 2017), 59.

the hands of the approaching forces, and the structures themselves could be made more suitable for major surgeries.

At its most efficient, the medical system was organised with specific points of access and evacuation. A typical medical journey from the frontline trench would begin with the stretcher bearers, who carried the wounded to Regimental Aid Posts, which were approximately 200–300 yards behind the frontline, usually in ruined buildings or dugouts but sometimes no more than a shell crater. The patient was then taken, typically by ambulance, to an Advanced Dressing Station, primarily for triage; then on to a Casualty Clearing Station, where most operations were carried out. Once stable, the wounded were transported, by ambulance train or barge, to a Base or Stationary Hospital situated in a large town or coastal port. In the event of extensive convalescence and rehabilitation, British and Commonwealth patients were transported back to Britain by hospital ship to one of the general hospitals across the country, some of which specialised in particular injuries.[27]

There have been two significant, overlapping developments in First World War medical scholarship in recent decades. The first stems from renewed attention, in the 1980s, to women's war writing, a move which refocused interest in some key female writers of the period whose work and legacy went well beyond associations with the First World War, such as Virginia Woolf, Edith Wharton, and Gertrude Stein. But alongside these well-known writers emerged some lesser known female voices, discussion of whom was stimulated by the republication, in 1988, of texts like Helen Zenna Smith's *Not So Quiet . . . The Stepdaughters of War*, and Irene Rathbone's *We That Were Young*, first published in 1930 and 1932, respectively. The renewed scholarly attention to these authors, in foregrounding the female voice of war, shifted the focus towards first-hand accounts of medical personnel. Resurging interest in women's stories countered the long-held belief that war writing had to fit a 'combat model':[28] in outlining his rationale for what was included in his 1929 anthology of war prose, John Brophy explained that the works included were only by 'men who waged and suffered it, not vicariously, but with their own bodies'.[29] That Brophy emphasised that the value of such war stories had to come

---

[27] Harrison, *Medical War*, 1–65.
[28] Das, *Touch*, 9.
[29] John Brophy, ed., *The Soldier's War: A Prose Anthology* (London: Dent, 1929), x, qtd in Das, *Touch*, 9.

from bodies that experienced the suffering, speaks to wider trends of discounting not only the perspectives of women but also the involvement of non-combatants, as well as demonstrating a fundamental misunderstanding about the experience of caregivers. Furthermore, that he discounts 'vicariously' acquired experience, reinforces the aforementioned long-term disregard for military-medical personnel's experiences.

The push in the 1980s onwards, with awareness for the need to capture the stories of those still living, such as Lyn MacDonald's *The Roses of No Man's Land* (1980), which anthologises nurses' experiences, gradually introduced more academic research into both the experiences and the writings of those in non-combatant roles. Margaret Higonnet's research has been particularly influential in foregrounding women's war writing, beginning with her co-edited collection of essays *Behind the Lines: Gender and the Two World Wars* (1987), followed by the carefully selected and curated collection of extracts from women's unpublished diaries and memoirs in *Lines of Fire: Women Writers of World War I* (1999), and *Nurses at the Front: Writing the Wounds of the Great War* (2001). Leading historian of nursing Christine Hallett has been a key figure in the collation of nurses' roles and experiences: *Containing Trauma: Nursing Work in the First World War* (2009), *Veiled Warriors: Allied Nurses of the First World War* (2014), with *Nurse Writers of the Great War* (2016) specifically engaging with nurses' writings. Although Hallett does not employ literary analysis, her source material often consists of nurses' personal memoirs and diaries, which she approaches with attentive detail to the impressions of the first-hand caregivers. Both Higonnet's and Hallett's research has been invaluable in understanding nurses' writings, and how this can be developed to look at other medics' writings.

The shift towards a focus on nursing experiences coincided with an increasing interest in First World War medicine, focusing on the details of medical resources and infrastructure. There has been considerable scholarship identifying the significance of First World War medicine, for example Leo van Bergen's *Before My Helpless Sight: Suffering, Dying and Military Medicine on the Western Front* (2009) and Mark Harrison's *The Medical War: British Military Medicine in the First World War* (2010). Further work which engages with medical personnel has tended to focus on one role rather than a range of experiences, such as Ian Whitehead's *Doctors in the Great War* (1999) and more recently Jessica Meyer's *An Equal Burden* (2019), which focuses on stretcher bearers within the Royal Army

Medical Corps. These studies, among many others,[30] account for historical engagement with the medical roles in question, rather than engaging with medics' own representations of events, or the literary qualities of their writing. Ultimately, the shift to explore women's writings, and the inevitable focus on the writings of nurses and some ambulance drivers, has been significant, but it also demonstrates how there remains little literary scholarship on the writings of other caregiver roles, namely doctors, orderlies, stretcher bearers, and male ambulance drivers.

As Paul Fussell and Ian Isherwood have noted, there were two significant publishing booms of war books between 1914 and the 1930s.[31] Both combatant and non-combatant narratives proved popular: audiences craved personal war accounts, up until a slight lull from 1919, then again between 1929 and the mid-1930s. The popularity of war books diminished, but did not disappear, in the quieter periods. These trends seem to have been mirrored across the Atlantic, with a major attempt to publish American experiences between 1915 and 1919. The texts discussed throughout this book conform to these trends, mostly having been published between 1915 and 1919, or 1927 and 1933. My sources also include some rediscovered, forgotten, or lost diaries, recently published for the first time, alongside republications of several landmark texts, as well as unpublished archival material, such as Irene Rathbone's 1918 diary.

Existing historical scholarship offers important explanations of the medical infrastructure, and details of the processes involved in medical care. While many of these studies draw on medics' personal accounts, the personal narratives are used as evidence rather than acting as sources for the multiple dimensions of experiences. For example, prominent modern military-medical historian Emily Mayhew offers a style of narrative history in *Wounded: The Long Journey Home from the Great War* (2014) that rewrites the diaries and testimonies of caregivers along the medical journey. The effect is one which concisely conveys the caregivers' experiences in a way

---

[30] For example, David Durnin, *The Irish Medical Profession and the First World War* (Cham: Palgrave Macmillan, 2019); Alexia Moncrieff, *Expertise, Authority and Control: The Australian Army Medical Corps in the First World War* (Cambridge: Cambridge University Press, 2020); Paul E. Stepansky, *Easing Pain on the Western Front: American Nurses of the Great War and the Birth of Modern Nursing Practice* (Jefferson, NC: McFarland, 2020).

[31] Paul Fussell, *The Great War and Modern Memory* (New York: Oxford University Press, 1975); Ian Isherwood, 'The British Publishing Industry and Commercial Memories of the First World War', *War in History* 23, no. 3 (2016): 328–32.

that is accessible to a popular audience but which does so at the price of subordinating the medics' own words. Overall, there is still very little consideration of the lived experience of caregiving, especially through close attention to personal voices and testimonies. There is a gap that needs bridging between literary approaches to war writings and studies of the different medical personnel. Only then can military-medical writings find their place within the wider context of war literature and the literature of medicine, and thus intervene in the current trajectory of critical medical humanities scholarship. In the specific context of caregiving narratives, close attention to the details of different representations offers new knowledge and perspectives on the truth of the experience for the individuals concerned. For example, close attention to metaphors, as in Chapter 2's discussion of layered, spatial identities, can help us grasp the multiple dimensions of experiences. Metaphors encourage us to rethink both the tenor and the vehicle, enhancing our understanding of how experiences may be perceived, and how they are consequently represented.

It has been vital in this line of research to look at experiences of each of the caregiving roles, and thus consider narratives from the first-hand caregivers at each point in the medical system. Throughout this book, I explore experiences recorded by stretcher bearers, ambulance drivers, orderlies, nurses, and doctors/surgeons. It is significant, however, that such roles are not always clearly distinct from one another: the medical roles, like medical spaces, tend to overlap. Female ambulance drivers often provided nursing when needed, and sometimes male ambulance drivers performed tasks often associated with orderlies. There is also a gendered aspect here which assumes that women are nurses while men are orderlies, though they are often performing similar tasks. It is in part for this reason that I do not separate accounts according to role in this book but embed the experiences of each kind of caregiver at every point in the system.

My selection of narratives is only a fraction of the published and unpublished first-hand material on medical care during the war, in memoir, diary, and semi-fictionalised form. There is a wealth of rich narrative material beyond the sample of accounts on which I have focused. While I draw on some contemporaneously translated texts from French and Russian caregivers, the majority of my chosen narratives are in English, from British, American, and Canadian caregivers. These sources draw on some experiences in Russia and Romania, but the main focus is on the Western Front, with some examples of general hospitals in Britain. A great deal more material remains untranslated. It is also significant that previously lost or unknown personal accounts are still being found: the centenary commemorations generated renewed interest in retrieving and protecting family stories, on which some publishers have been keen to capitalise. Archives have also become more alert to the possibility of hidden stories within their stacks, promising that more lost stories will come to light. This pattern will no doubt recur in the next ten to twenty years with respect to the medical narratives from the Second World War.

The basis of my selection of texts has been to get a full cross-section of experiences, from the stretcher bearers and ambulance drivers who are typically regarded as closest to the frontline of fighting, to the nurses, orderlies, and doctors/surgeons who work in the aid posts, clearing stations, field hospitals, and general hospitals. Engaging with accounts from all of these spaces allows for an overarching view of the different kinds of medical spaces, in order to contextualise the spatial conditions and the spatial associations of specific narratives.

Literary Context: Medicine, Modernism, and the First World War

Literature of the First World War is deeply tied to the characteristics of modernism. The metanarrative of this relationship insists that modernism inherited from the war the fracturing and fragmentation, dehumanisation and alienation which so marks the texts as literary modernism. It is widely accepted 'that the First World War helped bring literary modernism into being',[32] but there has often been uncritical acceptance that writing of the war is automatically modernist in nature. Trudi Tate, in *Modernism, History and the First World War* (1998), finds the label of 'modernism' helpful though imprecise: 'it remains a useful description of writings which were self-consciously avant-garde or attempting to extend the possibilities of literary form in the late nineteenth and early twentieth centuries'.[33] Yet, she goes on to highlight that 'rarely is the fiction

---

[32] Ann-Marie Einhaus, 'Modernism, Truth, and the Canon of First World War Literature', *Modernist Cultures* 6, no. 2 (2011): 298.

[33] Trudi Tate, *Modernism, History and the First World War* (Manchester: Manchester University Press, 1998), 2.

of Woolf or Lawrence read alongside the war memoirs of returned soldiers such as Blunden or Graves'.[34] Tate resituates war memoirs within the context of modernism, arguing for the inevitable impact of total war on society and culture. However, in her discussion on the canonicity of war literature, Ann-Marie Einhaus highlights how much of the literature to emerge from the war was not aesthetically modernist. Einhaus points out that 'the majority of writing that directly addresses the war is strikingly conventional and isn't formally experimental, opting as it does for a thoroughly realist mode of representation'.[35] This further adds to the debate that we cannot consider modernism as singular but instead think of modernisms, plural. Angela Smith argues that in doing so, there are texts which might be considered 'accidental modernism(s)', and this 'forms an important link between the experience of the First World War and the emergence of a wider modernist practice'.[36] To regard all war texts as modernist, or to suggest that it is only oblique modernist texts that are worth focusing on, is to lose a wealth of material. This is especially important given the immediate trend for narratives between 1915 and 1919, works which perhaps read more traditionally because they are written not within a high modernist culture but following literary models of the Victorian and Edwardian period. The impulse for modernist expression may explain why such texts as Arthur Martin's *A Surgeon in Khaki* (1915), David Rhodes Sparks's *Red Poppies* (1918), or Sophie Botcharsky's *They Knew How to Die* (1931) have received so little attention.

While this book focuses on the distinct experience of medics, by nature of writing within and of combat, there are overlaps with the imagery and impression given by combatant writings. At times, I draw out this continuity by making brief comparisons with combatant memoirs, such as Siegfried Sassoon's *Memoirs of an Infantry Officer* (1930) and Frederic Manning's *Her Privates We* (1929). There are common tropes which bind many combatant narratives, as Jay Winter has demonstrated with regards to cultural myth.[37] These tropes and imagery bleed into medics' writing too, as seen in Chapter 2's discussion of antediluvian and apocalyptic imagery.

---

[34] Ibid., 2.
[35] Einhaus, 'Modernism', 298.
[36] Angela K. Smith, *The Second Battlefield: Women, Modernism and the First World War* (Manchester: Manchester University Press, 2000), 71.
[37] Jay Winter, *Sites of Memory, Sites of Mourning: The Great War in European Cultural History* (Cambridge: Cambridge University Press, 1998).

There has been some initial discussion of some of these medical writings in relation to modernism. Allyson Booth's *Postcards from the Trenches* (1996) and, more recently, Alice Kelly's *Commemorative Modernism* (2020) both engage with nurses' writings in their consideration of proximities to death and remembrance. Modernist scholarship more broadly has begun to engage with medicine, through the works of such writers as Virginia Woolf, Dorothy Richardson, D. H. Lawrence, and Samuel Beckett, by Hermione Lee, Peter Fifield, Elizabeth Barry, Laura Salisbury, and Ulrika Maude.[38] Modernism's extensive focus on the body, embodiment, and senses sets itself up nicely to the surfacing of medicine as a locus around which to develop these concepts alongside critical medical humanities.

While this book does not focus on the literary context of modernism, or enter into debates around its origins and development, my literary starting points are considered exceptionally modernist texts, especially within the canon of nurses' writings. Mary Borden's *The Forbidden Zone* (1929) and Ellen N. La Motte's *The Backwash of War* (1916) offer particularly idiosyncratic styles of writing, with fracturing and experimentation, which has recently regained literary attention, especially with their republications in 2008 and 2014, respectively. Borden established and worked at L'Hôpital Chirurgical Mobile No. I at Rousbrugge, Belgium, where she worked with La Motte, and L'Hôpital d'Evacuation at Bray-sur-Somme. La Motte trained as a nurse at Johns Hopkins, specialising in tuberculosis nursing, but she was also a journalist, writing particularly for the *Atlantic Monthly*, where some of her stories were initially published. Her collection of short stories *The Backwash of War* was published in 1916, but the shocking subject matter led to the book being banned in Britain and France, and once the USA had formally entered the war, its marketing there was censored too.[39] Although written at the same time, Borden's *The Forbidden Zone* was not published until 1929, at the peak of the second wave of interest in war books. Borden had attempted to publish in 1917, but censoring rules

---

[38] For example, Laura Salisbury and Andrew Shail, eds, *Neurology and Modernity: A Cultural History of Nervous Systems, 1800–1950* (Basingstoke: Palgrave Macmillan, 2010); Peter Fifield, *Modernism and Physical Illness: Sick Books* (Oxford: Oxford University Press, 2020).

[39] Margaret R. Higonnet, 'Introduction', in *Nurses at the Front: Writing the Wounds of the Great War* (Boston: Northeastern University Press, 2001), x–xiv.

inhibited what she could say.⁴⁰ Despite the time gap, and despite the huge success of such key combatant narratives as Erich Maria Remarque's *All Quiet on the Western Front* (1929), Borden's writing was also met with criticism and censorship, deemed too shocking and repulsive. Such a reception suggests that it is one thing to depict the violence of warfare with brutal honesty, but it is another to show and critique the medical side of war, and that a line is crossed when a woman presents such shocking images, and in such a style. Perhaps it is no wonder that very little attention has been given to the writing of medics, especially these robustly honest and authentic of accounts, which are intimately personal and revealing.

It is important, however, to highlight that these two texts do not typify either nurses' writings or the work of other medics. Einhaus argues that within the recent interest in non-combatant war literature, Borden has received a disproportionate amount of scholarly attention, and *The Forbidden Zone* must not be read as emblematic of war writing by any means but instead contextualised.⁴¹ It is important to note, then, that both Borden and La Motte were immersed in avant-garde social circles prior to and after the war, via Borden's relationship with Wyndham Lewis, and La Motte's long-term friendship with Gertrude Stein, thus writing with awareness of literary trends taking place around them.⁴² In fact, Borden and La Motte visited Stein's home in Paris, which, Margaret Higonnet suggests, may have influenced the 'cubist vision' of their work.⁴³ Beyond this literature, I discuss a range of familiar and unfamiliar medic writers, including those with different levels of experience and success in their writing careers. As much as Borden's and La Motte's work impresses, there are numerous writers discussed throughout this book whose work is just as captivating, enthralling, and powerful but as yet has not reached larger audiences, and many of their works have not been republished in the twenty-first century, including, for instance, Maud Mortimer's *A Green Tent in Flanders* (1917), Elizabeth Walker Black's *Hospital Heroes* (1919), and Lesley Smith's *Four Years Out of Life* (1931).

---

⁴⁰ Jane Conway, *A Woman of Two Wars: The Life of Mary Borden* (n.p.: Munday Books, 2010), 77; Andrew Frayn, *Writing Disenchantment: British First World War Prose, 1914–30* (Manchester: Manchester University Press, 2015), 226.
⁴¹ Einhaus, 'Modernism', 303.
⁴² Ibid., 305; Smith, *Second Battlefield*, 84.
⁴³ Margaret Higonnet, 'Cubist Vision in Nursing Accounts', in *First World War Nursing: New Perspectives*, ed. Alison S. Fell and Christine E. Hallett (New York: Routledge, 2013), 158.

Literary Context: Medical Memoirs

While this book emphasises the experiences of medical caregivers in the early part of the twentieth century and within a specific context, it coincides with significant recent trends in contemporary medical memoirs and associated scholarship. There is strong established scholarship which has explored illness narratives, such as Anne Hunsaker Hawkins's *Reconstructing Illness: Studies in Pathography* (1993) and Arthur Frank's *The Wounded Storyteller* (1995), to name just a couple. However, there has been little in the way of similar conceptualisations of caregivers' experiences. The differentiation is difficult to mark, of course, given the flurry of memoirs by medical practitioners (most often doctors) who find themselves patients: arguably Paul Kalanithi's *When Breath Becomes Air* (2016), about his terminal cancer diagnosis, has been a significant watershed moment in this regard. Yet, what little critical reception this has garnered has resulted in a disappointingly reductive response concluding 'doctors are human too'. Such reception seems to see such texts as utilising a more humanised approach to medical practice, especially once situated within medical education.[44] While this recognises the practitioners' inherent humanity, it downplays their distinctive contribution to illuminating phenomenological, embodied, and affective dimensions of caregiving. More attention has, historically, been given to medics' memoirs if they have also been fiction writers, such as Arthur Conan Doyle, Anton Chekov, Mikhail Bulgakov, or William Carlos Williams. This focus misses a wealth of biographical and semi-biographical works which should be given greater inclusion within literary studies, which can aid understanding of the ways truth, testimony, authenticity, and memory can be expressed, with attention to the representational decisions and characteristics adopted to tell personal stories. More inclusion of these works would, importantly, diversify whose personal writings are regarded as significant.

Especially in the US, there has been a steady stream of, mostly physician, memoirs from the mid-twentieth century onwards. The field-defining work in narrative medicine by Rita Charon and the narrative focus of Kathryn Montgomery have sustained the importance of medical narratives within medical education and practice.

---

[44] Ann Jurecic and Daniel Marchalik, 'Breathing Lessons: Paul Kalanithi's *When Breath Becomes Air*', *The Lancet* 388, no. 10062 (10 December 2016): 2859.

Suzanne Poirier's engagement with medic memoirs, too, has illustrated their role within reflective practice.[45] Despite these studies engaging with contemporary and historical moments of clinical practice, they are less a literary study and more a demonstration of narrative structures, evidencing the value of narrative thinking and reading in medicine, with cross-pollination in, for example, the case history. Scholarly engagement with medic and caregiver narratives so far has focused less on the lived experience of the caregiver and more on the portrayal of a life in medicine.

Interest in medical practitioners' experiences and narratives has especially grown in recent years, with widespread publication of medic memoirs. In the UK particularly, these include retired medics looking back on their careers, such as surgeons Henry Marsh (*Do No Harm* (2014), *Admissions* (2017)) and Stephen Westaby (*Fragile Lives* (2017), *The Knife's Edge* (2019)), as well as memoirs of practising doctors, such as Rachel Clarke (*Your Life in My Hands* (2017), *Dear Life* (2020), *Breathtaking* (2021)) and Aoife Abbey (*Seven Signs of Life* (2019)). Of course, it is not just doctors; there is also interest in the memoirs of other healthcare roles, including nurses and paramedics, such as the nursing memoirs of Christie Watson (*The Language of Kindness* (2018), *The Courage to Care* (2020)). These recent publishing booms in personal medical writing, of the 2010s and 2020s, is part of a bigger interest in employment memoirs, but it also demonstrates interest in the 'frontline' of demanding yet often invisible or misunderstood roles.

Increasing attention to such narratives simultaneously illustrates the growing recognition for the value of life writing in general. A focus on medical life writing is one facet of life writing studies that can in turn revolutionise narrative studies, and aid the scholarly engagement with varied and emerging narrative forms and genres, such as diaries, semibiographical and semi-fictionalisations, autoethnography, autofiction, fictional autobiography, and letters and correspondence, and help clarify the hybridity, identification, and

---

[45] Rita Charon, *Narrative Medicine: Honoring the Stories of Illness* (Oxford and New York: Oxford University Press, 2006); Rita Charon et al., *The Principles and Practice of Narrative Medicine* (New York: Oxford University Press, 2016); Kathryn Montgomery, *Doctors' Stories: The Narrative Structure of Medical Knowledge* (Princeton, NJ: Princeton University Press, 1991); Kathryn Montgomery, *How Doctors Think: Clinical Judgement and the Practice of Medicine* (New York and Oxford: Oxford University Press, 2006); Suzanne Poirier, *Doctors in the Making: Memoirs and Medical Education* (Iowa City: University of Iowa Press, 2009).

labelling of such works. The purpose of this book is not to provide a value judgement on the popularity of such medical writings but to demonstrate how they have previously been overlooked for their literary attributes and underestimated in how they can convey deep insight. This work intends to mark a significant step in arguing for critical attention to the form, genre, and content of medic memoirs, and medical life writing more broadly.

Structure

This book has three sections. The first section begins with a particular focus on the literal space and landscape of the military-medical environment. Chapter 1, 'Corpography: Reconceptualising Somatic Geographies', establishes the medic's relationship with the war landscape: from the stretcher bearers and ambulance drivers at the frontline to the orderlies, nurses, and doctors distributed at the various aid posts and hospitals. The roles are intensely physical, relying at every point on phenomenological perception and knowledge. The medic is mentally and bodily immersed in the environment, in the sense of responding immediately to conditions as they arise, from shellfire and potholes to quick triage decisions or alertness to sudden haemorrhages. The chapter title signals my adoption of Derek Gregory's geographical concept of 'Corpography', which explains that the body in the war environment must change, adapting to the transformed surface of the earth, alert to the topographies of the trench and battlespace. I extend this concept specifically to the experience of medics, an area in which it has not been invoked previously, arguing that like combatants, the medics' bodies are directly affected by the spatial and sensuous geographies of the war landscape, which extends into the overlapping medical spaces. The corpographic body is not only physically altered; it also undergoes a reconfiguration and reprivileging of the senses in relation to its environment, in order to use perceptual resources in more effective, efficient, and life-saving ways.

In Chapter 2, 'Layering: Appropriating Medical Spaces', I focus on the literal spaces in which medical care takes place, and unearth the relationship between the physical environment and its figurative and emotional associations. There are multiple layers of associations in these spaces, which I explore by introducing the image of the spatial palimpsest. I consider medical spaces and battlespaces within a legacy of warfare and pain, situating the immediacy of experience within a wider context of memory. Considering the palimpsestic identities of space, by invoking Walter Benjamin's 'double ground', we can not only consider how traces and memories persist but also in turn explore how their persistence impacts experiences in the present. The effect is one of abiding incongruity and juxtaposition, often with uncanny consequences, as when a writhing soldier lies under the glittering light of a chandelier. But it is not just the past that impacts on spatial identity: by drawing on Lefebvre's *The Production of Space*, I consider how the power of metaphor informs the ways social activities inscribe or superimpose varying identities on a space. The consequent identities of the spaces are made up of both past and contemporaneous associations: thus the palimpsest continues to acquire further layers.

The central section of the book focuses on the wounds of patients, the breakdown of bodily boundaries, and the subsequent effect this has on the medic applying care, who must sometimes intrude on the spaces of the body. Chapter 3, 'Protrusions, Openings, and Depths: A Medical Grotesque', centres on the spatial and somatic connections between the body of the medic and the body of the wounded, where boundaries are threatened and visibly collapse, threatening the integrity of selfhood. I consider the representations of wounds and wound care in medical narratives through a theoretical prism of disgust, abjection, and the aesthetic grotesque. Close attention to these representations allows us to see the accumulating tensions held in the body of the medic, who must abject, dissociate, and disentangle themselves from bodily waste and bodily wreckage, as well as from bodies beyond care. I develop the idea of a 'medical grotesque', characterised by the tensions between bodily protrusions and intrusions, which pervades the discourse by which medical personnel critique their own roles as caregivers. The medical grotesque is a vehicle for self-reflection on the conflicting dimensions of caregiving, from the anxieties of repulsion and disgust to dilemmas of medical violence and ethics of intrusion. Rethinking the clinical gaze through a lens of a medical grotesque helps to illuminate the representational strategies these medics adopt in order to convey the complexities and tensions of medical care. It is vital that we do not accept an unreflective view of the medic as a figure of power but instead acknowledge that their position compounds complex negotiations between empathy and detachment, care and self-care.

The latter part of the book moves into the realm of psychological and imaginative landscapes, to examine complex emotions, trauma, coping, and survival. Chapters 4 and 5 are paired, centring on trauma and suffering with regards to the representation and articulation of painful experience. Chapter 4, 'Countering: Representing Coping Strategies', explores techniques of countering trauma and distress through the psychological movement between real and imaginary spaces. I appropriate Foucault's sociological concept of heterotopias to a psychological context, arguing that these imaginative spaces, traversing boundaries between the real and the unreal, are evident in pervasive theatrical images, such as the stage or film set, and can be considered psychological 'counter-sites': places experienced in parallel, with one supplying psychological refuge. By psychologically 'moving' into a place of refuge, the medics are able to shift their perspectives and self-reflect. Images of sight and vision, especially those drawing on various technologies of seeing, pervade these narratives, and are drawn out in order to explore the relationship between perception and representation.

Finally, Chapter 5, 'Surfaces: Articulating Pain and Trauma', focuses on textual spaces, and explores the psychological and emotional landscapes of the articulation of distress, trauma, and suffering. I address the narrative shape of these accounts directly, in order to consider what is absent and present in the communication of difficult and traumatic experiences. I introduce a spatial image of these texts as representational surfaces, in order to explore how gaps in representation are themselves features of representation. Existing trauma theory and scholarship suggests that 'gaps' and 'blanks' are symptomatic of trauma; yet it is my contention that by exploring the 'blank', we can discover in it a mode of articulation, and so further our understanding of pain and suffering. By interrogating existing notions of symptomatic writing, I explore how silences can be resources for new modes of storytelling, adopted as creative responses to the crisis of representation; for example, the aesthetic of blunted affect often used to express the complexities in medical care. Building on this idea, I explore the intricate role and responsibility of witness testimonies: the professional duty as caregiver and witness to testify for victims, as well as the humane instinct to testify on behalf of a greater understanding of war, pain, and suffering. The elaboration of these spatial concepts across the chapters of this book gradually adds detail to the picture of the medical space, and to the psychological landscapes of the medics working within it.

The narratives discussed in this book are at different times and to different degrees shocking, disturbing, graphic, upsetting, alarming, yet tender, humorous, thankful, and humane. It has been important in this work not to shy away from gruesome and unflinching representations but to allow the medics to speak for themselves and for the truth of their experiences. I hope this work places the caregivers' experiences in a new light. All too easily we eclipse caregivers' experiences by focusing on the one obviously in need of care. It is the medical and caregiving imperative to focus on the patient – it is after all their purpose in the relationship – but at what cost do we continue to turn a blind eye to those providing help, treatment, solace, and care?

Chapter 1

Corpography: Reconceptualising Somatic Geographies

The military-medical caregiving role necessitates, and generates, a particular connection between body and landscape. The military-medical landscape and the bodies of medic and combatant are mutually implicated, whereby the bodies are directly affected by the landscape, and the landscape is affected by human action. This chapter is concerned with the somatic and sensuous situation of the medic, in relation to the intersections of military and medical spatial geographies.

In discussing the modern experience of battle, Derek Gregory has developed the neologistic concept of 'corpography', explaining that

> the radically different knowledges that the war-weary soldiers improvised as a matter of sheer survival [constitute] a corpography: a way of apprehending the battle space through the body as an acutely physical field in which the senses of sound, smell and touch were increasingly privileged in the construction of a profoundly haptic or somatic geography.[1]

As Gregory's concept implies, the intensity of experience in the battlefield environment produces intimate physical continuity between the landscape and the bodies within it, with this immediate relationship being essential to surviving and navigating the battlespace. Such a concept can usefully be extended to the situation of the military-medic, so I propose to appropriate it in order to uncover the complex dimensions of care in relation to bodies and landscape. Here, I also

---

[1] Derek Gregory, 'Gabriel's Map: Cartography and Corpography in Modern War', in *Geographies of Knowledge and Power*, ed. Peter Meusburger, Derek Gregory, and Laura Suarsana (Dordrecht: Springer, 2015), 91.

develop a framework that considers the phenomenology of caregiving, which is specific to this war environment but also applies to further medical environments. For both combatant and medic, the body is at stake in an environment that compels the development of somatic geographies negotiating between the spatial and the sensory.

Corpography is in some ways similar to Santanu Das's 'phenomenological geography' and 'geographies of sense' in *Touch and Intimacy in First World War Literature* (2005), which is one of the few studies to explore the relationship between space and scape alongside senses in this specific, military context.[2] Das explains that the battlespace is 'a landscape not understood in terms of maps, places and names, but geography as processes of cognition, as subjective and sensuous states of experience'.[3] The concept of 'corpography' allows for a reconsideration of the somatic and phenomenological dimensions of the battle experience, with specific and significant inclusion of the role of the landscape; however, as this discussion will demonstrate, there is still a place for 'maps', 'places', and 'names' as components of cognition. The war experience is larger than the soldier's situation in a trench, and the spatial, somatic, and sensuous geographies involved have multiple phenomenological dimensions.

Gregory's approach to the phenomenology of the battlespace argues that 'surviving the [battle-space] required a "re-mapping", the improvisation of a corpography rather than a cartography'.[4] The concept invokes the navigational and cartographic structures of warfare to interrogate the experiences, but it is more than simply a metaphor or analogy: crucially, it involves a shift from third-person to first-person perspective; from objectivity to first-hand immersion. Significantly, the manifestations of corpography are processes (of cognition, affective response, sensation), and take place through a continual negotiation between the somatic and spatial. Gregory appears to build on John Keegan's mountaineering analogy of war, from *The Face of Battle* (1978).[5] Bodily investments and immersion in mountaineering, vulnerable to the (literal) 'exposure' of the rock face, provide an analogy for the exposure of involvement in war. Gregory draws out through his own concept how figurative,

---

[2] Santanu Das, *Touch and Intimacy in First World War Literature* (2005; Cambridge: Cambridge University Press, 2008), 73.
[3] Ibid.
[4] Derek Gregory, 'The Natures of War', *Antipode* 48, no. 1 (2016): 9.
[5] John Keegan, *The Face of Battle* (London: Penguin, 1978), 304.

immersive map-making and map-reading determines somatic awareness and actions.

The 're-mapping' dimension of Gregory's corpography performs the function of cartography, which to an extent overlaps with the concept of 'regridding' within Gilles Deleuze and Félix Guattari's 'smooth and striated spaces'.[6] The landscape must undergo a 'regridding' in order to counter the destruction of the visible and known landscape and space, and recover a recognisable sense of place. The rapidly changing war landscape makes navigation increasingly difficult; regardless of the figurative overlap of battle and medical spaces, for the medic who must move within and between them, some kind of definition and demarcation of areas is needed. The effort is to make the unmappable, mappable. In order to function and act in the world, the body must, as Maurice Merleau-Ponty suggests, 'build into the geographical setting a behavioural one, a system of meanings outwardly expressive of the subject's internal activity'.[7] Only by knowing the geography, can the forms of behaviour and behavioural instincts develop.

The space of battle forces the body to adapt, and demands that the relationship between the body and earth be transformed. This is particularly evident in the case of sniper attacks, where those in the trenches must be constantly aware of where exactly their body is, to avoid the slightest part appearing over the edge of the parapet. As combatant A. P. Herbert describes, '[soldiers] hated the "blinded" feeling it produced; it was demoralizing always to be wondering if one's head was low enough, always to walk with a stoop'.[8] This method of survival relies on a constant negotiation between body and earth, but the effect is by no means only a physical strain on the body. The soldiers' constant vulnerability to annihilation enforces a continual self-monitoring that is much more wearing than the physical strain involved. It has a transformative effect on the senses and the psyche, in which the body is wholly implicated in critical details of the spatial environment.

The interior and exterior of the body thus undergo a 're-mapping', of spatial relationships, somatic boundaries, and sensuous configurations. This chapter builds on some of these established

---

[6] Gilles Deleuze and Félix Guattari, *A Thousand Plateaus*, trans. Brian Massumi (1987; London and New York: Bloomsbury Academic, 2016), 551–81.

[7] Maurice Merleau-Ponty, *Phenomenology of Perception*, trans. Colin Smith (1945; London and New York: Routledge Classics, 2005), 129.

[8] A. P. Herbert, *The Secret Battle* (1919; Barnsley: Pen & Sword Books, 2009), 45.

ideas, extending and adapting them specifically to the medical experience. The concept of corpography has yet to be explicitly applied to the experiences of the medic, but such a move certainly warrants exploration. As combatant, the body of the soldier is vulnerable; it is intensely experienced as a situated body in a spatial environment, and an extended body in relation to that environment. For the medic, however, there is a redoubling of this somatic situation: their own body is at stake, to varying degrees, as well as the body of the wounded in their care. The medic's experience is like that of the combatant, in which their own body is vulnerable and threatened, but this threat is multiplied, given their position as caregiver. The medic is responsible for more than one body. Their embodied awareness of environment is both direct and vicarious, so that the physical and psychological effects of embodiedness are intensified. In Havi Carel's theorising of the phenomenology of illness, she illustrates that the ill person's experience of space changes and in turn 'shared meanings and concepts change as well'.[9] We can see an interpretation of this playing out for medics, who, while there to perform specific imperatives of caregiving, are too susceptible to the psychological and physical damage that renders them ill and injured. While the physical spaces evolve and adapt, the understanding and interpretation of those spaces require something extra of the medic's body and mind.

The military-medical spaces must be considered in connection to somatic and haptic geographies, which, as Das explains, are 'particularly useful for understanding the world of the trenches, drawing on a "common" sense to translate the different kinds of sensory stimuli impinging on the consciousness'.[10] Crucially, active combat is not confined to an explicitly demarcated space: the battlefield extends, and boundaries between areas collapse. The classifications of battle and medical spaces, and their relations to each other, are physically and psychologically complex. In her highly modernist work *The Forbidden Zone* (1929), volunteer nurse Mary Borden labels the medical space the 'second battlefield':

> It seemed to me that the crazy crowded bright hot shelter was a beautiful place. I thought, 'This is the second battlefield. The battle now is going on over the helpless bodies of these men. It is we who are doing the fighting now, with their real enemies.' And I thought of the chief

---

[9] Havi Carel, *Phenomenology of Illness* (Oxford: Oxford University Press, 2016), 9.
[10] Das, *Touch*, 74–5.

surgeon, the wizard working like lightning through the night, and all the others wielding their flashing knives against the invisible enemy.[11]

This is unquestionably a comment on the acts and duties of the medical personnel, recognising the battles, struggles, and dangers inherent to the medical space. She likens the role of the medic to that of the combatant, in conflict with the new, and real, enemies: pain and death. In this metaphor of the hospital as a battlefield, it is ambiguous if 'second' connotes simultaneity or subsequence. Given the cyclical role of medical care within the larger domain of the war effort, on call to provide medical attention whenever it is needed, there is a sense in which we can understand this as a concurrent battlefield. Yet, part of the metaphorical combat of war is the combat between medics and wounds, and in this sense the 'second battlefield' is the domain of a consequential stage of war. The soldiers literally move from the first, combatant battlefield to the subsequent but continuous environment of military-medical care.

Borden's 'second battlefield' has further resonance, then, if we consider the medical space not as separate from the frontline but as overlapping with it. It is difficult to delineate the boundaries of these military and medical spaces: although there are distinct military-medical spaces (Regimental Aid Post, Casualty Clearing Station, Field Hospital), the idea of demarcating the military space from the medical is practically and conceptually problematic. 'Battlefield' is in fact a difficult term, its scope open to question, in the literal as well as figurative sense. On the one hand, the 'battlefield' needs to be tangible in order to be a functional, 'humanitarian construct', defining mutually understood areas of exclusion for non-combatants.[12] On the other hand, 'battlefield' is also used, or inferred to mean, more metaphorically, a general area of combat.[13] In 'War and the Vanishing Battlefield' (2011), Frédéric Mégret explains:

---

[11] Mary Borden, 'Blind', in *The Forbidden Zone* (1929; London: Hesperus Press, 2008), 97. The quotation has been noted by many in discussion of Borden's work, and even inspired the title of Angela K. Smith's monograph *The Second Battlefield: Women, Modernism and the First World War* (Manchester: Manchester University Press, 2000), but as yet no one seems to have interrogated Borden's statement and the imagery it inspires. Smith's work seems to adopt 'second' as a means of the inclusion of female perspectives and writings.

[12] Frédéric Mégret, 'War and the Vanishing Battlefield', *Loyola University Chicago International Law Review* 9, no. 1 (2011): 138.

[13] Ibid., 136.

The concept of the battlefield has long structured the understanding of war. A battlefield is typically an area, limited in space and time, upon which a battle occurs. The battlefield may be created by the chance encounter of enemy troops, but it may also be agreed upon by opposite armies. The battlefield is not a clearly defined space, not even in the most traditional battles. It is 'an imaginary arena in which the bounds are seen to be the edges of the territory occupied by the two armies during the course of the fight'. But it is space nonetheless, one that has a core and a periphery and whose existence is premised on the ability to distinguish between what occurs within it and what is beyond it. For that space to have any meaning, however, it must be inscribed in a series of understandings about its purpose and its rules. The battlefield is, in other words, as much an idea as it is a space, and only when one understands the assumptions underlying the idea of the battlefield can one understand how the battlefield today has come under threat.[14]

If, as Mégret explains, the battlefield 'is premised on the ability to distinguish between what occurs within it and what is beyond it', then no such distinction separates the trenches and no man's land from the roads and fields between them and the medical spaces behind. If the mark of the battlefield is the acts of violence within it, then these roads and fields, and indeed the medical huts, tents, and hospitals they link, remain within the sphere of influence of conflict. The foci of battle and the spaces of medical care do not exist in wholly discrete spaces.

The concept of the battlefield in the modern period has certainly become increasingly complicated, with the increase in aerial warfare one of the most defining complications. My contribution to the discussion rests on the central idea that the area of war can no longer be considered a battlefield but rather a battle*space*. In discussing the work of Paul Virilio, Stuart Elden points out that 'aerial warfare in World War I opened up new senses of battle*space*, rather than just a battle*field*'; in fact, the military space must be thought of in terms of volume rather than area.[15] While the medical effort does not seem directly affected by this vertical extension of the warzone (after all, there was not yet any aerial evacuation), the fact is that medics within the vastly extended battlespace are subject to the consequences of aerial warfare, and the misleading concept of 'battlefield'

[14] Ibid., 132–3.
[15] Stuart Elden, 'Secure the Volume: Vertical Geopolitics and the Depth of Power', *Political Geography* 34 (2013): 36.

no longer seems appropriate. Delineating the spaces individually is difficult and counter-intuitive; I argue that such spaces overlap, and that this recognition enables us to perceive the enduring ramifications of warfare. We cannot comfortably separate medical aid from battle acts, especially given that medical advances are themselves a part of the technological arms race, and medical infrastructure is a key resource for each nation and alliance. Given the fluid boundaries of such spaces, they mutually implicate the body of the medic in their common atmosphere, regardless of traditional assumptions about relative proximity to centres of war. Recognising that these spaces overlap with one another is important for the realisation that there is crisis at every stage, and that the body of the medic is situated within a continuous war landscape. To mark a divide where conflict ends and care begins is to understate not only the role of military medicine but the embodied engagement of medics providing care. This, I think, is what Borden is pushing towards with the 'second battlefield' analogy and its suggestion that conflict enters the spaces of caregiving.

In this chapter, I argue that the body of the medic, too, is immersed within the battlespaces. Like the combatants, their bodies must also change, adapt, and 're-map' in order to function in this setting. 'Corpography' provides a clear conceptual framework within which to explore the situation of the medic in the war context, and I use Gregory's concept to structure my argument around the phenomenology of the medics' bodies. By considering how their bodies are immersed in the space, we can specifically articulate how medics interact with the landscape and their spatial environments, and thus how they respond to changes in that environment. The medic, through an immersive understanding of space, must read and interpret external stimuli: both the signification of the space itself, and that presented by the patients, to be translated into specific medical knowledge, which elucidates phenomenological aspects specific to caregiving. The chapter culminates by considering the body of the medic as a mediating body, as well as a navigational instrument, sorting through bodies. The medic's body mediates between the earth and the wounded bodies, through profoundly multisensory and intensely somatic, immersive geographies; by attending to every part of their body, the medic makes sense of the spatial and medical situation before them, and of its psychological and physical impact.

Immersion and Being

In his memoir *Ambulancing on the French Front* (1918), Edward Coyle illustrates the physical and psychological challenges of navigating through the trenches:

> Crouching, we advanced some fifty yards. In passing one place that was particularly low, we were observed and the next second brought a hail of machine-gun bullets which kicked up the dust all about us. In front of us, some fifteen or twenty feet away, I noticed another spot where the side walls of the trench did not afford much protection and at the same instant, or just long enough for a man to proceed from one opening to another, came a stream of machine-gun bullets in front of us.
>
> It was a case of being between the devil and the deep sea; all we could do was to remain in the position where we were protected. We finally decided that by crawling on our hands and knees we could get past the second opening.[16]

Coyle provides an example of a very physical kind of problem solving; the body of the individual is intensely subject to the conditions of his environment, and reliant on his adaptation to the features of the surrounding earthworks. In pursuit of his objective he depends on a reciprocity between body and cognitive judgement, made acute by fear and the immediate threat to his physical safety. Coyle's description foregrounds the altering of posture and the intimate relation to the earth, upon which self-preservation depends. The successive negotiations with space – what to hide behind, where to avoid, when to run – are emblematic of the trench experience, and of immersion in the battlespace more generally. In negotiating their environment, the medics cannot wait for the bullets as stimuli because then it is too late; instead, they must deal in lines of sight and lines of fire, which are not direct perceptions but extrapolations from their situation in the landscape. The individual's spatial awareness, their synthetic sense of environment and body, becomes a paramount psychological attribute.

In Coyle's illustration we can begin to register the intuitive interpretation of landscape that combatants and caregivers in this particular battle context must instinctively develop. This is a convincing

---

[16] Edward R. Coyle, *Ambulancing on the French Front* (New York: Britton, 1918), 117.

example of Gregory's corpography, where the connection between space, body, and somatic sensations must be alert to external stimuli. As he points out,

> the remote orderings of military violence were never autonomous projections onto a pure plane; they also depended on the bodies of soldiers whose apprehension of the battle space was always more than visual. In part, this was a matter of affect, but it was also a matter of knowledge – of what I call a corpography rather than a cartography – whose materialities also inflected imaginative geographies of militarised nature.[17]

This spatial and somatic intuition, then, is a combination of affect and knowledge; the body, with all its perturbations (emotive, psychological, and embodied), combines these stimuli *through* and *as* judgement. Emotions and judgements are intertwined, and as Martha Nussbaum argues, 'emotions always involve thought of an object combined with thought of the object's salience or importance; in that sense, they always involve appraisal or evaluation'.[18] It is in light of this that we can appreciate the importance of the affective dimension of experience as integral to perception, and thus adopt a more rounded view of the knowledge gained from an environment. Knowledge of the battlespace is gathered through a symbiosis of somatic, embodied response and emotional, affective response. The immediacy of bodily immersion in a highly charged space and landscape has significant intuitive and affective dimensions. Coyle's description, along with many others, demonstrates the capacity for navigation and deduction that emerges from immersive experience. Given that '[t]he world is not what I think, but what I live through',[19] knowledge of the landscape and its import for the body can only be gained by being *in* it. Living 'through' and being 'in' are crucial doorways in this discussion, helping to establish the importance of the experiential and immersive in the demanding role of the caregiver.

Knowledge and awareness in the medical space involves the spatial and sensuous experience of the world, navigated and negotiated through perceptual and bodily investments. Ambulance driver Katherine Hodges offers a perfect example of how corpography informs the experience of driving: 'it sometimes became necessary to

---

[17] Gregory, 'Natures', 4.
[18] Martha Craven Nussbaum, *Upheavals of Thought: The Intelligence of Emotions* (Cambridge: Cambridge University Press, 2001), 23.
[19] Merleau-Ponty, *Phenomenology of Perception*, xviii.

stop, get out of the car, and on one's hands and knees feel the surface of the road for a few yards, get in again, drive the distance explored, and then repeat the process'.[20] Hodges literally crawls in the dark to find her way, reinforcing Gregory's conception of corpography as a bodily intimacy with the earth. Flattening her body against the earth to feel her way through, Hodges apprehends the surrounding geography in terms of a very physical, somatic knowledge and embodied cognition of topographies. Preconceived, imaginative geographies are subordinated, and the emphasis is placed on experiential navigation and interpretation of space. This proves, in part, 'the untenability of mind/body dualism and emphasises the centrality and importance of the body to understanding human experience',[21] and the primacy of embodied knowledge. External stimuli instruct the body, which responds accordingly.

Stretcher bearers and ambulance drivers experience the force of such somatic immersion with utmost immediacy, but it is also in these specific caregiving roles that the combatant/non-combatant distinction is most obscured. It is important to remember that stretcher bearers and ambulance drivers were explicitly non-combatant; in fact, they were sometimes pacifists or conscientious objectors, their roles either voluntary or enforced. The blurred line between combatant and non-combatant is a consequence of their relationship to the war environment, rather than their role, although they certainly did not bear arms. Numerous accounts demonstrate the demands of bearing patients from no man's land and the trenches, and the intensity of their relationship to the objects and surroundings of the battle landscape. Writing in her memoir *Flanders and Other Fields* (1964), ambulance driver and sometime stretcher bearer Elsie Knocker (published under her married name of Baroness de T'Serclaes) explains, 'We had to bend double to keep below the level of the earthworks (and so avoid the rifle-fire which the Germans had opened up on us) while carrying two horribly wounded men on stretchers.'[22] Similarly, stretcher bearer James Braid explains how in retrieving the wounded soldiers, 'we were up to the knees in water and it was awful. We could hardly walk ourselves, let alone carry the stretchers [. . .] It is trying, as we are always under fire and have to keep dropping down

---

[20] Katherine Hodges, 'A Driver at the Front', Private Papers of Miss K Hodges, Imperial War Museum Collections, Documents.1974, 143.
[21] Carel, *Phenomenology of Illness*, 7.
[22] Baroness de T'Serclaes, *Flanders and Other Fields* (London: George G. Harrap, 1964), 42–4.

to keep out of sight.'[23] It is evident here how in bearing the wounded the medic has to contend with the landscape of the trenches, and the obstacles it presents, maintaining an awareness of the ongoing rifle fire for their safety while simultaneously protecting and evacuating the wounded to safety. There is the physical strain of bending double; the fear of injury or fatality; and the continual imperative to perform their duty and care for the wounded with skill, swiftness, and precision.

J. H. Newton, in *A Stretcher Bearer's Diary: Three Years in France with the 21st Division* (1931), articulates the physical experience of stretcher bearing:

> The trenches are narrow in places, and it is difficult at times to get along as only two can carry at one time, and the rear bearer cannot see where he is putting his feet. In daylight the front bearer can warn him of broken duck-boards, but at night it is a case of stumbling and struggling along as well as you can.[24]

Newton conveys the numerous demands of stretcher bearing on the body, evoking the constrained environment of the trenches and the inevitable debris littering the often narrow route, impeding quick movement. The stretcher bearers struggle to see where they are going and manage the heavy weights of the bodies, as well as carrying without causing further injury or pain. These are not easy weights to bear, or actions to perform:

> The shell-fire, and the mud, are simply beyond description, and it is a miracle that any escape being hit. We have to carry the wounded shoulder high, the only way it can be done, because of the mud. Our shoulders are made raw by the chafing of the stretcher handles, although we wear folded sandbags under our shoulder straps. Sweat runs into our eyes, until we can hardly see.[25]

Not only must the stretcher bearers hold the weight of the wounded, they must also adjust the stretcher's angles and levels in order to navigate the enclosed spaces of the trench. In her examination of Royal Army Medical Corps (RAMC) stretcher bearers, Jessica Meyer suggests that 'While the negotiation of war- and weather-damaged

---

[23] James Braid, 'Unpublished diary', The Liddle Collection, University of Leeds Special Collections, LIDDLE/WWI/GS/0185, 2.

[24] J. H. Newton, *A Stretcher Bearer's Diary: Three Years in France with the 21st Division* (1931; London: Arthur H. Stockwell, 2009), 199–200. Kindle.

[25] Ibid., 244–5.

landscapes required a noticeable physical effort, it was the basic act of lifting and carrying wounded men that had the greatest physical effect on bearers.'[26] The weights could be exceptionally high, quickly exceeding the 12 stone per stretcher which they had been trained to carry.[27] Newton further describes how

> The trench had been knocked in here and there, and it was very difficult to keep the stretcher level when getting it over those mounds of earth. We managed it at last, but the patient must have received a good shaking, although he made no complaint.[28]

While awareness of and familiarity with the topographies of such space must develop, and stretcher bearers undergo intense physical strain, having to navigate both the topographical challenges of these narrow and dangerous routes themselves, they must also maintain awareness of and consideration for the patient on the stretcher, protecting the wounded in their care.

What is most crucial in Newton's accounts is the reiterated concern for the patient: 'When a barrage comes we must keep on and take no notice, as even if we could find cover, there is none for the man on the stretcher.'[29] Here the imperative to protect the wounded takes precedence over their own safety. Navigating through the trench network, with a heightened concern not only for their own bodies but also for the body of the wounded soldier in their care, they acquire a doubled somatic relation to their environment. The wounded Other must be treated as if connected to their own, able body, and their vigilant sensations are extended to encompass a doubled somatic perspective. It is a reciprocal somatic negotiation between space and body, and body and body.

Such a doubled somatic perspective is also necessary for the ambulance driver, whose navigation of dangerous routes is informed by intuitions accumulated in the course of their immersion in such situations: 'only actual experience under such shell fire enables them to become expert in their judgment as to slowing down or shooting on the gas when the condition is met with'.[30] In some cases this develops into an extended embodiment connecting the driver's body

---

[26] Jessica Meyer, *An Equal Burden: The Men of the Royal Army Medical Corps in the First World War* (Oxford: Oxford University Press, 2019), 100.
[27] Ibid., 100.
[28] Newton, 149–50.
[29] Ibid., 244–5.
[30] Coyle, *Ambulancing*, 41.

and the vehicle, as they navigate the landscape. A striking example is provided by David Rhodes Sparks in *Red Poppies* (1918), describing a situation in which he lies on the vehicle to aid navigation: 'The chief drove with W- on the seat beside him as I lay forward on the fender in an effort to see the road [. . . I] moved only to squeeze in tight to the hood away from a few skidding camions.'[31] Lying on the fender to guide the driver, Sparks enacts another, slightly different, kind of corpographic immersion. With his body lying prone on the fender of the vehicle, he is unusually exposed to the consequences of the vehicle's movement. The vehicle becomes an extension of the body: not only in the sense of augmentation but also in that it synthesises the multiple agency of Sparks and the driver. The vulnerable body, external to the vehicle, underlines the sense that steering the vehicle involves awareness of its field of movement like that of one's own body, so that it does not scrape on the wall or hit another vehicle or person, developing an extended proprioception to be aware of movement and location. The vehicle is not anthropomorphised, nor is the body mechanised: instead, the matter of the vehicle connects with the matter of the body. Thus, the doubling is sometimes extended even beyond bodies, to incorporate the material structures, like the ambulance car, which mediate their environment.

As the ambulance drivers attempt to navigate the torn roads and dodge artillery, they are conscious of the wounded passengers, who scream and cry with every jolt, bump, and sudden turn. Inflicting such pain is beyond the drivers' control to an extent, given their constrained route options, but the need to limit their patients' suffering weighs heavily upon them:

> for half a mile in open view of the Boche trenches the road was shot completely to pieces, I tried to go fast, for full daylight had come, and I was horribly afraid. But the beggars in back all roared so that I could find no heart to make their agony greater. So we plugged along in 'first'.[32]

The desire to get away from danger as quickly as possible gives way to sympathy for the agony of the wounded. Coyle, too, highlights the difficulty of transporting the wounded when every bump and hole in the road furthers their agony, but speed is a matter of life and death:

---

[31] David Rhodes Sparks, *Red Poppies* (Cambridge: Privately Printed, The Riverside Press, 1918), 60–1.
[32] Ibid., 73.

> The trips to the hospital with emergency cases are sometimes very trying to a sensitive driver. A man on a stretcher, shot through the abdomen and suffering unbearable agony, shouting '*tout doucement, mon Dieu, tout doucement!*' ('Go slow, my God, go slow!'), while another man, with both hands off at the wrist, and realizing that only a quick trip can save his life, screams '*Viet, Conducteur, viet,*' meaning 'Fast, driver, fast,' will tax one's powers and sympathy to the limit. Another screams incoherently from sheer pain.[33]

A rapid evacuation to the aid posts would give the wounded the best chance at life, yet it often conflicts not only with the reality of the conditions but also with humane concern for the pain of the wounded. Coyle's comment presents the complexities of care for the bodies of others, and the dilemmas it presents. The effort to provide effective care sometimes requires ignoring the appeals of the wounded:

> It is the desire, of course, for the man at the wheel to do each man's bidding, but, under such conditions, the pleadings of the unfortunate must be disregarded. This might seem harsh, but when one realizes that he is doing his very best, he becomes, after a while, hardened to the work.[34]

In these moments it is not only the pain and discomfort of the wounded in the back of his ambulance that informs the driver's actions but also his acquired medical knowledge of the state of their wounded bodies. Coyle emphasises the psychological hardening that is required of the individual at the wheel, but we must also recognise that this derives from the same motive of care that it seems to override. The 'sensitive driver' is exactly what they become: not only empathetically attuned but also acutely perceptive to the imperatives of their own and their patients' situation.

In her account of ambulance driving, *Golden Lads* (1916), Helen Hayes Gleason describes how 'It was the writhing and moaning of men that communicated their pain to me.'[35] The wounded body transfers its signals in ways that alert the medic to the depths of their pain. The communication of the pain becomes physical for the driver: a vicarious experience of their patients' suffering, which is intensified by the awareness that their welfare is precisely the driver's responsibility. Ana Carden-Coyne suggests that such communicated

---

[33] Coyle, *Ambulancing*, 38–9.
[34] Ibid., 39.
[35] Arthur Gleason and Helen Hayes Gleason, *Golden Lads* (Toronto: McClelland, Goodchild & Stewart, 1916), 1586–8. Kindle.

pain demonstrates that the 'sensory and emotional effects of working with the wounded were deeply personal. Observing, studying, and reflecting on a soldier's wounds indelibly inscribed something of his pain in the minds and memories'[36] of the caregivers. And such emotional alignment of course takes its toll. We might interpret these examples as exhibiting a phenomenological second-person perspective. Carel suggests this is when a parent of a sick child is neither the person experiencing the discomfort, nor the detached, clinical observer: they are instead caught up within the embodied experience, and suffer for their child.[37] While the relationship between patient and caregiver here is necessarily different, these examples show how part of what is felt by the wounded soldier is also felt by the medics, in their second-person perspective, and the imperative to pay attention to movements affecting the bodies in their care.

Such experience is inscribed in the mind and memory of the caregivers, but it is also inscribed on their bodies. In *Behind the Wheel of a War Ambulance* (1918), Robert Whitney Imbrie feels the jolts from the road more profoundly, knowing that it harms the wounded: 'every bump and jolt seems to tear your flesh as you think of those poor, stricken chaps in behind'.[38] It is a visceral and intensely embodied reaction, like sympathy pains for the crying men, produced by imagining the suffering of others, such that the driver experiences the obstacles of the journey as if himself an extension of the wounded patients. Sympathy between driver and wounded becomes an affective connection, experienced as a physical reciprocity between bodies. In such situations the bodies are mutually implicated, in the haptic and affective connections between them within a hostile landscape.

Reading and Interpreting

Medics become cartographic instruments through a corpography in which their bodies negotiate the intricacies of the battlespace, as well as the somatic topographies of self and other. Literal negotiations of the battlespaces require a reciprocal physical and psychological

---

[36] Ana Carden-Coyne, *The Politics of Wounds: Military Patients and Medical Power in the First World War* (Oxford: Oxford University Press, 2014), 18.
[37] Carel, *Phenomenology of Illness*, 54.
[38] Robert Whitney Imbrie, *Behind the Wheel of a War Ambulance* (New York: Robert M. McBride, 1918), 41.

re-mapping, directly affected by the changes to the landscape. This is immersive map-reading, which compels improvised map-making, and specifically re-mapping of the space in terms of the somatic relationship to that space. The immersive experience directly determines the caregivers' explicit negotiations between somatic and environmental topographies, and their invocation of cognitive and affective maps. Given that at this time '[l]andmarks vanished, maps lost all accuracy',[39] it was increasingly necessary to re-map through somatic and sensuous means, and this need is especially evident in the identification of contingent landmarks.

In order to read 'a topography without a frame of reference',[40] medics needed to combat displacement through improvised landmarking. Becca Weir has discussed battlefield topography in terms of Deleuze and Guattari's two kinds of space, striated and smooth, in '"Degrees in nothingness": Battlefield Topography in the First World War' (2007). Weir's article moves away from a discussion of smooth and striated space in terms of nomadic and State territories, towards an exploration of the smooth and striated in relation to fixed points and regridding, uncovering the distinct modernity of the First World War battlefield. I wish to develop the concepts in the direction of such 'regridding' and explore how a consideration of the smooth and striated can aid our understanding of corpographic navigation.

The loss of one's bearings and the struggle to navigate through a collapsed landscape is a source of anxiety, causing a crisis of placement. Borden exemplifies this crisis of placement, in her sketch 'The City in the Desert', rhetorically asking, 'Down where? How do I know? I'm lost. I've lost my way. The road was slippery. There were no landmarks.'[41] The landscape has become smooth space, unmarked by identifiable markers or significant landmarks, and has thus become unmappable. This sense of the environment as a mutable landscape is intensified in Borden's narrative by her subsequent conception of the hospital as a desert. According to Deleuze and Guattari, the desert is an archetype of smooth space, because it is unlimited with no fixed features:

> Smooth space is filled by events or haecceities, far more than by formed and perceived things. It is a space of affects, more than one

---

[39] Paul Virilio, *War and Cinema: The Logistics of Perception*, trans. Patrick Camiller (1984; London: Verso, 1989), 70.
[40] Becca Weir, '"Degrees in nothingness": Battlefield Topography in the First World War', *Critical Quarterly* 49, no. 4 (2007): 40.
[41] Borden, 'The City in the Desert', in *Forbidden*, 74.

of properties. It is *haptic* rather than optical perception. Whereas in the striated forms organize a matter, in the smooth materials signal forces and serve as symptoms for them.⁴²

This is a helpful context within which to interpret the mutable landscape of battlespaces rendered smooth by warfare, given their loss of recognisable organising structure and regulation. The need, however, is to striate the space, and by doing so recover a sense of place. Identifying the smooth is itself a step towards the perception of order: 'Wilderness needs to be "pointed out," nudged towards striation.'⁴³ Subsequently a negotiation of striations can take place, through the corpographic relations between body and land, enabling a regridding of the landscape, and so re-establishing a field of reference.

In the battlespace the traditional landmarks of buildings or topographical features have ceased to be mappable, and so are supplanted by often disturbing alternatives. This is strikingly illustrated in William Boyd's memoir *With a Field Ambulance at Ypres* (1916):

> One is very apt to miss this path on a dark night, but fortunately just at the point where it commences a dead horse lies in the ditch. Judging from the physical signs, it must have lain there for many months, and, however dark the night, I have never heard of any one who has missed that landmark.⁴⁴

It is indicative of the sheer desperation for recognisable features that he finds it 'fortunate' to come upon the rotting carcass of a long-dead horse. Both combatants and non-combatants are continually forced to make points of reference out of the extrinsic, because 'battlefield topography forces [them] to do the "impossible" and discriminate one wilderness from another'.⁴⁵ Combatant accounts often show how in the trenches a half-buried, dismembered leg or arm helps identify a particular trench or direction, indicating how the necessity of spatial improvisation negotiates with powerful affective disturbances. As one account shows, 'Our landmarks were provided for us in the back areas, or by such debris as wrecked aeroplanes, derelict tanks, dead horses and even dead men nearer the front line.'⁴⁶ As

---

⁴² Deleuze and Guattari, *Thousand Plateaus*, 557.
⁴³ Weir, '"Degrees"', 42.
⁴⁴ William Boyd, *With a Field Ambulance at Ypres* (Toronto: Musson, 1916), 95–6.
⁴⁵ Weir, '"Degrees"', 40–1.
⁴⁶ Rogerson, qtd in Ross J. Wilson, *Landscapes of the Western Front: Materiality During the Great War* (New York: Routledge, 2012), 114.

with Boyd's dead horse, the implication is that grotesque and ghastly sights acquire navigational value because they dominate perceptual experience and memory. Such objects are also charged with a sense of *memento mori*, so that navigation proceeds hand in hand with reminders of death, vulnerability, and mortality.

Such reliance on landmarks is specifically necessary for stretcher bearers and ambulance drivers, who regularly had to traverse the smoothness of the shelled landscape on roads between the front-line and medical bases. The experiences of stretcher bearer Charles Horton with the RAMC have been edited into the memoir *Stretcher Bearer!* (2013), in which he explains:

> From our vantage point, we look upon a manmade desert stretching to the horizon on which we can distinguish no landmarks but clumps of what were once trees clustered round little hamlets, but now lifeless sticks, bereft of branches, with no sign of any human habitation remaining above ground.[47]

Again, we find the image of the 'desert', an example of smooth space in need of regridding. A new mode of map-making and map-reading develops as a means to the process of land marking; a new code, with its own kind of measurement, involving idiosyncratic scales in order to seize on any foundation for a field of reference. When the only recognisable features are things that no longer resemble their original form, 'lifeless sticks' and 'clumps', a striating of the space is necessary, however provisional or disturbing the available features may be:

> We pass our own post and press on toward the road, feeling with our feet what have become familiar 'landmarks'. One is a discarded bag of Mills bombs with one grenade showing above ground and already polished with the passing of feet; then the rump of a buried body, which gives a little to the heavy pressure of a boot.[48]

The material and human debris of war itself is foregrounded, placing an emphasis on the extent to which the natural environment has been obliterated by human acts. Recognition and navigation here is explicitly haptic, the medics 'feeling with [their] feet', closely adhering to the haptic character of geographies emerging from the interaction between body and landscape. These sensory signals, which tell

---

[47] Charles H. Horton, *Stretcher Bearer!*, ed. Dale Le Vack (Oxford: Lion Books, 2013), 56.
[48] Ibid., 58.

the body to adjust and beware, are directly connected with fear: the encounter with dangerous objects (actual bombs and grenades) and their deadly human consequences intensifies the body's reaction. Such signals establish strong connections between cognitive and affective dimensions of the immersive evaluations needed to function in such environments.

The identification of landmarks and specific sites is also a way of introducing newcomers to an environment, notionally to ease their transition: 'A kindly finger points out the "sights" – my first view of trenches gashed in the flats along the roadside and of barbed wire entanglements, all the landmarks of a long drive later to become so poignantly familiar.'[49] More than physical navigation is already involved in this evocation of significant sights; there is evidently also affective navigation, engaged with sites of memory and sites of emotion. The urgent imperative, however, is to establish a sense of ordered space sufficient for common understanding and effective communication. It depends on the possibility of recognition which 'results from a sense of ordered space: it is the moment when one knows how a given point relates to other points, an exposure of striation'.[50] The fragility attending these efforts is illustrated in Evadne Price's pseudonymous novel *Not So Quiet . . . Stepdaughters of War* (1930), published under the name Helen Zenna Smith. Commissioned as a female *All Quiet on the Western Front*, it is the story of female ambulance driver Smith (influenced by the real firsthand diary of Winifred Constance Young, since lost). Due to loss of this source, we can never be sure how much of Smith's novelisation is factual, but it is a stimulating portrayal of ambulance work, as well as of a female perspective of war service. At a point in the novel when a new driver shadows Smith's shift, she struggles to navigate through the weather and poor visibility:

> How am I going to point out landmarks when they are all snow covered? The black tree-stump on the left that leads to Number Eight, the shell-hole that indicates the turning to Number Five, and so on. Familiar as the landscape is to me, it takes me all my time to keep my bearings.[51]

---

[49] Maud Mortimer, *A Green Tent in Flanders* (New York: Doubleday, Page, 1917), 47.
[50] Weir, '"Degrees"', 47.
[51] Helen Zenna Smith, *Not So Quiet . . . Stepdaughters of War* (1930; London: Virago, 1988), 73.

The snow returns the route to the smooth space, undoing the striations of recognition, and figuring the mutability of the war landscape itself. It is made evident that, '[f]amiliar as the landscape is', its striations, represented as 'landmarks', are fluid and susceptible to change. Smith's scene suggests the need for a continual process of re-mapping in the consistent attempt to recover bearings not just for the self but also in order to direct others. Following this passage she describes the intuition and improvisation involved in such spatial orientation as having to play 'the role of human road map',[52] an image that echoes Ross Wilson's idea of 'mental maps', improvised by soldiers and others 'from the material of the conflict that littered the way to the front'.[53] Regridding the space requires that affective connotations be transformed into knowledge, in order to renew the space and re-establish some striation. As a 'human road map' the caregiver is both a corpographic and cartographic instrument, whose body is invested in a circuit of affective and cognitive response.

Significantly, such mapping is not just visual but involves the entire body and all of the empirical senses. For example, Imbrie explains, 'Our directions for finding the place were "to go to the fifth smell beyond Verdun," – directions inspired by the group of rotting horse carcasses which were scattered along the way.'[54] The rotting carcasses provide an olfactory landmark, or 'smellmark' (which I will return to later in the chapter), enabling an acquaintance with the space. They navigate through smell, creating and apprehending a sensory map familiar to themselves and shared with their colleagues.

Such techniques of mapping extend to the reading of the body, and the skill of diagnosis. The immersive experience of reading bodies is integral to the immersive learning of triage. As a fundamental technique for effective treatment, triage is underpinned by a foundational notion of organisation; 'triage' deriving from *trier*, Old French for 'pick, cull', denotes sorting out according to quality, and has become a methodology of sorting and hierarchising wounds and complaints. It is widely considered that formal battlefield triage systems were first introduced by Napoleon's chief surgeon Baron Dominique-Jean Larrey in 1812. He was the first medic to insist on the categorisation of wounds during the battles, treating and evacuating the wounded as soon as it was needed. With his introduction of 'flying ambulances', he began to treat numerous wounded on the

[52] Ibid., 75.
[53] Wilson, *Landscapes*, 114.
[54] Imbrie, *Behind*, 98.

battlefield, including amputations, with the remit that 'those who are dangerously wounded should receive the first attention, without regard to rank or distinction'.[55] The triage system was further developed by British naval surgeon John Wilson who, in 1846, argued that the most effective organisation prioritised treatment for those who had the best prospects of survival, while wounds that seemed most probably fatal, even with treatment, should be deferred. It was not until the First World War, however, that the term 'triage' was formally used in a military-medical context. Although following similar remits to Larrey and Wilson for the most part, the approach triggered tensions and disputes over the prioritising of the minimally wounded, in order to be returned to combat quickly.[56] Discussions of the intricacies of triage often focus on the politics of the system, and overlook the immersive and thus corpographic aspect of its organisation.

Arthur Martin, in *A Surgeon in Khaki* (1915), offers up a poignant description of the triage process as a 'sieve':

> It has to sift the lightly wounded from the seriously wounded and the serious cases from the desperate cases. In this process of sifting a large collection of wounded men, it discriminates between those who are fit to be sent to the Base and those who must remain for a longer or a shorter period.[57]

It is an apt metaphor for the triage procedure; the method sorts and sifts through the bodies, their symptoms, and their wounds. As a system with in-built criteria of evaluation, it organises the wounded according to priority and specific need. Borden also comments on the method and process of such sorting, in 'Blind':

> It was my business to sort out the wounded as they were brought in from the ambulances and to keep them from dying before they got to the operating rooms: it was my business to sort out the nearly dying from the dying. I was there to sort them out and tell how fast life was ebbing in them. Life was leaking away from all of them; but with some there was no hurry, with others it was a case of minutes. It was my business to create a counter-wave of life, to create the flow against the ebb [. . .] I had to watch, to see if they were slipping, being

---

[55] Baron Dominique-Jean Larrey, qtd in Kenneth V. Iserson and John C. Moskop, 'Triage in Medicine, Part I: Concept, History, and Types', *Annals of Emergency Medicine* 49, no. 3 (2007): 277.

[56] Iserson and Moskop, 'Triage in Medicine, Part I', 277.

[57] Arthur A. Martin, *A Surgeon in Khaki* (London: Edward Arnold, 1915), 137.

dragged away. If a man were slipping quickly, being sucked down rapidly, I sent runners to the operating rooms [...] It was my business to know which of the wounded could wait and which could not. I had to decide for myself. There was no one to tell me. If I made any mistakes, some would die on their stretchers on the floor under my eyes who need not have died. I didn't worry. I didn't think. I was too busy, too absorbed in what I was doing.[58]

Borden repeats 'it was my business' to great effect, not only conveying the repetitive nature of her actions but also confirming the business-like manner of treatment. Initially, this reads as symptomatic of the detachment necessary for professionalism, especially given its echo of one of Borden's earlier phrases, 'the business of killing and the business of living'.[59] The sorting of patients is sometimes considered frustrating and inadequate, involving a certain coldness and thus carelessness. Yet, the repetition of 'my' reiterates the personal and individual burden of responsibility; that such decisions come down to one's independent interpretation of signs and quick decision making.

Repeated images of water and fluidity pervade the whole of Borden's text but especially this passage with its 'ebbing', 'leaking', 'counter-wave', 'flow', 'slipping'. She adopts an extended tidal metaphor:

> It was like a tug of war with the tide. The ebb of life was cold. When life was ebbing the man was cold; when it began to flow back, he grew warm. It was all, you see, like a dream. The dying men on the floor were drowned men cast up on the beach, and there was the ebb of life pouring away over them, sucking them away, an invisible tide; and my old orderlies, like old sea-salts out of a lifeboat, were working to save them.[60]

The analogy is itself fluid and inconsistent, however, as this passage particularly demonstrates; the water in which the men are drowning is also the 'life' receding from them. The continual back-and-forth movement conveys the instability and precariousness of life for the wounded but also the rhythms of the periodically saturated and overrun space of care. Such intense imagery of water is especially evocative of the triage process itself when we consider it in relation to Martin's sieve metaphor. The fluid metaphors represent

---

[58] Borden, 'Blind', 95.
[59] Ibid., 'The Square', 18.
[60] Ibid., 'Blind', 95.

indeterminacy, and smoothness, which is contrasted with the necessary categorical order of triage decisions. The framework of order is desired in this context, so that the smooth can be countered by striations: 'Whereas in the striated forms organize a matter, in the smooth materials signal forces and serve as symptoms for them.'[61] Triage becomes the 'form' which organises matter, striating the smoothness which is represented by the ebbing life in these wounded bodies: life is the 'force' of which the symptoms need to be read and translated into the system of triage. Order is not only desired but a prerequisite for effective medical care in this environment.

Triage is a system of order that can be likened to the order (or semblance of order) provided by the map. From this understanding of the triage system, and its consequences, we can begin to explore triage and diagnosis in terms of another map analogy, between the reading of the physical environment by soldiers and medics and the diagnostic dimension of identifying symptoms. The medic is both a cartographic and corpographic instrument, creating the map, and a map-reader – where the patient's body is the map. The idea of medical practitioners as map-readers is not a new image: as John Donne writes in 'Hymne to God, my God, in my sicknesse' (1635), 'Whilst my Physitians by their love are growne / Cosmographers, and I their Mapp'.[62] While on the one hand this image relates to the idea of the clinical gaze, and the construction of the body as a semiotic system (discussed in Chapter 3), the map metaphor also suggests the search for recognisable features for symptoms as landmarks.

When looking at a map we search for familiar sites by which to establish our bearings, and the same can be said for viewing the wounded body. This is vividly evoked in *Four Years Out of Life* (1931) when nurse Lesley Smith discusses the experience of treating burn victims. She describes how her burn patients have become so familiar to her that she is not alarmed by their burned faces: 'The burned faces in my own ward were not masks, they were almost painfully individual; each crack, each scarlet patch was a landmark, and most of the sightless eyes had opened and smiled at me at least once or twice.'[63] Again we see the significance of 'landmarks' here, symbols of familiarity with the patients as individuals, but also the devastating signs of the extent of injury to the skin (arguably this

---

[61] Deleuze and Guattari, *Thousand Plateaus*, 557.
[62] John Donne, 'Hymne to God my God, in my sicknesse', in *The Divine Poems*, ed. Helen Gardner (1952; Oxford: Clarendon Press, 1959), 50, lines 5–6.
[63] Lesley Smith, *Four Years Out of Life* (London: Philip Allan, 1931), 234.

is all the more striking because we have moved from the surface of the earth to the surface of the body). There is an inherent tension, however, between the notion of familiarity and the process of diagnosis: the significance of 'symptoms' is their marked deviation from norms, even their notable unfamiliarity. Such 'landmarks' facilitate both diagnosis and the treatment aimed at removing them.

The idea of cartographic reading also extends to the specific systems for diagnostic reading of wounds. The Carrel-Dakin method of advanced wound care, in which tubes were inserted into the skin with flowing antiseptic solution, was introduced part way through the war, and extensively used for treating wounds. Discussing the treatment in *The Politics of Wounds* (2014), Carden-Coyne reminds us that 'this was not a single-process treatment; it required continuous irrigation combined with Alexis Carrel's method of surgical debridement and modern pathology to determine when the wound should be closed'.[64] The modern pathology consisted mainly of monitoring the wounds, and measuring the extent of infection and healing by means of a specific framework and chart for comparison. Coyle provides an explanation and description of the chart:

> [Carrel] and his associates compiled a chart or card, which recorded the age of the patient, the square inches or area of the wound, and such other facts as enabled them, through the handling of so many cases, to establish and chart lines of healing showing the progress of the wound from day to day in its course of treatment, and giving such other information as the proper time of closing the wound and the discontinuing of irrigation, etc.
>
> So accurate did this chart work out that it enabled them to control all cases by its use. Thus, in the event that a wound had not progressed properly in its healing by a certain day to the requirement shown on the chart, the deduction was that the case required special treatment and so it was immediately given the requisite attention.[65]

In its pathological context the chart provides a standardised way of reading the wounds and assessing them, the ability to 'chart lines of healing', clearly suggestive of an analogy between diagnosis and cartography. The chart, as a guide, performs the function of a map, whereby the doctor can immediately recognise the markers of infection and respond with necessary treatment. In Coyle's explanation it is telling that he draws our attention to the chart's 'lines', which

---

[64] Carden-Coyne, *Politics*, 124.
[65] Coyle, *Ambulancing*, 45–6.

play a dual role as markers of both conformity and idiosyncrasy. The lines of the wound and healing skin are akin to the contour lines on maps, revealing the topographies and morphologies of the wound. Reading wounds is an analytical corpography which 'discriminates' between signs according to systems of pathological knowledge, and enables the medic to make sense of symptoms beyond appearances.

Sense Making and Mediating

The different kinds of reading for signs, of a map, of a body, begin with visual orderings, and involve all of the senses. But although the embodied senses are the basis of our perception, they are not independent of affective and psychological qualities, especially in the context of the stress this specific environment elicits. Paul Rodaway's *Sensuous Geographies* (1994) establishes a dual focus on 'the senses both as a relationship to a world and the senses as in themselves a kind of structuring of space and defining of place'.[66] This is the perspective I wish to bring to the reconfiguration and reprivileging of the senses in representations of military-medical space.

The battle environment puts a great deal of strain on an individual's nerves, which is evident in many combatant and non-combatant accounts. The sensory system is a part of the nervous system, but the seemingly interchangeable use of 'nerve' and 'sense' or 'sensation' in these texts demonstrates that there is a feedback loop between meanings of 'nerve' that equate with the sensory system and meanings that equate with affective states. For example, on commencing his medical work, Imbrie 'speculated on just what my sensations would be and wondered whether my nerve would hold when confronted with the conditions I had come to seek'.[67] There is a fundamental, physical impact of such work on the medic, and a unique strain on the senses in consequence of such psychological stress, sometimes resulting in changes to the working of the senses. The intensity of wartime medical experience is compounded by the 'different kinds of sensory stimuli impinging on the consciousness'.[68]

The vulnerability of the physical body is not distinct from the

---

[66] Paul Rodaway, *Sensuous Geographies: Body, Sense and Place* (London: Routledge, 1994), 4.
[67] Imbrie, *Behind*, 23.
[68] Das, *Touch*, 75.

vulnerability of the psychological and emotional body: there is an embodied experiential relation between nerve as sensation and nerve as affect. Given the sheer sensory overload of the environment, there are numerous strains pulling medics towards the limit of their nerves: 'When one is continually under fire one sometimes feels like shrivelling up. Even if one is not hit the effect on the nervous system is trying.'[69] This 'trying' effect encompasses how the whole body responds to threats, suggesting that it recoils inwards, 'shrivelling up'. The body is vulnerable and exposed – as if the nervous system lay outside of the body rather than being internally protected by its frame. We get the sense of a dissolution of the boundary between the nerve endings and the environment, as if the nerves were exposed and raw. Helen Dore Boylston experiences this as 'wearing' on the nerves: 'it is a bit wearing, to be scared for so long at a time'; 'the general nervous strain is wearing us down'.[70] Such an extreme sensitivity serves as a method of self-defence, but it simultaneously heightens anxieties. The main system of bodily control, the internal nervous system, is thus exposed and under unprecedented stress, becoming compromised in new and serious ways.

We witness these men and women getting closer and closer to the edge of their nerves: there are recurrent references in these texts to the 'edge', in both subtle and highly figurative forms, which generate poignant insight into the medics' general psychology and wellbeing. Early in her text, Borden movingly describes how the physical threshold between the trenches and mutilated land is 'just a bleeding edge',[71] the vivid connotations of which pervade the reading of her own text and many others. Borden's use of 'bleeding edge' derives figurative force from its meaning in cartography and printmaking, where it refers to an image or map that extends beyond the page's margins. But the overlap of space, and the blurred boundaries of the battlespace, now also applies to the nerves, in a further figurative sense. The specifically *'bleeding* edge' suggests a porous boundary, where tactile experiences bleed from body to mind. There is no secure boundary between the mind and body, or between body and environment. The 'bleeding edge' is not only physical but also an image of the experiential quality of work at the frontline: these men and women are on the edge of ordinary life, and on the edge of their nerves.

[69] T'Serclaes, *Flanders*, 78.
[70] Helen Dore Boylston, *'Sister': The War Diary of a Nurse* (New York: Ives Washburn, 1927), 103, 131–2.
[71] Borden, 'Belgium', in *Forbidden*, 7.

There are numerous ways in which this idea of 'the edge' emerges in relation to the nerves, especially if we think of being 'on edge' or 'edginess'. Julia Stimson's *Finding Themselves* (1918) offers some explicit comments on nervousness and exhaustion:

> My nurses are beginning to show the effect of the emotional strain. Their nerves are a bit on edge [...] they are not standing the strain and loss as well as they did the last time we were so busy. I have had about a dozen of them weeping, so I am hunting about for more forms of diversion. The continuous rainy, damp weather, the accumulating emotional strain, and the real hard work are having an effect upon them all that is bothering me [...] Naturally I cannot do any weeping here, since I have to be wept on; but there are times when it would be such a comfort to be braced myself.[72]

Stimson acknowledges her own and other nurses' psychological and emotional distress in terms relating physical exhaustion to nervous exhaustion. In the position of Matron she cannot succumb to the emotional strain, and must take care of the nurses in her charge, as well as persisting herself as a caregiver to the wounded. Stimson also recognises that 'It isn't only the women that are affected by these things, the men don't weep often, but they come near to it. And they get just as edgy.'[73] Here is that word 'edgy' again, which speaks directly of the nerves.

The extent of these 'edge' metaphors indicates the pervasiveness of such a sense of the literal and symbolic physicality of raw nerves. The strain on the nerves is succinctly remarked on in Frederic Manning's combatant novel *Her Privates We* (1929), where he explains that 'every sense seemed to be stretched to an exquisite apprehension'.[74] Not only does this make clear the fraught alertness of the nerves, it also vividly conveys an idea of the nerves as matter 'stretched'. The nerves are material, exposed to the onslaught of external stimuli. This is further evident in Gleason's observation that 'bruised nerves refuse to listen to reason, and again and again I ducked as I heard that high wail, believing I was about to be struck'.[75] The nerves conceived as 'stretched' and 'bruised' convey pain and somatic strain, giving a strong indication of the physical pressure involved. Although such hypersensitivity and attentiveness originates as a

---

[72] Julia Stimson, *Finding Themselves* (New York: Macmillan, 1918), 92.
[73] Ibid., 93.
[74] Frederic Manning, *Her Privates We* (1929; London: Serpent's Tail, 1999), 244.
[75] Gleason and Gleason, *Golden Lads*, 858–9.

means of self-protection, it becomes itself a major cause of distress to the psyche, as evident through the discourse on shell shock and neurasthenia, and the significant developments in the psychology of these conditions after the war.

Many accounts, from both combatants and non-combatants, note that the silence and absence of the noise of artillery is more trying on their nerves than the sounds of bombs; that hearing the attack is preferable to suffering the anticipation: 'It was this uncertainty which gave the place a tense, uncomfortable atmosphere so that even when there was no shelling the quiet was an uncanny quiet which was almost harder to bear than the shelling itself.'[76] It is in waiting, and anticipating, with its unbearable expectancy and dread, that the nerves are so stretched and bruised. The nerves are primed for such hypersensitivity by the 'phenomenology of the sound of shelling in an exposed position: the perception of every sound as a physical collision and possible annihilation'.[77] The preference to hear the shells is equally understandable given the old wives' tale that '"The shell that will kill you you won't hear coming. So you'll never know."'[78]

For medics, such conditions present specific challenges given that their nerves and senses need to be minutely attentive. Stimson suggests that she 'needed to use continuous alertness of mind to keep up with the details'.[79] It is only with alertness and attentiveness that they are able to continue to perform their caregiving duties, regardless of the strain on their bodies and minds. In *We That Were Young* (1932), Irene Rathbone describes how during night duty it was 'Difficult not to imagine things [...] under these conditions. Shadows flickered. Wasn't there an alteration in the breathing? She leant forward, every sense alert.'[80] In her caregiving and monitoring role she must remain attentive, and ready to react to subtle changes indicative of the needs of the wounded. The senses, and the overall body, form a receptive device for perceiving what is going on in the environment and in the bodies of the patients. To an extent, the senses are both reactive and protective, involving a reciprocal somatic response between the outward signs given by the wounded body and the moment of recognition in the medic's own body.

---

[76] Imbrie, *Behind*, 58.
[77] Das, *Touch*, 81.
[78] Gleason and Gleason, *Golden Lads*, 688–9.
[79] Stimson, *Finding*, 196.
[80] Irene Rathbone, *We That Were Young* (1932; London: Virago, 1988), 286.

Again, the bodies are doubled: the medics perceive for themselves and for their patients.

In this environment, medics are exposed by their reliance on receptiveness to sensory signifiers. This is particularly visible with regards to the changing influence of sound, as illustrated in Vera Brittain's *Testament of Youth* (1933):

> The noise of the distant guns was a sense rather than a sound; sometimes a quiver shook the earth, a vibration trembled upon the wind, when I could actually hear nothing. But that sense made any feeling of complete peace impossible; in the atmosphere was always the tenseness, the restlessness, the slight rustling, that comes before an earthquake or with imminent thunder.[81]

This is an intensification and reconfiguration of the senses, with sound becoming something she feels throughout her body; more haptic than auditory. In fact, it becomes 'a strange sensory phenomenon – the experience of sound as something tangible [. . .] Sound waves, after a certain volume and intensity, literally touch the surface of the body.'[82] The experience is a kind of synaesthesia, where multiple senses are experienced simultaneously, confusing sense-knowledge;[83] the physical impact of sound is thrown into high relief: 'a shell exploded near us with a sound that convulsed us'.[84] Sound becomes an environmental violation of somatic boundaries, invading the individual's body, where 'every sound impinged on our shrinking sensibilities'.[85] The 'shrinking sensibilities', reminiscent of 'shrivelling' in the earlier example, is a response to the environment's encroachment on the self, in which the nerves are 'impinged' on. Like the 'senses stretched to a new apprehension' and 'bruised nerves', there is physicality to the experience, evoking a direct material contact between environment, sense, and nerves. It effects a transformation in the texture of the senses, manifesting the pervasive fear and anxiety of war, and the exposure of human vulnerability.

Yet, it is significant that such reconfigurations of the senses are not entirely, or always, destructive; they are also built-in mechanisms of self-protection, developed out of communication between

---

[81] Vera Brittain, *Testament of Youth* (1933; London: Penguin Books, 2005), 372.
[82] Das, *Touch*, 79.
[83] Rodaway, *Sensuous*, 6.
[84] Coyle, *Ambulancing*, 79.
[85] Smith, *Four Years*, 34.

the psyche and the nervous system, alert to the 'bleeding edge' of sensation. This is not to suggest that there are no debilitating consequences to the stress of warfare, sometimes permanent, as is clear from the substantial body of evidence and numerous cases, not least from the First World War itself. However, I wish to draw out some details of the functional reconfiguration of the senses, to explore the extent to which it can offer valuable, purposeful, and pragmatic means of functioning.

In some cases the privileging of another sense, whether hearing, touch, or smell, over that of sight is a practical necessity, especially in an environment where visual information is increasingly unstable and unreliable. The reprivileging of the senses here provides for the acquisition of new sense knowledge. As Gregory's 'corpography' shows, 'surviving the [battle-space] required a "re-mapping", the improvisation of a corpography rather than a cartography, *in which other senses had to be heightened* in order to apprehend and navigate the field of battle'.[86] The field of medical care is also apprehended and navigated through a 're-mapping' of the senses. While the senses are strained, this effect on the sensory nervous system can also yield useful diagnostic tools. In some ways this process conforms to Rodaway's concept of sensory 're-assignment', a process in which 'one or more senses (or features of a sense) are marginalised, whilst one or more other senses (or features of a sense) gain prominence'.[87] Sometimes touch, rather than sight, can speed up diagnosis and treatment; for example, Martin describes the spread of gas gangrene, common in many of the wounds encountered, explaining that 'As the organism spreads up the limb it produces a gas of its own, and by pressing on the skin one can feel this gas cracking, like tissue paper, under the fingers'.[88] Touch here becomes a sensory key to identifying the presence of the bacilli and diagnosing the condition. A further example, again depicting the value of touch, can be seen when Borden explains:

> My hand could tell of itself one kind of cold from another. They were all half-frozen when they arrived, but the chill of their icy flesh wasn't the same as the cold inside them when life was almost ebbed away. My hands could instantly tell the difference between the cold of the harsh bitter night and the stealthy cold of death.[89]

---

[86] Gregory, 'Natures', 9 (italics added).
[87] Rodaway, *Sensuous*, 146.
[88] Martin, *Khaki*, 185.
[89] Borden, 'Blind', 95–6.

We can see how swift knowledge of the waning of life would aid the process of triage and the organisation of care when faced with high numbers of casualties. The reiterated fact that it is the hand of the medic, in both examples, emphasises the value of haptic communication. For Borden, distinguishing the coldness of frost from the coldness of life 'almost ebbed away' is a specific learned skill, complementing cognitive processes focused on other signs and needs.

Haptic geographies are not restricted to the hands, however. Imbrie offers a further example of the value of haptic senses, drawing attention to the fact that touch is a sensory resource throughout the body: 'The nights during this period were especially dark. In the pitchy streets of Verdun with the debris piled high on either side it was impossible to see a bayonet thrust ahead. Eyes were of no avail; one steered by *feet*.'[90] The situation of navigating oneself in the dark, and having to rely on haptic clues to aid movement, is an example of feeling topographies; the recourse to feeling with the 'feet', as we have seen with the reorganisation of landmarks, is a means of striation in an otherwise smooth space.

The changing impact of sensory phenomena is especially prominent in the case of sound, which is reconfigured and reprivileged. It is significant that 'sound is not just sensation: it is information',[91] and in this crucial cognitive sense it is increasingly valuable. Das explains the role of 'shell-sense', present in numerous combatant memoirs, as 'a new cognitive category that seems to combine perception of sound, danger and space', whereby 'the ability to judge the direction of a coming shell prevented the psyche from being battered repeatedly with the possibility of death'.[92] Such an ability was not confined to the combatants, but is also evident in numerous medics' narratives. For example, in *The White Road of Mystery* (1918), ambulance driver Philip Dana Orcutt acknowledges how their 'ears are constantly strained to catch the first augmentation of the distant thunder of the guns, and to determine from which end of the sector it comes'.[93] By attuning to this phenomenon, they are aurally locating the direction of incoming shells, and mapping their probable location, in order to determine when and where to move;

---

[90] Imbrie, *Behind*, 123.
[91] Rodaway, *Sensuous*, 95.
[92] Das, *Touch*, 83, 73.
[93] Philip Dana Orcutt, *The White Road of Mystery* (New York: John Lane, 1918), 113.

such a reconfiguration of the use of the senses is a protective strategy used by combatant and medic alike. The difference between listening and hearing is foregrounded here; only in listening can the auditory sense provide information. The nature of sound and specifically the soundscape of shellfire is such that the listening ear can only attain information from a receptive stance, but the absence of the investigative agency this implies does not equate with passivity: 'The auditory self is an attentive rather than an investigatory self, which takes part in the world rather than taking aim at it.'[94] The listening individual does not go in search of the sounds but must wait for auditory signals and deduce the information from them.

The wounded body also offers distinctive sounds; for example, 'a gurgling noise would tell me that it was too late to hurry this one'.[95] Or, like the cracking tissue paper mentioned by Martin, gas gangrene produces 'little crackling noises [...] like bubbles'.[96] These crackling bubbles provide a distinctive 'soundmark', which, like a landmark, provides a specific and shareable reference point.[97] Its meaning is understood in a specialised way: according to Rodaway, 'sense or meaning is derived from previous experience of the same or similar sound and from the context of our experience, activity or intention'.[98] The indexical quality of the soundmark signifies infection and thus points to diagnosis. Similarly, while monitoring her patients Borden remarks, 'I went from hut to hut again, listening for the little sounds of uncertain fluttering life. Was this one slipping away or that one?'[99] Such readings of the medical landscape rely on the reciprocity and reactivity of the medic, who is subject to the sensations of the patients' bodies and the events taking place in them. Smith poignantly describes the auditory signals of death:

> the silence crept in to my very bones, so that I was thankful when No. 6 began muttering and tossing, and I had to hold his hands and talk gently to him. Anything to break the deathly silence [...] I wonder who first used that adjective for silence, and for the first time I realised its force. All other silences are merely passive, the silence

[94] Steven Connor, 'The Modern Auditory I', in *Rewriting the Self: Histories from the Middle Ages to the Present*, ed. Roy Porter (London: Routledge, 1997), 219.
[95] Elizabeth Walker Black, *Hospital Heroes* (New York: Charles Scribner's Sons, 1919), 217.
[96] Ellen N. La Motte, 'Alone', in *The Backwash of War* (1916; London: Conway, 2014), 51.
[97] Rodaway, *Sensuous*, 87.
[98] Ibid., 88.
[99] Borden, 'Enfant de Malheur', in *Forbidden*, 60.

of death is active – it impinges on one's sense of hearing. Something seemed to pluck my arm gently from behind and I found myself constantly turning to look over my shoulder. I could not leave No. 6's hand for one moment or he became restless and excited, and a blind panic was slowly surging up within me.[100]

Through immersion in the environment, Smith learns the distinguishing features of silences, in a specialised and space-specific field of reference. While 'crept into my very bones' might be a common metaphor, almost to the point of cliché, it is not to be overlooked lightly: the metaphor reiterates the very physicality of such a presence. As we have seen with the idea of nerves as matter, the reciprocity between bodies presents itself as touch. The effect is suggestive of the seeming absence of 'silence' as something tangible. As well as identifying silence as a signal, Smith's comment also offers an insight into the embodied presence of death. Death is experienced on the one hand as knowledge and inevitable expectation, but it is also a sense presence, which is haunting – feeling/hearing/smelling death – and begins to offer an insight into the intuitive and hard-to-define qualities of working in such an environment.

Like the olfactory landmark (or smellmark) we saw earlier – '"the fifth smell beyond Verdun," – directions inspired by the group of rotting horse carcasses'[101] – smell can also aid one's apprehension of the environment, spatially and somatically. Both sound and smell supplement the privileged sense of sight, and can aid and quicken diagnosis. There are certain smells which recur throughout these narratives: putrefying wounds, charred flesh, acids and antiseptics, distinctive smells of death. Imbrie regards the growingly familiar scent as a 'war smell': 'that compound of anaesthetics, blood and unwashed bodies'.[102]

Although at different times we can see the respective aid of smellmarks or soundmarks, it is not that the medics attend to these senses above others but rather that they must reprivilege touch, smell, and sound to become as significant and instructive as vision. In such a sensuously saturated space, where '[t]he tang of carbolic and ether competes with a ghastly smell of putrefaction',[103] they must differentiate *within* the sense clues. When it is '"difficult to take a shallow

---

[100] Smith, *Four Years*, 18.
[101] Imbrie, *Behind*, 98.
[102] Ibid., 105.
[103] Smith, *Four Years*, 4.

pulse with all that smashing and crashing"'[104] it is necessary to isolate different sensory signals. They must close off their ear to the noise of bombs to listen to breathing; they must exclude the smell of antiseptic in order to smell the signs of abdominal perforations. Through 'abstraction', 'a process of reduction of the range of a sense dimension which is perceived, that is a restriction of its definition to a limited number of features',[105] they must separate sensuous markers in order to distinguish and diagnose. Often, it is through a symbiosis of senses that they are able to negotiate and navigate. This is especially the case in accounts of treating gas gangrene, where the distinctive smell and sound are foregrounded. The smell becomes 'a specialised olfaction',[106] which aids diagnosis. It is a learned field of reference, specific to this war context, which works alongside a filtering of the senses.

The filtering out of the senses by no means separates them, hierarchically or corpographically, but rather employs them as a set of discrete channels of information. Borden suggests that her categorisation and organisation must work through the co-operation of sensation and knowledge: 'I had to judge from what was written on their tickets and from the way they looked and the way they felt to my hand.'[107] This is a symbiotic gathering of knowledge, supplementing the bureaucratic and systematic label with the evidence of sight and touch, a synthesis of multiple signals.

Such an employment of the senses and instincts is only effective through the reciprocity between mind and body. The nature of phenomenological perception is such that we cannot pin down a clearly defined input, thus the interplay between perception and interpretation is indistinct:

> We arrive at sensation when we think about perceptions and try to make it clear that they are not completely our work. Pure sensation, defined as the action of stimuli on our body, is the 'last effect' of knowledge, particularly of scientific knowledge, and it is an illusion (a not unnatural one, moreover) that causes us to put it at the beginning and to believe that it precedes knowledge.[108]

---

[104] Ibid., 222.
[105] Rodaway, *Sensuous*, 146.
[106] Ibid., 69.
[107] Borden, 'Blind', 95.
[108] Merleau-Ponty, *Phenomenology of Perception*, 43.

It is the senses which structure our knowledge of the world, and how we must in turn behave and act: 'Perception becomes an "interpretation" of the signs that our senses provide with the bodily *stimuli*, a "hypothesis" that the mind evolves to "explain its impression to itself".'[109] The body is the occasion of perception, and intuition and interpretation follow. And in this unique space, the body and environment are mutually implicated in the interpretation of meaning, and response. The role of the medic involves a specific phenomenological relationship with this environment, relying on external stimuli to realise internal, cognitive significance.

While general discussions are often reluctant to acknowledge the many similarities between the experiences of combatants and non-combatant medics, it cannot be denied that the effects on their bodies are occasionally identical. The concept of corpography is vital to an understanding of the demands made upon the body in this setting, and is a valuable way of relating the body not just to the spatial environment but also to somatic and sensuous geographies. The mutual implications between body and landscape, and body and body, determine the distinct somatic and sensuous experience of war and, more specifically, of military-medical care. We cannot, and should not, categorically separate the soldier figure from the medic figure, both of whose bodies are affected by the war landscape. The bodies in the war zone are forced to alter, and relate to the landscape in different and heightened multisensory ways. The movement and action of the individual relies on bodily and perceptual investments in a crucially volatile, unstable landscape.

In this environment all bodies are forced to adapt themselves in order to survive and navigate the landscape, but this need is amplified for medics, who are also responsible for bodies in their care. The medic's experience is necessarily different from that of the combatant, specifically in relation to other bodies. Their bodies, while adapting out of caregiving necessity, are also receivers of involuntary phenomenological disruption: vulnerable to injury and illness, to direct and vicarious trauma, and affective care for the bodies of others. The body of the medic must adjust in response to a mutable topography, but this extends to the bodyscape of the patients; the medic must be alert to the ways in which patients' bodies present injury and healing. Even in a non-military context, it is vital that medics can respond attentively and react to the needs of the patient. In the unstable, often improvised conditions that attend the treatment of wounded patients

[109] Ibid., 39.

in a war environment, there must be an 'alertness of mind that can keep up with the details' of an intense phenomenological onslaught, details which sometimes conform to, and sometimes deviate from, medical expectations. Medicine is not just action but *reaction*, drawing on all perceptual resources in order to diagnose, treat, care.

Chapter 2

Layering: Appropriating Medical Spaces

The physical sites of military-medical care, from swiftly erected field hospitals to commandeered existing buildings, can be understood as spaces of palimpsestic identity. These are places which are disrupted and altered in order to be adapted for medical uses, and they thus acquire different, often contrasting, associations. Different spatial identities are layered literally and figuratively upon the space, drawing attention to its history and in turn affecting how the space is understood. Multiple associations are inscribed on the site, which influence how it is perceived and experienced by those within it. The layering of different functions and identities on the space results in complex interactions between layers of memory and layers of meaning. By considering these polytemporal intersections, we can begin to understand how the spaces are experienced by the medics who interact with them, and consequently represent them. This chapter examines the connotations of literal medical spaces, particularly focusing on the polytemporal, and often conflicting, identities encapsulated within these spaces, and drawing attention to how the layers of spatial identity persist through their interaction with one another.

Of especial interest are those sites which have been co-opted for medical use: places which in civilian hands held altogether different uses but have now been repurposed as hospitals. It is perhaps well known that many stately homes across Britain were used for the rehabilitation of wounded soldiers, but there were also incongruously appropriated hotels and casinos and many improvised sites frantically erected in France and Belgium. The depiction of these sites in the writings of the caregivers who worked in them often reveals the overlapping uses and histories of the space, and allows us to explore how these conflicting associations affect the medics and patients. The visible layers of history within the spaces suggest that the spatial palimpsest is directly concerned with time. We cannot discuss space without paying attention to its relationship with time, so it is necessary to consider these medical spaces through their polytemporality. Within first-hand medical narratives we can often see the interconnected nature of space and time; the experience of each space is informed by its history as well as the present spatial details.

Walter Benjamin and Max Silverman treat spaces as sites of memory. In particular, Benjamin's *The Arcades Project* (1982) sheds light on how place can trigger the intersections of memory and experience:

> The street conducts the flâneur into a vanished time. For him, every street is precipitous. It leads downward – if not to the mythical Mothers, then into a past that can be all the more spellbinding because it is not his own, not private. Nevertheless, it always remains the time of childhood. But why that of the life he has lived? In the asphalt over which he passes, his steps awaken a surprising resonance. The gaslight that streams down on the paving stones throws an equivocal light on this double ground.[1]

Benjamin reflects on the way walking a particular street can be a trigger for memories to flood in. The physical journey along the paving stones triggers a mental journey into the past, producing a 'double ground'. The 'double ground', as Silverman remarks, 'is evocative of the Proustian stumble',[2] a temporary slippage through different layers of consciousness to an unstable other ground. A single site has the potential to accommodate different levels of consciousness; it is not quite being in two places at once but rather a reciprocal relation between the physical site and the psychological terrain of the triggered memory. The 'double ground' has the potential to shed 'equivocal light' on that which has been hidden:

> It is not that what is past casts its light on what is present, or what is present its light on what is past; rather, image is that wherein what has been comes together in a flash with the now to form a constellation. In other words, image is dialectics at a standstill. For while the

---

[1] Walter Benjamin, *The Arcades Project*, trans. Howard Eiland and Kevin McLaughlin (1982; Cambridge and London: The Belknap Press of Harvard University Press, 2002), 416.

[2] Max Silverman, *Palimpsestic Memory: The Holocaust and Colonialism in French and Francophone Fiction and Film* (New York: Berghahn Books, 2013), 25.

relation of the present to the past is a purely temporal, continuous one, the relation of what-has-been to the now is dialectical: is not progression but image, suddenly emergent.³

The 'double ground' enables the reciprocal figural relation between past and present in the 'constellation'. By considering Benjamin's 'double ground' and the 'constellation' of past and present brought together in a 'flash', it becomes increasingly clear that we can think of figurative polytemporality spatially. Silverman argues that 'Benjamin's "image" or "constellation" is one of the most profound descriptions of this overlapping of spatio-temporal sites in which personal and collective memory and the conscious and unconscious collide.'⁴ The dialectical image is beyond time; that is, it remains in each time and place. With Benjamin's monumental 'flash' we are able to consider the polytemporality of identities impinging on one space, and explore how memories can be manifest in the contemporary moment, in order to reconceptualise and understand contemporary events.

Building on Benjamin's thesis, Silverman explains how the exposure of traces and superimpositions 'draws [. . .] together and creates correspondences between different elements so that the "oppositions" between the fragment and the totality, past and present, here and elsewhere, and movement and stasis are not in fact oppositions but in permanent tension'.⁵ When history is made visible in the present moment, it impacts how the space is experienced both in its present inhabitation and in the future recollection of personal or cultural memory. If multiple temporal events occur in the same space, our attention is drawn towards the relationship current events have to the past, present, and future: 'one can be seen within the other, just as history must be made visible (recognizable) in the present moment'.⁶ Recognising that each space is a 'double ground' allows us to be fully aware of the ongoing temporal tensions across the spatial layers.

In this chapter I want to develop the idea of the palimpsest, Silverman's term for the spatial notion of memory, as a way to understand the overlap and coexistence of layers, times, and identities. Silverman's work on palimpsestic memory frames how we might explore the polytemporality of space:

---

³ Benjamin, *Arcades*, 462.
⁴ Silverman, *Palimpsestic Memory*, 26.
⁵ Ibid.
⁶ Ibid.

the present is shown to be shadowed or haunted by a past which is not immediately visible but is progressively brought into view. The relationship between present and past therefore takes the form of a superimposition and interaction of different temporal traces to constitute a sort of composite structure, like a palimpsest, so that one layer of traces can be seen through, and is transformed by another.[7]

Silverman emphasises the overlap of temporal attitudes, drawing out the relevant ways in which different temporalities emerge and interact with one another. Vital to the image of the palimpsest is the fact that its different layers interact and affect one another. The figurative palimpsest is fundamental to our understanding of how traces, hauntings, and superimpositions directly impact the experience of space, and significantly how they impact a specific moment of time in that space. Each layer is transformed by another, with 'different temporal traces' coexisting, interacting, and amassing to create a polytemporal, spatial palimpsest.

This chapter is organised around the different layers which make up the spatial palimpsest, drawing on discussions from Silverman, in conjunction with Benjamin, Freud, Lefebvre, Spivak, and Derrida, to explore the palimpsestic nature of wartime medical spaces, and the significant relations between the multiple layers of the spatial experience. Appropriated buildings and improvised medical spaces draw attention to unsettling incongruities between old and new uses. As a result of the polytemporal interactions there is, sometimes consciously, sometimes incidentally, a curious juxtaposition between prior and present uses. Incongruities often emerge aesthetically in descriptive contrasts between decoration, materiel, and medical objects, as well as figuratively, through personal and cultural associations with the space. Such incongruities are not confined to interior spaces but can also be found in commentary on contrasts within the natural environment. In *The Doctor's Part* (1918), James Robb Church describes the incongruous nature of the ruined landscape, which is a useful starting point from which to consider juxtaposition:

> There is an incongruity about a battleground in a cultivated country. It seems all wrong somehow; not to belong; as though some black hideous excrescence had appeared on a flowering plant. There yet remain enough of the landmarks of happy peace to show what had existed before the scorching breath of war and passion had swept

[7] Ibid., 3.

over everything turning the green to brown and breaking and twisting into fantastic shapes all the homely marks of normal existence.[8]

Church's poignant acknowledgement here echoes the previous chapter's discussion on the consequences of war on the landscape; yet it goes further, recognising the pre-war traces which persist and remain, demonstrating the explicit and often shocking incongruities of war and nature. Unlike the landmarks previously explored, these remaining 'landmarks of happy peace' are not navigational markers but traces of the past. Explicitly, Church focuses on nature, namely the fields and farmland which become the sites of battle. The pastoral is corrupted by the influence of war, and while the familiar is being destroyed, there are memories and faint traces of the life before. Church contrasts the fecundity of nature, with the 'black hideous excrescence' of war, its greenery with the war-torn blasted ground. Enough faint traces of 'what had existed before' remain for him to feel the juxtaposition of previous beauty and peace with the corruption that war has brought to the country and to the land. While Church comments on war's effect on the natural environment, we can build on his images and impressions to consider how imposed medical spaces affect their spatial and temporal sites.

The 'cultivated' earth is significant in Church's comment; in a landscape designed for cultivation and the repeated turning and churning of the soil, we are given the impression that the earth has little to conceal. The earth is directly related to the means of living: its cultivation is a comfort, a familiar process, in which human actions mirror nature's cycles. Cultivation of the earth is designed to inspire growth and fruition; war, on the other hand, brings corruption and barrenness. The 'homely' is broken and twisted, corrupting the memory and perception of 'normal existence', so that the familiar is made strange. Church's description evokes uncanniness: the 'homely', *heimlich*, is distorted and corrupted, becoming unfamiliar and *unheimlich*. The war landscape, twisted and coated in 'hideous excrescence', conveys the impression that nature and individuals can no longer 'belong'. Yet, there is an inherent tension, and potential contradiction, in the multiple meanings of *unheimlich*: the uncanny is not only the familiar turned unfamiliar but also 'applies to everything that was intended to remain secret, hidden away, and has come out in to the open'.[9]

---

[8] James Robb Church, *The Doctor's Part* (New York: D. Appleton, 1918), 200–1.
[9] Sigmund Freud, *The Uncanny*, trans. David McLintock (1919; London: Penguin Classics, 2003), 132.

The *unheimlich* is also that which is unfamiliar because it was never known. Freud's notion of 'unhomeliness', *unheimlich*, 'was more than a simple sense of not belonging; it was the fundamental propensity of the familiar to turn on its owners, suddenly to become defamiliarised, derealized, as if in a dream',[10] and of the propensity for the hidden to emerge. Such psychological disturbance resonates here, especially when we take into account Church's feeling that 'it seems wrong'. The experience of the uncanny arises with the polytemporal layering of the space and the consequent jarring incongruities and juxtapositions.

This chapter moves on from juxtaposition and the uncanny to invocation and superimposition. Alternative associations can change how we relate to a space; the palimpsest is built up over time, from traces of the past, but also accumulates imposed associations, which are not always unequivocally tangible. These traces, events, and legacies are fundamentally social, and a result of human interactions with a site. Henri Lefebvre, in *The Production of Space* (1974), explains:

> Every social space is the outcome of a process with many aspects and many contributing currents, signifying and non-signifying, perceived and directly experienced, practical and theoretical. In short, every social space has a history, one invariably grounded in nature, in natural conditions that are at once primordial and unique in the sense that they are always and everywhere endowed with specific characteristics (site, climate, etc.).[11]

Use of the space and the ways in which it is interacted with (and on) amass numerous associations, ranging from the personal to the cultural, encompassing both material traces and the atmospheric resonance of past activity. Social action within a space is not always visible, in the present or in retrospect, but traces persist through metaphor and the analogical invocation of past action.

Metaphor encourages us to rethink that which is being invoked, and what is being analogised. The invocation of other times and places, through metaphor, allows us to rethink the relationship of the present to past events: 'The true power of metaphor is not that it simply substitutes one thing for another but that, by drawing together two distinct elements through a perceived similarity, it connects them

---

[10] Anthony Vidler, *Architectural Uncanny: Essays in the Modern Unhomely* (Cambridge, MA and London: MIT Press, 1992), 7.

[11] Henri Lefebvre, *The Production of Space*, trans. Donald Nicholson-Smith (1974; Oxford: Blackwell, 1991), 110.

[. . .] and, in the process, reinvents both.'[12] Metaphorically imposing different associations on a space creates opportunities to reconsider how the space is situated emotionally and culturally: 'Metaphor is a creative and transformative process in that it unsettles or defamiliarises habitual meanings, connects the most unlikely elements and, in doing so, reshapes our perceptions.'[13] Metaphor and analogy, comparison and contrast, foreground the presences which hover at the edges of experience. Exploring the metaphors invoked in association with the medical spaces encourages us to rethink past and present events and the relations between them.

Finally, the chapter examines the traces of the past that remain and re-emerge. The identities of the space do not fade away with each epoch of its use but instead become the layers that make up how the space is experienced, and how it is represented in memory and recollection. The ever-present trace of past existence insists that nothing can be entirely erased. One of the most defining metaphors of these narratives and experiences, one that epitomises the inherently complex tension between past and present, is that of ghosts and haunting. Spectrality is hinted at in a number of these narratives, but the image is explicitly invoked in Vera Brittain's *Testament of Youth* (1933), when she recognises her 'world for a kingdom of death, in which the poor ghosts of the victims had no power to help their comrades by breaking nature's laws'.[14] That the hospital space becomes 'a kingdom of death' is straightforward in its connotations, but what is particularly significant is the suggestion that the ghosts of former patients continue to reside in the hospital. The space is not just 'a kingdom of death' in terms of a place where many have died but is, and continues to be, the residence of deceased soldiers. The result is an image of the living and dead residing side by side. The medical spaces are haunted by 'the poor ghosts of the victims' who continue to walk these halls. Brittain does not refer literally to supernatural presences but rather, more figuratively, to the inability to escape what has taken place within these walls. The living are layered alongside the dead. Traces, memories, imprints of the deceased remain, ingrained on the figural

---

[12] Max Silverman, 'Trips, Tropes and Traces: Reflections on Memory in French and Francophone Culture', in *Anamnesia: Private and Public Memory in Modern French Culture*, ed. Peter Collier, Anna Magdalena Elsner, and Olga Smith (Bern: Peter Lang, 2009), 19.
[13] Ibid.
[14] Vera Brittain, *Testament of Youth* (1933; London: Penguin Books, 2005), 416.

site, adding layers to the palimpsest, and directly affecting how the space is experienced.

Juxtaposition

From the very beginning of the conflict, existing buildings and sites were reappropriated as improvised medical spaces: sites which included hotels, schools, asylums, châteaux, casinos, and racecourses. The reappropriation and improvised use of such sites often resulted in unusual incongruities and juxtapositions between, for example, the aesthetic surroundings and decor, and the medical objects, sterilisation, and the wounded bodies within. Church sums up the pragmatics of reappropriation by noting that The Hotel Palace, 'like many structures of that kind [...,] has changed its sphere of usefulness as the normal life of the state has been turned upside down'.[15] Both spaces of grandeur and spaces of habitual, quotidian routine are suspended in time, their ordinary, 'normal life' arrested by the change in their 'sphere of usefulness'. But the space is not just suspended for the duration, it is fundamentally changed, so that the story of the space is revised and extra narratives are added. As a result of this polytemporal overlap, the old and the new are contrasted, in often strange and unsettling ways.

Tensions between the old and the new are profound in 'The Beach', from Mary Borden's *The Forbidden Zone* (1929), which centres on a coastal casino reappropriated as a hospital. Borden illustrates the incongruity by adopting the casino-turned-hospital as a device to draw out the irrevocable changes caused by the war, and the conflicting perspectives of decadent excess and the broken wounded. True to Borden's literary style, the scene is darkly playful and ironic, as well as by turns euphemistic, highly satirical, and caustic in tone. This passage is not from Borden's first-person perspective but instead adopts the voices of a wounded soldier talking with his wife on the beach. We quickly realise that in fact this is not unambiguously their speech but perhaps instead their inner monologues, highlighting the disjunction between what can and cannot be said, and the strained communication between man and wife now that he is wounded beyond repair.

With the vividness of a filmic set piece, the woman muses on the beauty of the beach, the sea, and the sky, and ponders the creation of

[15] Church, *Part*, 109.

the beach over millions of years: '"How many millions of years has it taken to make the beach? How many snails have left their shells behind them, do you think, to make all this powdery sand? A million billion?"'[16] The scene immediately focuses on the issue of time: not only are we forced to consider prehistoric processes, we are also made to see the disjunction between before and after the war. The insurmountable changes it has brought are represented by temporal distance and strangeness, expressing the remoteness of the marriage and relationship the couple previously had, set against the backdrop of a world to which they cannot return. The wounded soldier, trying to smooth over the cracks rapidly widening in their relationship, invokes images of pleasure and leisure:

> 'A little jazz now and a baccarat table would make all the difference, wouldn't it? It would cheer us up. You'd dance and I'd have a go at the tables. That's the casino over there, that big thing; that's not empty, that's crowded, but I don't advise you to go there. I don't think you'd like it. It's not your kind of a crowd. It's all right for me, but not for you. No, it wouldn't do for you – not even on a gala night.'[17]

Trying to bridge the gap between them, he attempts to go back to the pleasures of normal life but only heightens the contrast with the present. The parallel between the uncanny transformation of the casino and the failing relationship locates the physical breakage of the wounded body within a temporal fracture between before and after. Here the scene descends most notably into the irony of juxtaposition: the temporal distance collapses when the scene focuses in on the present use of the casino. Pleasant memories or illusions are shattered by the mutation of the casino crowd into a hospital full of broken soldiers.

The power of Borden's remarkable passage is the overriding significance of the dramatic irony in the 'gala night' euphemism:

> 'They've a gala night in our casino whenever there's a battle. Funny sort of place. You should watch the motors drive up then. The rush begins about ten in the evening and goes on till morning. Quite like Deauville the night of the Grand Prix. You never saw such a crowd. They all rush there from the front, you know – the way they do from the racecourse – though, to be sure, it is not quite the real thing

---

[16] Mary Borden, 'The Beach', in *The Forbidden Zone* (1929; London: Hesperus Press, 2008), 33.
[17] Ibid., 35.

– not really a smart crowd. No, not precisely, though the wasters in Deauville weren't much to look at, were they? Still, our crowd here aren't precisely wasters. Gamblers, of course, down and outs, wrecks – all gone to pieces, parts of 'em missing, you know, tops of their heads gone, or one of their legs. When they take their places at the tables, the croupiers – that is to say, the doctors – look them over. Come closer, I'll whisper it. Some of them have no faces.'[18]

The uncomfortable euphemism of battle as 'a gala night' conflates war with social excess and indulgence. The casino is an incongruous setting for a hospital, a site of salvage for wrecked bodies imposed on one of recreation and pleasure. Borden employs the game metaphor to disturbing effect, paralleling the doctors with 'croupiers', insinuating the role of chance in war and survival. But it is an even more uncomfortable parallel than that: the suggestion that the doctors are dealers depicts them as complicit in the cruelty of chance. The description of the soldiers and their wounds is both conflated and contrasted with the social indulgence and corruptive effects of gambling. Comparable analogies between gaming and operations emerge in a number of places in these narratives: 'The billiard-room had become an operating theatre';[19] 'he is laid on the table which the wounded men call the "billiard-table"'.[20] Such a play on games and gambling is even more explicit in surgeon Fred Albee's declaration that 'The great casino [at Calais] was filled with the wounded, as well as the bathing houses. Where once the baccarat wheels had spun, the surgeons now gambled with death.'[21] The implication is not only that survival is a game of chance but also that venial moral corruption and exploitation becomes mortal in the context of war. The baccarat wheels become Fortune's Wheel, and the doctors, whose interventions are also a force of violence and corruption, are subordinate to chance and fate.

Borden simultaneously introduces issues of identity and privilege by bringing in a critique of class. The casino has a specific clientele, who must have the right of entry. Invoking this idea of the casino as an exclusive club, with a glance at the glorification of wounds,

---

[18] Ibid.
[19] Baroness de T'Serclaes, *Flanders and Other Fields* (London: George G. Harrap, 1964), 41.
[20] Georges Duhamel, *The New Book of Martyrs*, trans. Florence Simmonds (New York: George H. Doran, 1918), 169.
[21] Fred H. Albee, *A Surgeon's Fight to Rebuild Men* (New York: E. P. Dutton, 1943), 140.

Borden suggests that even the lowest ranking soldier, if he has the wounds, has the right to entry: '"All that's needed is a ticket. It's tied to you like a luggage label. It has your name on it in case you don't remember your name. You needn't have a face, but a ticket you must have to get into our casino."'[22] The medical label doubles as both a ticket of entry and a ticket to travel, becoming the proof of an individual's identity. The class-bound privilege of the casino clientele is overthrown, at the bitter cost of a new mark of status: the cultural perception of wounds as badges of honour. Because their wounds mark them as worthy, men who before would not have previously gained entry to the casino now have the right to enter this privileged space. This is not social progress, however, but a mark of how much the site itself is altered.

Borden leaves us in no doubt that the casino is 'funny' and 'queer', and that all things are being turned upside down:

> 'It's a funny place. There's a skating rink, you ought to see it. You go through the baccarat rooms and the dance hall to get to it. They're all full of beds. Rows of beds under the big crystal chandeliers, rows of beds under the big gilt mirrors, and the skating rink is full of beds, too. The sun blazes down through the glass roof. It's like a hothouse in Kew Gardens. There's that dank smell of a rotting swamp, the smell of gas gangrene. Men with gas gangrene turn green, you know, like rotting plants.'[23]

The juxtaposition of the grandeur and leisure of the 'skating rink', 'baccarat rooms', 'dance hall', 'crystal chandeliers', and 'gilt mirrors' with the rows of beds highlights the squalid present reality. The wounded can only be assimilated to this idea of place as rotting hothouse plants.

The scene also features in Borden's later, more traditional, autobiography *Journey Down a Blind Alley* (1946), which describes her first nursing experience in the Dunkirk casino, where 'The sick lay helpless under the great tarnished chandeliers of the gaming rooms, the rows of dingy beds were reflected to infinity in the vast gilded mirrors.'[24] There is something uncanny, almost grotesque, in the image of wounded bodies reflected in the glass under the crystal chandeliers. The wounded are made into spectacles 'reflected to

---

[22] Borden, 'The Beach', 35.
[23] Ibid., 36.
[24] Borden, *Journey Down a Blind Alley* (New York and London: Harper & Brothers, 1946), 8.

infinity', across time and space, an echoing revulsion made more forceful by contrast with the temporal, worldly pleasures of the casino. We can identify the Freudian 'uncanny' in this incongruity, in the turning of the familiar on its head 'suddenly to become defamiliarized, derealized'.[25] Once a place to show off wealth and excess, the casino has now become a spectacle from which to recoil, defamiliarised by its new 'sphere of usefulness'.[26]

A similar impression is suggested by Sarah Macnaughtan, in *A Woman's Diary of the War* (1916), where the concert-hall turned hospital offers a sight of incongruity:

> At night time the concert-hall, with its platform and gay pillars and the forgotten air of gaiety about it, always struck me as being particularly sad. It seemed like a living protest against the destruction of simple happiness in a big provincial town, where men and women had enjoyed music, and tea at little marble tables, and a concert-hall with singers in it. Now it was plunged in darkness, and nurses with tiny lights, going up and down between the straight little beds, had to listen to cries of 'A boire, mademoiselle,' all through the night.[27]

While the contrast is not explicitly uncanny, there is sadness and pause about the juxtaposing sights. The space clings faintly to its history of pleasure and recreation, but this is twisted by the contrast of 'a great arch of decorated ceiling, all gay with painted flowers'[28] above the beds of wounded soldiers.

The uncanny, which is evoked by this reappropriation, is not always inherently disturbing or frightening; in some cases the uncanniness is subsumed by irony or merely strange juxtaposition. The inhabitants are out of place, and time is 'out of joint', but the effect is not always straightforwardly fear or revulsion. Among the numerous auxiliary hospitals set up across Britain, in addition to the buildings appropriated in France and Belgium, one notable example was the requisition of Brighton's Royal Pavilion and Gardens Estate. The Pavilion is distinctive for its Asian architectural and decorative influences; its external minarets and domes are complemented inside by exotic designs and furniture with Japanese, Chinese, and Indian influences. The Pavilion Estate, including the lawns, the Dome, and

---

[25] Vidler, *Architectural Uncanny*, 7.
[26] Church, *Part*, 109.
[27] Sarah Macnaughtan, *A Woman's Diary of the War* (London: Thomas Nelson and Sons, 1916), 38.
[28] Ibid.

the Pavilion, became a military hospital for Indian soldiers from 1914 to 1916, and a hospital for Limbless Soldiers from 1916 to 1920. As a local newspaper observed at the time,

> Never surely, were there more beautiful hospital wards, with their decorated walls and ceilings, their wonderful chandeliers, their broad sheen of mirrors. All the morning sun streams in at those long windows, which open direct on to the eastern lawn. [. . .] There are some forty beds in the Banqueting Room and Music Room, and from fifteen to twenty in the others.[29]

The Pavilion Estate provided necessary space for the recovering wounded, but the choice of venue remains visually, and to an extent ideologically, disconcerting. The decision to use the site for Indian soldiers was partly necessity and partly founded on colonial intentions; some considered that the appropriation of this specific space would strengthen the Indian nationals' loyalty to the British Crown.[30] The patients were aware of the significance and history of the place, with many of the soldiers expressing 'pride and even shock that they were staying in a building once inhabited by the King'; but the fact that the Pavilion had ceased to be a royal palace long ago, and had since become a function hall, was kept from the patients.[31]

Although there are very few first-hand records of experiences in the Pavilion, in part due to censored correspondence, there is a short story by a hospital visitor, which provides insight into the juxtapositions produced by such a site acting as a hospital. After visiting, Alfred Ollivant penned 'The Indian Hospital' (1916) as part of a collection of short stories concerning the war. Ollivant particularly comments on the appearance of the building and the aesthetics of the adopted hospital space, describing how '[o]n the seats by the lawns under the elms [Indian soldiers] were sitting, strange indeed and yet not entirely out of place in that semi-Oriental environment.'[32] Instantly the 'strangeness' here is not so much the displaced function of the building but rather an encountering of the Other: Indian men. Of course, the Indian men are not 'out of place' in terms of the

---

[29] *Brighton Herald*, 28 November 1916.
[30] Samuel Hyson and Alan Lester, '"British India on trial": Brighton Military Hospitals and the Politics of Empire in World War I', *Journal of Historical Geography* 38 (2012): 19.
[31] Ibid., 29.
[32] Alfred Ollivant, 'The Indian Hospital', in *The Brown Mare, and Other Studies of England Under the Cloud* (London: George Allen & Unwin, 1916. Reprint, Leopold Classic Library), 85.

Layering 79

aesthetic setting, fitting in culturally with the oriental style of the Pavilion, but the interior juxtaposition of patient beds and gilded chandeliers intensifies the strangeness of the contrasts between patients and palace.

The juxtaposition is not only visual but a source of multisensory incongruities. Ollivant recalls the long history of the Pavilion, with echoes of previous visitors:

> These floors which of old answered to the nimble feet of courtiers, the swish of ladies' skirts, and the music of mazurkas and minuets, echoed now to the stump of crutches, the slither of slippered feet, and the shuffle of carrying parties bearing patients to and from the operating theatre set up in what was of old, perhaps, the royal pantry.[33]

There is auditory contrast here between the 'swish' and 'music' of the past and the 'stump' and 'shuffle' of patients now occupying the space. Ollivant also explicitly draws out the juxtaposition between the royal legacies of the place and the movement of the wounded soldiers throughout, with a list of previous occupants:

> In that vast gilded room where of old King George gossiped, and Fox drank, and Wilberforce expounded; where in our time General Booth has preached, and Paderewski played, and Lloyd George spoken, the floor to-day is white with beds. They are under the chandelier, against the organ, on the terrace, beneath the balcony – flocks of them. And in each white bed is a brown face, uplifted to the banyan-tree that by a happy accident decorates the roof.[34]

By identifying previous historical events, particularly political, Ollivant draws out the continuum of the space as a feature of history. Under the auspices of that same aesthetic and atmospheric grandeur, in the spaces where high-flung luminaries indulged, the soldiers and caregivers retrace the steps of notable figures.

The powerful juxtaposition of the Pavilion rooms can be seen in surviving photographs and magic lantern slides. Figure 2.1 depicts the Music Room as a ward, showing how the room is taken over by rows of beds, and boards are placed on the ground and put up on the lower half of the walls, separating the people from the adornment. But the abiding sight is the image of dangling chandeliers above the wounded lying in bed. The chandeliers are intricately fashioned to resemble exotic plants, with etched glass extending the ceiling

---

[33] Ibid., 87.
[34] Ibid., 90.

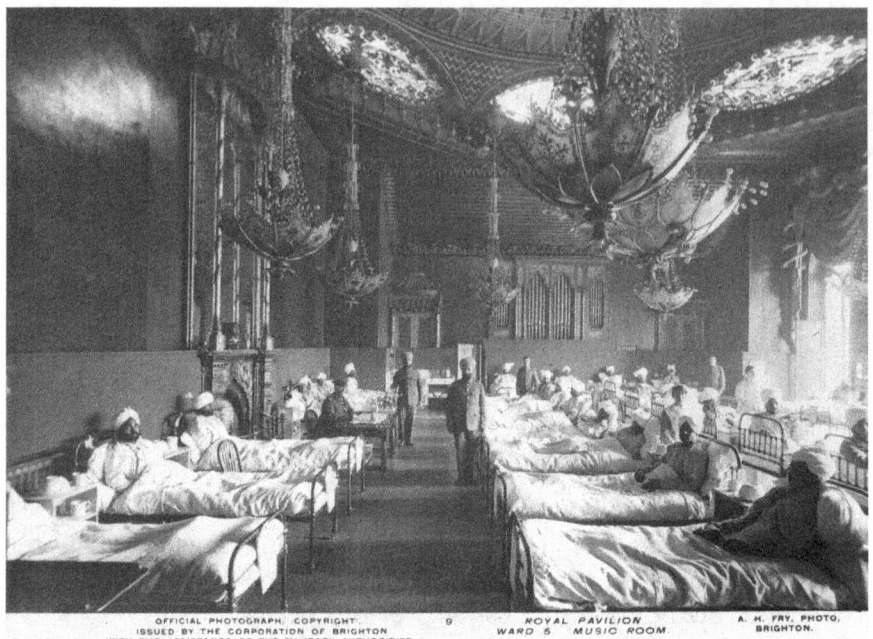

Figure 2.1 Magic lantern slide showing Indian soldiers in beds in the Music Room of the Royal Pavilion during its use as a military hospital, 1915. Royal Pavilion & Museums, Brighton & Hove. BY-SA 4.0 Creative Commons.

designs down into the room. Here we can get an idea of how the men reflected in the chandeliers and mirrors of Borden's casino may have looked. The monochrome of the image is only able to reveal the contrast between the white of the sheets, the patients' clothes and their turbans, and the grey of the rest of the room, when in reality the room is brightly decorated with bold reds, oranges, and gold.

Similarly, as Figure 2.2 illustrates, the Brighton Dome was taken over by rows of wounded soldiers. In 1850 the Dome, which had been used as riding stables, was sold off by the Crown to the town of Brighton, and it was used as cavalry barracks between 1856 and 1864, until it was renovated and reopened as a concert hall and assembly rooms in June 1867. The rich history of the Dome's use is dominated by performance and leisure, which is visible in the design and decoration of the space, as seen in Figure 2.2.[35] The

---

[35] Considering the multi-layered history of the Dome, particularly as a performance space, raises some interesting links across diverse epochs of time: in 1974 this

Layering 81

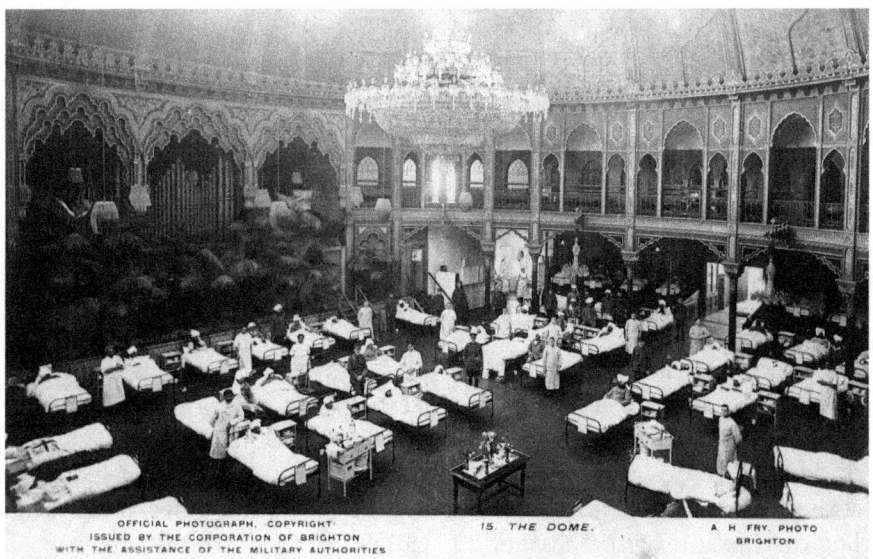

Figure 2.2 Monochrome photograph showing Indian soldiers in rows of beds inside the Dome during its use as a military hospital, 1915. Royal Pavilion & Museums, Brighton & Hove. BY-SA 4.0 Creative Commons.

building is set up to have a central staging area, to be seen from all positions: typically located in front of the palm trees, located on the left of the photograph, by the organ pipes. The Pavilion's oriental style continues in the Dome, with arches and pillars decorating the roof and walls, and with the expansive chandelier central to the Dome. Like the Pavilion photo, there is an extreme contrast between the chandelier and wounded men lying on beds. The Dome, as a space of performance and entertainment, exemplifies the unsettling juxtaposition of signs of decadence and signs of pain and injury. Precisely because of the building's style and decoration, as well as its royal legacy, the sight of soldiers occupying these spaces is particularly jarring, creating a tension between its different identities.

In a less uncanny, but still unsettling, example, Adelaide Walker further illustrates the jarring juxtaposition of a hotel-turned-hospital:

was the location of ABBA's Eurovision Song Contest victory, with 'Waterloo', and considering this in conjunction with its time as a military hospital raises even further examples of strangeness, juxtaposition, and an almost humorous uncanniness.

> My first experience at a Base hospital was at Versailles in August, 1914. The hotel 'Trianon Palace' had been converted into a hospital. The rooms (which in 1919 were used for the compiling of the peace terms) were full of terribly wounded men, dying of gas gangrene and tetanus. [. . .] It was a curious sight – almost unbelievable – the brightly lighted hall, scarlet carpeted stairs (there had been no time to remove the carpets), stretcher after stretcher being carried in with wounded men caked in mud and blood, some of whom had lain out for days before they could be got at. Beautiful bedrooms were filled with hospital beds, all occupied.[36]

The juxtaposition of the decor and grandeur with the 'terribly wounded' provides a visual conflict between sights of beauty and sights of pain. The urgency of the appropriation of the space precluded the removal of the richly luxurious decoration and features, with the result that the 'curious sight' is all the more unsettling. The distraction of the aesthetic features of the setting is interrupted by the 'wounded men caked in mud and blood' who occupy the luxurious space of the hotel suite. The hotel itself was relatively new, only built in 1910, but it had already played host to a number of significant political and cultural figures, and thus very quickly acquired multiple layers of identity. The 'Trianon Palace' is not only situated close to the Palace of Versailles but, as Walker proleptically acknowledges, would later be the site of the initial dictation of the terms of the Treaty of Versailles in 1919. Consequently, this is a place of immense contrasts not only aesthetically but in the historical 'constellation' of past, present, and future. Walker's proleptic aside describing what is to come in that place instils the idea that the identities of space are multidirectional. Not only are the identities of spaces comprised of new features interacting with new uses, they are retrospectively informed by subsequent instances of the overwriting of space, which overlay figurative and imaginative associations on the site of memory.

Overlaying

The overlaying of different associations on a space is not always an exclusively conscious or unconscious act. How we interact and associate with a space is as much about social actions as it is about

---

[36] Adelaide L. Walker, 'Experiences at a Base Hospital in France, 1914–1915', in *Reminiscent Sketches* (London: John Bale, Sons and Danielsson, 1922), 54.

cultural or personal connotations: 'The uncertain traces left by events are not the only marks on (or in) space: society in its actuality also deposits its script, the result and product of social activities.'[37] Social actions and interactions leave their marks on a space, which are abstract associations just as much as they are visible or tangible scars on the landscape.

An alternative atmosphere or environment may be invoked in order to alter, perhaps to ameliorate, the space in the minds of its inhabitants. In order to establish a sense of stability for a temporary space, there is a need to enrich its associations. This was apparent in the previous chapters' discussion of the mental remapping of landmarks, where associations are superimposed on something unfamiliar in order to establish a functional connection; but this can be extended to overlaying associations on a space. From one perspective, the overlaying of alternative associations might be an effort to conceal what is beneath: a repression for which we can appeal to the Freudian concept of 'screen memory', where one memory serves as a substitute for a more distressing one. Invoking alternative identities and memories may be an attempt to dilute revulsions, discomforts, and the overwhelming sense of the *unheimlich*. This may be done through a kind of familiarisation of unfamiliar and terrifying scenes, by superimposing alternative features in an effort to either re/acquaint with or ameliorate the emotions of the space; invoking associations of 'home', for example, to provide more pleasant and comforting associations.

The concept of 'home' can take on new meaning and symbolism for those experiencing the alien conditions of war. To an extent, home may be idealised, and a desire for the domestic increases the longer the individual is away from home comforts and the familiarity of their own country. But, by invoking the right associations, the distance between home and away can be bridged. We can consider this superimposition of home to be a reversal of the uncanny, but it is not as straightforward as simply undoing the *unheimlich*. Given that 'Freud was taken with this slow unfolding of the homely into the unhomely, pleased to discover that "*heimlich* is a word the meaning of which develops in the direction of ambivalence, until it finally coincides with its opposite, *unheimlich*"',[38] then we could extrapolate that the *unheimlich* becoming *heimlich* inevitably becomes *unheimlich* again. The unfamiliar can be made to be familiar, but in

---

[37] Lefebvre, *Space*, 110.
[38] Vidler, *Architectural Uncanny*, 25.

the process it inevitably becomes unfamiliar again. The concept of home is held in a tense vicious circle of known and unknown, and the superimposition of home cannot protect from every discomfort.

Transplanting the impression of home, with its inherent associations of comfort and security, to military-medical environments is an effort to ameliorate the setting, and distance it from the frontline. Initially, it may seem that these domestic images illustrate the natural desire for home – the unconscious invocation of the sanctity of home and hearth. To think of home is to recall not only the familiar but also safety and security. After all, home 'is the human's territorial core, providing stimulation, security, and identity',[39] and it is the 'territorial core' which the human instinct always tries to protect. For Gaston Bachelard, 'A house constitutes a body of images that give mankind proofs or illusions of stability.'[40] In the specific medical environment, it is imperative that the patients feel safe and secure, which is not easy in a traumatic context in which the guns often rage on around them. Yet, the invocation of 'home' is not only for comfort; grasping on to the association of home is also something that can be shared with others. While those involved are not picturing the same version of home, there is commonality in the associations of 'home', which allows the act of remembering to become a recollective communal bond.

It has often been noted that the medical space comes to resemble a family, with 'communities of men and women, at times mirroring the "family drama" of siblings and parents. Fellow wounded were "brothers"'; Matrons, mothers or teachers; doctors, fathers; and nurses, sisters or 'potential lovers'.[41] This is superficially confirmed in Olive Dent's nursing account, in a view expressed by one of her patients: '"I know now why you nurses are called 'sisters'. You *are* sisters to us boys"', and the ward is referred to as a 'family of sixty-five people'.[42] Julia Stimson, in her role as Matron, refers to the nurses in her control as her 'children'. She takes on the responsibility of an overall maternal figure, with an intense emotional investment: 'it is

---

[39] J. Douglas Porteous, *Landscapes of the Mind: Worlds of Sense and Metaphor* (Toronto: University of Toronto Press, 1990), 107.

[40] Gaston Bachelard, *The Poetics of Space*, trans. Maria Jolas (1958; Boston: Beacon Press, 1994), 17.

[41] Ana Carden-Coyne, *The Politics of Wounds: Military Patients and Medical Power in the First World War* (Oxford: Oxford University Press, 2014), 11.

[42] Olive Dent, *A Volunteer Nurse on the Western Front* (1917; London: Virgin Books, 2014), 37, 75.

worrying to have my children sick'.[43] Even as she identifies herself as the mother figure, she acknowledges her own desire for a maternal shoulder: 'I would have given a good deal myself to have had some one like Mother to weep on', but in her capacity as Matron, mother, and source of comfort, she must continue 'to be wept on'.[44]

The invocations of family are only a slight remove from the emotional security of home, which is mostly implied through images of domestic objects. It seems that it is the material environment of home which is most desired. Borden illustrates how the physical domestic object has a psychological and emotional impact: when a visiting General

> admired the white coverlets with their gay patterns of pink or red flowers [...] I said [...] that the coverlets came from Selfridges and cost two shillings apiece, and I thought they were worth it. They even [...] made the difference sometimes between a man's slipping away or back into the world when he woke.[45]

While Borden explains that these images of home aid the rehabilitation of the patients, we can also see how domestic objects serve to anchor the experience in something more familiar; to remove the imagination from the violence, chaos, and devastation of the trenchscapes, and to focus on images of stability and security.

Borden goes beyond the literal acquisition of domestic material to an effusive use of domestic metaphors, which complicate the depiction of the patients in partly contradictory ways. Borden's use of domestic metaphors can express an objectification of the wounded as, for example, when patients are 'pulled out of the ambulances as loaves of bread are pulled out of the oven', or are 'spread like a carpet'.[46] Her domestic images include an extended comparison between the soldiers and items of clothing:

> Just as you send your clothes to the laundry and mend them when they come back, so we send our men to the trenches and mend them when they come back again. You send your socks and your shirts again and again to the laundry, and you sew up the tears and clip the ravelled edges again and again, just as many times as they will stand it [...] We have all the things here for mending, the tables and the

---

[43] Julia Stimson, *Finding Themselves* (New York: Macmillan, 1918), 97.
[44] Ibid., 92.
[45] Borden, 'The Priest and the Rabbi', in *Forbidden*, 105.
[46] Borden, 'Conspiracy', in *Forbidden*, 79; Borden, 'Blind', in *Forbidden*, 101.

needles, and the thread and the knives and the scissors, and many curious things that you never use for your clothes.[47]

Borden equates familiar, typically feminine, domestic chores with the care of patients, but the effect of her comparison between the sewing of shirts and the sewing of bodies is disturbing, not consoling. Ultimately, the familiar becomes unfamiliar. Unassuming tasks such as cleaning, laundry, or mending clothes are uncannily twisted into the evidences of warfare. Such domestic imagery takes on new and more sinister meaning when viewed in relation to the grotesque, as the next chapter will explore. In the desire for home comforts we can see the tension which the atmosphere of the uncanny exploits, disrupting the invocation of the security of the hearth.

Home can have a myriad of meanings and associations for different people, extending from the domestic sphere to nationhood. Various combatant accounts demonstrate how soldiers attempted to familiarise themselves with the alien space and invest foreign fields with personal or emotional value through a 'process of naming and renaming sites' known as 'Tommification', for example by christening trenches 'Piccadilly' or 'Knightsbridge'.[48] It was psychologically important for soldiers to develop a personal sense of place, and so combat the strangeness of their environment. This overlaying of familiar place names evidences a kind of screen memory, buffering the impact of the strangeness and unfamiliarity of the war environment: not just because it is a different country (for many) but because the landscape itself is inherently unsettling. While psychoanalytic thought on screen memories might focus on the conflict between memories, or on the idea of traumatic experience resisting the imposition of a more positive screen, in the context of this discussion it proves more useful to consider Michael Rothberg's comment that screen memory 'more closely resembles a remapping of memory in which links between memories are formed and then redistributed between the conscious and unconscious'.[49] This interpretation of Freud's psychoanalytic memory concept invokes a specifically spatial conception of the processes of memory and cognition. 'Remapping' occurs between and across the different layers. Appropriated to the current context, 'remapping' becomes a more helpful way

[47] Borden, 'Conspiracy', 79.
[48] Ross J. Wilson, *Landscapes of the Western Front: Materiality During the Great War* (New York: Routledge, 2012), 121.
[49] Michael Rothberg, *Multidirectional Memory: Remembering the Holocaust in the Age of Decolonization* (Stanford: Stanford University Press, 2009), 14.

to understand how these individuals relate to space, both in the moment and through recollection.

Invoking a pleasant recollection can certainly be an attempt to lessen the power of the strange and uncanny place, but it does not erase what fundamentally disturbs. The overlay of home, as an ameliorating association, itself takes on new connotations in its new relation to the warzone – and, to some extent, the contrast between the warmth of familiar home and the coldness of the strange and hostile place is increased. Invocations and superimpositions in the work of these medic-writers do not always aim at amelioration or familiarisation. In fact, many such metaphorical associations are invoked in ways that force us to rethink both what is invoked and what is analogised. Rather than overlaying an association that familiarises and comforts, the analogy is intended to disrupt and unsettle. Examples of such metaphors and similes in the accounts include the image of hospital wards as 'subterranean caves or catacombs',[50] and their being 'more like a charnel-house than a place of succour'.[51] In these instances there are Gothic connotations, making the hospital space threatening and harmful, and increasingly strange and Other. It is not exactly memory that is being invoked, but rather the reference draws out relationships which ensure we reconsider both it and the Other. For Borden, the casino-turned-hospital becomes 'like a hothouse in Kew Gardens. There's that dank smell of a rotting swamp, the smell of gas gangrene.'[52] The image forces upon us a feeling of sensuous saturation, but also ensures we do not experience the invoked Kew Gardens hothouses in the same way again.

Invocation through metaphor has the power to force us to reconsider both the tenor and vehicle of the analogy, enabling us to see each of two, often divergent, associations in a new light. By building on Silverman's discussion of metaphor at the start of this chapter, we can see that,

> In relation to memory, metaphor allows a past sensation, and, as Proust says, all its associations, to flood into the present, creating new relationships between past and present and, hence, forcing us to rethink both. Metaphor does not simply collapse one element into the other so that they become the same; nor does it leave both

---

[50] Elizabeth Walker Black, *Hospital Heroes* (New York: Charles Scribner's Sons, 1919), 48.
[51] T'Serclaes, *Flanders*, 53.
[52] Borden, 'The Beach', 36.

elements intact and separate. Its beauty lies in the fact that it creates correspondences through similarity while maintaining differences.[53]

We rethink the association and in turn rethink the relationship between its terms, old and new. The creation of 'new relationships between past and present' is key here: in the invocation of metaphor an association is overlaid on the space, but this in no way erases what is underneath. The invocation and overlaying of meanings and associations constitutes a figurative palimpsest, which is made up of often abstract, typically emotive associations. Yet, the figurative palimpsest only gains such power by the very tangible presence of the historical palimpsest. The overlaying of different layers is further affected by the emergence of the marks underneath, which always exist and, once they present themselves, can never be erased.

Traces

The 'different temporal traces' of the spaces include the continued visibility of the past, evidencing that 'the historical and diachronic realms and the generative past are forever leaving their inscriptions upon the writing-tablet, so to speak, of space'.[54] Like Freud and Silverman, Lefebvre also invokes the image of the palimpsest, to illustrate that marks of action do not disappear over time but instead remain in traces left behind.

In the midst of war, the quintessential pastoral scene of farmland and fields is deeply disturbed by the effects of military actions. The exploding artillery, the military presence, and the scars on the land infect and corrupt nature, churning it inside out. Poignantly, Church illustrates

> the contrast between the struggle of man in his passion and the struggle of nature to hold to her own inflexible order the things that are hers. And finally, nature will conquer, for when the 'shouting and the tumult dies, the Captains and the Kings depart' all this will come back to the purpose for which it was designed and the scars of man will heal on the landscape and remain as faint evidence of spent passion.[55]

---

[53] Silverman, 'Trips', 19.
[54] Lefebvre, *Space*, 110.
[55] Church, *Part*, 213–14.

This becomes especially resonant when taken in conjunction with Church's quote at the start of this chapter, which contrasted pre-war natural beauty, still evident in 'landmarks of happy peace', with war's corruption of the land. Nature, however violently disrupted, outlasts and persists. But it also becomes evident, in slight tension with Church's description here, that 'nature', in whatever form we might conceive of it, is intrinsically caught up in the 'struggle of man'. Church quotes Kipling's poem 'Recessional' (1897), the origin of those eternally monumental words 'lest we forget', underlining the importance of memory while emphasising the difficulty of the persistence of traumatic memories and traces in the psychological or physical environment. There is no guarantee that 'the scars of man will heal on the landscape', since history has proven that there does 'remain [. . .] evidence of spent passion'; the traces of human action persist.

Many things may remain: 'the present contains traces of the past'; 'these traces could be anywhere – in everyday objects, in a piece of music, in a sound, in a taste – because they are, in fact, in ourselves'.[56] There is a complexity to 'traces of the past' because there are two kinds of 'trace': first, those manifest in tangible revenants and remainders of the past, and second, those that persist in personal and cultural perceptions of the past ('in ourselves'). The following discussion foregrounds examples of the physical perseverance of history, demonstrating that these are often inextricably entangled with traces within cultural memory. Acts on the surface reveal what lies underneath; past and present mix so that not only are the spaces palimpsestic with previous epochs of their existence, they reveal themselves as simultaneously polytemporal spaces.

Borden's 'The City in the Desert' is most evocative of the enduring traces of the past, bringing together the destruction of the landscape with the frantic erection of another field hospital: 'What is this city that sprawls in the shallow valley between the chalk hills? Why are its buildings all alike, gaunt wooden sheds with iron roofs? Why are there no trees, no gardens, no pleasant places?'[57] The 'city' represents the erected field hospital, frantically imposed on the site of a destroyed village. Borden emphasises the contrast by recalling personal memories of the village:

---

[56] Silverman, 'Trips', 18.
[57] Borden, 'The City in the Desert', in *Forbidden*, 73.

> Queer, isn't it? This new city where there was a snug town huddled round a church with cafes, little tables under the trees, schoolboys in black pinafores playing on the church steps. The inn, I remember, was famous for its cuisine. What has become of the fat landlord who watched the plump succulent fowls turning on a spit and dripping?[58]

Borden foregrounds the strange contrast between the now-ruined town of the past and what has been imposed in its place: 'Now, there's this place that looks like a mining town or a lumber camp, only it can't be.'[59] Borden both names and refuses the appearance of the new development, the significance of which is belied by its resemblance to a 'mining town' or 'lumber camp'. Everything about this site has been twisted: it has become an uncanny ruin yet still in the process of change. Instability is the keynote of this scene, which not only evokes the site's unsettling transformation but also conveys the influence of place on selfhood. As argued in the previous chapter, to be unaware of your surroundings is to lose your bearings, compromising your somatic and spatial relationship; but the confrontation with flux and discontinuity, as this scene foregrounds, also has the quality of an encounter with the unreal, the 'derealized', and the threatening; its insistent absurdity is that of a dreamscape. The depiction of the transformed landscape, the ruin of the past and the marks of that ruination, epitomises Freud's 'encounter with a derealized world': 'In the traces left behind, an excess of matter is produced, serving to remind the visitor that beyond the appearance of presence, uncanniness and otherness coincide with an abnormal mode of embodiment.'[60] Borden's 'The City in the Desert' perfectly captures this idea; the ruin constantly hints at an 'excess of matter', unassimilable to the incomprehensible surface of the present.

The 'desert', the quintessence of smooth space, as explored in the previous chapter, produces displacement and uncertainty. Borden's incessant questions reiterate the loss of her bearings, evoking the search for something stable within this quicksand-like pit:

> The village I used to know at the cross-roads was gone. Everything was sliding in the mud and all the villages that I knew here once upon a time had slipped clean out of sight, and now all the men and horses

---

[58] Ibid., 74.
[59] Ibid.
[60] Dylan Trigg, *The Memory of Place: A Phenomenology of the Uncanny* (Athens, OH: Ohio University Press, 2012), 275.

in the world with wagons and motor lorries seem to be pouring after them into a gulf.[61]

She is faced with the ruin of a village she once knew; more than a spatial loss of bearings, this is also a temporal disjunct. Dylan Trigg suggests that 'a parallel intercession occurs in the appearance of ruins, whereby we witness a *reciprocity between the destruction of the past, the lapse in time thereafter, and the unexpected persistence of damaged materiality in the present*'.[62] In this site, time collapses in on itself; the past merges with the present and future, 'pouring [. . .] into a gulf' in time. The collapse of the village and all its pleasant places, gardens, and people, is not the only consequence, however: 'Ruination is [. . .] not simply the erosion of materiality, but also the preservation of a past, manifest not by the fulfilment of that past, but through its decay.'[63] Even in the collapse of previous structures, the past is preserved and survives in the present, as 'damaged materiality' and decay.

Borden's pervasive imagery of fluidity represents both the literal and metaphorical damage and wreckage of war. The vulnerability and instability of the landscape is evoked by mudslides and quicksand; the violence and weaponry of war has destabilised nature, to the point where the earth needs to be 'tied [. . .] down with wire'.[64] Water also represents the destructive power of war, with the roar of guns evoking the crashing of waves: 'You tell me there is no sea over there. But the roar? Surely there are waves breaking, and this desert is wet as if a great wave had just receded.'[65] Borden invokes the beach and shoreline with a composite of overlapping images, depicting the shoreline, coastal processes, and the crash of artillery. This story features in the second part of her text, entitled 'The Somme', so it seems this scene is located not near the coast but further south, likely a depiction of her field hospital at Bray-sur-Somme. The sound of the sea is a metaphor for the 'roar' of war. The effects of artillery are likened to the effects of tidal erosion or flooding, encompassing dual images of natural and unnatural abrasion of the landscape.

One of the more complex aspects of Borden's passage concerns the paradoxical image of the Flood as both cleansing and destroying. Equating the war with the Flood is not unusual, appearing for

---

[61] Borden, 'The City in the Desert', 74.
[62] Trigg, *Memory*, 268 (italics in original).
[63] Ibid., 269.
[64] Borden, 'The City in the Desert', 74.
[65] Ibid., 73.

example in Brittain's reference to her 'friends who went down in the Flood'.[66] Borden's story contains definite biblical connotations, with references to Noah and the suggestion of a second momentous event on a biblical scale: 'Perhaps there has been a new flood, since Noah, and you and I slept through it.'[67] The destructive import of Flood imagery is clear, but parallels also develop with the idea of retribution for human violence and sin depicted in the Genesis story:

> Now the earth was corrupt in God's sight, and the earth was filled with violence. And God saw the earth, and behold, it was corrupt; for all flesh had corrupted their way upon the earth. And God said to Noah, 'I have determined to make an end of all flesh; for the earth is filled with violence through them; behold, I will destroy them with the earth.'[68]

Adoption of the Flood narrative allows for a comment on the state of mankind, but what makes Borden's images far more complex is the sense that it offers no resolution. According to God's covenant, the biblical Flood is a one-off event: '"I establish my covenant with you, that never again shall all flesh be cut off by the waters of a flood, and never again shall there be a flood to destroy the earth"',[69] but the war underlines the failure of the Flood event in cleansing and punishing. A crisis of faith is introduced in the suggestion that there is still violence beyond God's power, and even beyond this new Flood, in the city built in its ruins: 'some strange industry, some dreadful trade is evidently being carried on here', 'to serve some queer purpose'.[70] However, this bleak image of the field hospital is balanced against a sense of the place as a site of refuge. Despite the destruction of the town, a place of refuge has at least been hastily established, offering sanctuary to the 'lost men, wrecked men, survivors from that other world that was here before the flood passed this way, washed up against the shore of this world again by the great backwash'.[71] That 'other world' has been washed away by war, but the 'survivors' cast up here, in this 'city of refuge', have at least some hope of being 'saved for this world'.[72]

[66] Brittain, *Testament*, 411.
[67] Borden, 'The City in the Desert', 75.
[68] Genesis 6:11–13, English Standard Version.
[69] Ibid., 9:11.
[70] Borden, 'The City in the Desert', 73.
[71] Ibid., 76.
[72] Ibid., 77.

Yet, the passage presents a complex and inconsistent representation of life, with primordial images intensifying throughout. Borden insists at first on the barrenness of nature and absence of life: 'No sign of life, no fish fossils, or rotting seaweed, no plant of any kind, not a blade of green; a dead sea must have lain here.'[73] The picture becomes more complex, however, when she introduces life, or versions of life: 'Perhaps a new race of men has been hatched out of the mud, hatched like newts, slugs, larvae of water beetles.'[74] Borden offers unsettling connotations of distorted and corrupted evolution, perhaps even into a degenerative breed. These scenes articulate an evolutionist narrative, in which 'human existence has its remote origins in the "primordial slime" from which all life was said to arise. In the minus narrative of devolution, sliminess may be posited as well as the logical terminus of mutable human identity'.[75] Borden represents 'a scene of extinctive degeneration',[76] while simultaneously evoking a kind of Sartrean protoplasmic slime as an 'image of destruction-creation'.[77] Borden continues, saying, 'But slugs who know horribly, acutely, that they have only a moment to live in between flood tides and so built this place quickly.'[78] These are images of primitive life, a transient breed of men who will not last long: bred to act and fight, and to be destroyed by the next wave of attack. If the remnants and final traces of life are hereafter a mutated 'new race of men', human identity is irredeemably degenerate. Such an atmosphere of degeneration is disturbing, showing that 'When "something that should have remained hidden" does come to the opening, then the shock of the uncanny becomes a battleground between possession of oneself and oneself as being possessed'.[79]

---

[73] Ibid., 73. This is reminiscent of Liam O'Flaherty's combat narrative *Return of the Brute* (London: Mandrake Press, 1929), which is dominated by primordial and primitive imagery, such as the description of 'the mysterious gloom of the primeval earth, where no life had yet arisen; no sap of growing things; nothing but worms and rats feeding on death' (ibid., 23).

[74] Borden, 'The City in the Desert', 74–5.

[75] Kelly Hurley, *The Gothic Body* (Cambridge: Cambridge University Press, 1996), 34.

[76] Sarah Cole, *At the Violet Hour: Modernism and Violence in England and Ireland* (New York: Oxford University Press, 2012), 65.

[77] Jean Paul Sartre, qtd in Mary Warnock, *The Philosophy of Sartre* (London: Hutchinson, 1965), 102.

[78] Borden, 'The City in the Desert', 75.

[79] Trigg, *Memory*, 301.

The scene risks succumbing to a 'revenge of matter'[80] on body and psyche.

The degeneration narrative is apocalyptic, but Ariela Freedman characterises Borden's perspective more appropriately when she suggests that Borden 'situates herself and this place not as post- or pre-apocalypse, but between apocalypses, in the moment between flood tides, in the interim quiet'.[81] The situation is urgent, tense, and momentary because 'in the wet desert, where a flood has passed and another will come',[82] nature and life are contingent and unpredictable. This profound loss of solid ground is evident in other war texts, for example Henri Barbusse's *Under Fire* (1916), one of the earliest First World War combat novels published, which includes many water and flood images:

> We see lakes, and between the lakes there are lines of milky and motionless water. There is more water even than we had thought. It has taken everything and spread everywhere [. . .] There are no more trenches; these canals are the trenches enshrouded. It is a universal flood. The battlefield is not sleeping; it is dead.[83]

For Barbusse, there is little worse than this mass of water and its encroaching presence. The 'universal flood' gestures towards the biblical Flood narrative, hinting at the idea of cleansing – but this flood is no blessing; the fear of being engulfed overwhelms any connotations of renewal. The imagery parallels that of Borden's passage, especially her reference to a 'dead sea'.[84] Although Barbusse's landscape is not the same as the one Borden depicts, it is equally a landscape transfigured by war. Barbusse's evocation of 'sullen Stygian immensity'[85] is echoed in Siegfried Sassoon's later description of the 'Stygian significance of war';[86] and although Borden does not use images of Styx, Hades, or the Underworld, her repeated reference to

---

[80] Santanu Das, *Touch and Intimacy in First World War Literature* (2005; Cambridge: Cambridge University Press, 2008), 51.
[81] Ariela Freedman, 'Mary Borden's *Forbidden Zone*: Women's Writing from No-Man's-Land', *Modernism/modernity* 9, no. 1 (2002): 115.
[82] Borden, 'The City in the Desert', 75.
[83] Henri Barbusse, *Under Fire*, trans. W. Fitzwater Wray (1988; Floating Press, 2009), 526–7.
[84] Borden, 'The City in the Desert', 73.
[85] Barbusse, *Under Fire*, 544.
[86] Siegfried Sassoon, *Memoirs of an Infantry Officer* (1930; London: Faber and Faber, 1997), 72.

the Christian God, 'wrath of God', 'angry Eye of God'[87] does imply a parallel with hell, confirming the idea that 'hell is water'.[88]

Jay Winter's reading of Barbusse argues that 'Only after the Flood, when devastation is universal, can men turn away from the abominations of war and of the societies that made it.'[89] The Flood narrative provides 'an apocalyptic language in which [Barbusse] could locate his yearning for a world without war'.[90] It is not implausible to read in Borden's passage the similar employment of the apocalyptic image of the flood, but her suggestion of another flood, of being in-between tides, does not imply a fresh or clean slate, but rather the expectation that human acts of violence are nowhere near their end; the flood tides will recur just as successive attacks, successive wars occur. 'Every social space has a history, one invariably grounded in nature, in natural conditions that are at once primordial and unique in the sense that they are always and everywhere endowed with specific characteristics':[91] in the derealised space of war landscape, an 'excess of matter' continues to enact permutations of its 'revenge'. Even the cleansing Flood is not powerful enough to erase the traces of human action.

Earthly traces and memories are also strikingly manifest through a figurative microbiology. Arthur Martin makes reference to the bacteria embedded in the earth of the battlespaces, imagining continuity between wars in terms of bacterial infection:

> The hardships of the Crimean trenches – cold, rheumatism, and frostbite – have been repeated on the Yser. Gangrene was rampant amongst the wounded of Wagram, Austerlitz, and Borodino, and amongst the French and British wounded at Vittoria, Salamanca, Badajos, and other great battles of the Peninsula, and it has startlingly reappeared on the Aisne and in Flanders.
>
> Historians of that day refer to it as hospital gangrene, or the gangrene so common after any surgical operation or wound of that time. It may, on the other hand, have been the same gas gangrene that has ominously complicated so many of our wounds in France and Flanders. The bacillus which produces this gangrene may belong, for all we know to the contrary, to a very old family of bacilli, who would look upon pedigrees dating to William the Conqueror with an

---

[87] Borden, 'The City in the Desert', 75, 77.
[88] Barbusse, *Under Fire*, 532.
[89] Jay Winter, *Sites of Memory, Sites of Mourning: the Great War in European Cultural History* (Cambridge: Cambridge University Press, 1998), 186.
[90] Ibid.
[91] Lefebvre, *Space*, 110.

aristocratic contempt when his own stretched back to the beginning of time.⁹²

Martin's comment links contemporary events with history along the lines of bacteria and disease, and makes use of his scientific knowledge of infection to comment on the continuum of war. Martin illustrates the power of natural history to dwarf human action, as a genealogical lineage beyond the scope of human agency. He combines images of the spread of infection to trace a medical history of previous warfare and then, with 'very old family', 'pedigrees', and 'aristocratic', translates human pretensions to ancestry to a much vaster biological timescale. While the present war is culturally and symbolically informed by the traces of past conflict, he suggests, it is literally connected to them via the traces of infection and disease. In a comparable way, we continue to see the remnants of the First World War a century on, with the Iron Harvest and the continued yield of human and animal remains and unexploded ordnance.⁹³ Conflict leaves its residues on the field, the psyche, and the page. Thus, we continue to inherit the infected earth.

By inheriting this figuratively infected earth, the present moment is haunted by the ghosts of past conflicts. Precisely because 'the act of remembering is always in and of the present, while its referent is of the past and thus absent',⁹⁴ its motion is to draw the past into the present. Drawing together different epochs of French conflict, Church describes the adoption of the Château de Compiègne, former seat of royal government, built by Louis XV and restored by Napoleon Bonaparte. It is now

> a Military Hospital for medical cases. The tri-color hangs over the gate and French soldiers are on guard in the courtyard, and sick in the interior. And so the summer palace of the kings and emperors has come under the rule of the present master of France, – War with all its stern necessities to satisfy. I wonder if the shade of the Empress Marie Louise flits through the salons which once were hers, but now

---

⁹² Arthur A. Martin, *A Surgeon in Khaki* (London: Edward Arnold, 1915), 194.
⁹³ Experts believe that it will take another 500 years for all ordnance to be found and destroyed. Belgian bomb disposal warn that much of the ordnance continues to be dangerous, carrying huge, often toxic, payloads. DOVO-SEDEE, Guided Tour, Houthulst, Belgium, 4 July 2018.
⁹⁴ Andreas Huyssen, *Present Pasts: Urban Palimpsests and the Politics of Memory* (Stanford: Stanford University Press, 2003), 3–4.

are wards for the descendants of the soldiers who helped to place in power her liege lord, the great Napoleon?[95]

Again, we can recognise the juxtaposed realities of wounded soldiers and the former royal palace in which they are being treated. Becoming a military hospital is only the latest layer of the building's identity and history. The legacy of the building's past is not faded but resurges in this new stage in its history, where past and present come together. In the act of reappropriating an existing place, especially one with a rich history, it is inevitable that ghostly traces of the past persist. The sick and injured who occupy the palace are now superimposed on the traces of its previous use; the wounded inhabit the same space as the 'Empress' shade', which haunts the space. The uncanny effect of the juxtaposition and incongruity is crystallised in the ghost who 'flits through salons which once were hers'.

Such a sense of haunting and ghostliness frequently emerges in these narratives. In a curious image, Martin invokes the concept of the 'séance' as expressive of his surgical role: 'At the agreed time everything was certain to be prepared, and I just had to scrub up, put on my sterilised apron, cap, and rubber gloves, and be ready for my part of the *séance*.'[96] The comparison between surgery and séance is unsettling, casting a suspicious light on the surgeon, consolidated in an overriding sense of ritual: 'at the agreed time', 'everything [...] prepared'. He hints that the function he is about to perform is conversing with or reinvoking the dead. On the one hand, the limbs he is about to amputate are already 'dead', and are perhaps unquiet ghosts: as the figure leading the séance, he can ease their passing. On the other hand, ghostliness in relation to amputations evokes the phenomenon of phantom limbs, which Martin could be alluding to here, commenting on the fact that he is creating more phantoms through amputations. It is also possible that Martin's use of 'séance' is punning on its ordinary use, in French, for 'sitting, session' (interspersions of French language are common in many of these narratives). The 'séance' also relates to issues of memory; by invoking the dead it attempts to recover the presence of something which has passed. The séance is an active recalling of ghosts, and memories, within the contemporary moment, and layers the living and the dead together. Ghosts come to inhabit the same space as the living, in the present moment.

[95] Church, *Part*, 122.
[96] Martin, *Khaki*, 181.

In this 'kingdom of death', as identified by Brittain, the ghosts of other soldiers sit beside the patients. By recounting their stories and conversations, Brittain relates how this is also experienced by the patients:

> 'if that ain't the chap I 'elped Jim to bury more'n a week agone'
> [. . .]
> 'Do you really mean that in the middle of the battle you met those men again whom you'd thought were dead?' [. . .]
> 'Aye, Sister, they're dead right enough. [. . .] And it's our belief they're fightin' with us still.'[97]

These men are dead, and yet somehow they are still present, returning to their comrades and '"fightin' [. . .] still"'. This may be taken as a supernatural phenomenon of haunting; or it may instead express the persistence of the past, psychologically manifesting itself as a spectral presence. Those whose lives have been inscribed so intensely on a space are never really gone; though dead, they persist in memory and their layered continuity with the continuing action of the spatial palimpsest. Brittain's memory of this conversation is triggered when reading E. A. Mackintosh's 'Cha Till Maccruimein' (1917): 'And there in front of the men were marching, / With feet that made no mark, / The grey old ghosts of the ancient fighters / Come back again from the dark . . .'.[98] Here it is not simply ghosts that are invoked but ghosts returning; yet we cannot ignore the irony that they certainly do make and leave a 'mark': 'the ghost presents itself as a trace of that which no longer exists'.[99] Their absent-presence is itself such a trace.

The return of ghosts is made possible by the 'tension between discontinuous and continuous modes of time';[100] they emerge through the temporal ruptures that dominate the experience of the space. As Trigg elaborates, 'the ghost occupies a particular relationship with the place it haunts, in the process of articulating its desires in and through space. In this way, the ghost's dwelling-in-place shatters the linearity of time, its legacy one of repetition and returning.'[101] This shattered linearity of time corresponds to the polytemporal overlap of every space, in which memory reaches back, and forward, rewriting every epoch of its existence.

[97] Brittain, *Testament*, 415–16.
[98] Ibid., 416.
[99] Trigg, *Memory*, 318.
[100] Ibid., 319.
[101] Ibid.

Every space is made up of what is and is not present. In fact, the present of each space is 'under erasure', in the sense invoked in Jacques Derrida's concept of the inherent absence of presence. In prefacing her translation of Derrida's *Of Grammatology* (1976), Gayatri Chakravorty Spivak explains that 'Derrida's ~~trace~~ is the mark of the absence of a presence, an always already absent present, of the lack at the origin that is the condition of thought and experience.'[102] This concept of the ~~trace~~ gains particular traction because of its *sous rature*: 'This is to write a word, cross it out, and then print both word and deletion.'[103] The spaces discussed here retain traces (in the form of aesthetic aftermaths, figurative associations, and hauntings, etc.) of their previous life. The casino-turned-hospital, for example, illustrates a twist on the *sous rature* trace: in becoming a hospital, its identity as the casino is crossed out: signs of its previous existence are pushed aside, but crucially in their negation they are not entirely erased. The casino exists simultaneously with the hospital. When a reappropriated space (school, casino, hotel, etc) is cast as a hospital, it is simultaneously emphasised that the site is not really a hospital. Consequently, 'Things that are assumed present are now witnessed as absent, things hitherto thought to be homely emerge as unhomely, and entities we once thought dead materialize as being quite undead',[104] hence the unremitting sense of unease which is fuelled by witnessing the literal and figurative contrasts and juxtapositions.

Looking back on her war experiences, and reflecting on the changed relationship that she and her fellow caregivers have with the spaces of caregiving, E. C. Fox illustrates that it is difficult, often impossible, to return to them:

> Very few among the many who worked there during the war would, I think, choose to return to that hotel to spend their summer holidays. To go back to the hotel would revive too vivid memories of suffering and tragedy in which the place was often steeped during the war: sleep might easily be troubled with dreams of ambulances rolling slowly but steadily all through the night to the hospital, each disgorging its load of wounded men.[105]

---

[102] Gayatri Chakravorty Spivak, 'Translator's Preface', in *Of Grammatology*, by Jacques Derrida (Baltimore: Johns Hopkins University Press, 1976), xvii.
[103] Ibid., xiv.
[104] Trigg, *Memory*, 28.
[105] E. C. Fox, 'An Officers' Hospital in France During the War', in *Reminiscent Sketches*, 61.

Fox illustrates the common consequence for those involved in war: that they cannot return to the same places with a clean slate; while the memories and ghosts may sleep, they cannot be fully erased. The space, in this case the hotel-turned-hospital, can never be experienced as only a hotel again. The landscape of these places changes irrevocably: the layers of its identity, once altered and added to, are eternally connected to these events, which are not easily forgotten. Perhaps, then, there is something more to the trace in this context: the absent-presence of what the space was never meant to be. The casino was never meant to be anything other than a casino. The hotel was never meant to be a hospital. Consequently, its episode as a hospital is crossed out, but not erased, so the ambulances, each one with 'its load of wounded men', will always continue to roll up.

Such aftermaths are the inverse of the medics' original experience of these spaces as diachronic: however familiar or unfamiliar they might be with the space in its previous incarnation, the medic can only ever experience the reappropriated space as exactly that: re-appropriated. In the redesignation of the space as hospital, attention is continually drawn to the fact that it was not always a hospital, nor will it always be one. And the traces, ghosts, and associations from other times, past, present, and future, will always re-emerge, build up different layers, and interact in ways which affect the spatial identity.

The spaces discussed here, which have been experienced as reappropriated medical spaces, demonstrate the multidirectionality of the 'double ground' and that the traces of the past can be experienced both abstractly and through visible remainders. Accessing the 'double ground' does not always require the Proustian stumble, or at least that stumble can manifest itself in different ways. The overlap of different layers, particularly through the visible contrast between past and present uses, becomes unsettling; the sight of wounded men is made all the more chilling overlain on the discordant previous nature of the space. The contrasts between the elaborate decoration and the writhing of bodies in pain; the juxtaposition of the fragility of the wounded body with a place of royal and political distinction; and the backdrop of historical mutability to the site of refuge, all result in the emergence of uncanny difference. The contrasts and tensions between layers is what makes the experience of space uncanny, often derealising, and inherently ironic. The different spatial layers do not sit comfortably alongside one another; they maintain a 'permanent tension', continually transforming each other, and thus transforming individual relations to the space's polytemporality. In the incongruous clash of different characteristics, something emerges: 'an excess of matter' comes to the surface. Something that once remained hidden is now visible – never to be hidden again. The ever-present trace, more particularly, exudes and rewrites the identity of the space, and consequently the spatial experience. The ever-present trace foreshadows how the world is irrevocably altered by the events of the war, changes that cannot be undone.

Chapter 3

Protrusions, Openings, and Depths: A Medical Grotesque

Although wounds and injury are inevitable in the war environment, traditional war narratives rarely foreground medical encounters with wounds, and we are seldom encouraged to consider the intimate moments of medical intervention. Enid Bagnold, in *A Diary Without Dates* (1918), deplores the sanitised view of the war wounded afforded to those outside of the medical profession, who do not see the wounds or consider the realities of medical treatment: 'O visitors, who come into the ward in the calm of the long afternoon [. . .] when the men look like men again and smoke and talk and read . . . if you could see what lies beneath the dressings!'[1] Beneath those dressings are the reality of the medical landscape and the evidence of lengthy, arduous, medical encounters: the dressings cover transgressions of bodily boundaries, where the body exceeds its margins or the medic is required to intrude on the internal spaces of the body. These encounters are invisible to those outside of the medical space, and thus often go unexamined; but for the medics, they are deeply affecting, with complex emotional consequences. These are difficult experiences to articulate, fraught with conflicting emotions, especially given that the confrontation with weeping wounds and mutilated limbs can be repulsive, and that medical acts can be perceived as themselves invasive or violating. This chapter looks 'beneath the dressings', to explore the medics' representation of the protrusions, openings, and depths of the body.

By discussing the depictions and representations of wounds, I shall examine the medics' confrontations with the broken boundaries

[1] Enid Bagnold, *A Diary Without Dates* (London: William Heinemann, 1918), 103.

of the body, and the impact of the internal body exceeding itself. Specifically, the chapter looks at how the spaces of the body are represented from the viewpoint of medics who touch and enter these spaces; it uncovers the challenging ways in which the mutilated and exposed body affects the medical witness. This exploration opens a discussion on the roles of, and relationship between, protrusion and intrusion, and how and why care necessarily involves a brutalisation of the medical space.

The self-reflexivity and self-consciousness in these narratives reveals how the medics become increasingly aware that their actions, and the assertion of medical power, can be experienced as harm or violence, often directly increasing the patients' pain and distress. Sophie Botcharsky, in *They Knew How to Die* (1931), illustrates the array of conflicting emotions produced by participation in invasive procedures:

> Pitroff with a quick movement swept his knife the full circle of the man's leg. It left a bright red ribbon, and as the colour flamed on the human flesh a frantic protest rose in me that to do such a thing to a man's leg was butchery. It was unnatural. [. . .] You could not turn a human body into a dreadful, lopped fragment of a man. Pitroff whistled the 'Merry Widow' waltz, and angry pulses beat all through me. I could hear the thin scrape of the saw, and I glanced down to see that the leg was off. The orderly, arrested with horror, held it without moving [. . .] I was overwhelmed with revulsion.[2]

While the surgeon is cast as almost villainous, Botcharsky and the orderly, assisting in the procedure, are themselves both observers to and complicit in the act of 'butchery'. In this evocative scene, Botcharsky encapsulates the multiple factors affecting the medical witness: the strangeness of the body is manifest as it is opened and broken, and the unsettling incongruity is intensified by the repulsive juxtaposition of the surgeon whistling as he saws. As the patient's body bleeds, the nurse's body sympathetically reacts, so that her ethical and emotional recoil seems grounded in vicarious feeling and suffering with the patient. While the medical system may be felt as impersonal by the patients, it is overwhelmingly personal for the caregivers who must perform and witness the infliction of further pain on those already hurt. These narratives give us access to the affective

---

[2] Sophie Botcharsky and Florida Pier, *They Knew How to Die: Being a Narrative of the Personal Experiences of a Red Cross Sister on the Russian Front* (Edinburgh: Peter Davies, 1931), 10.

landscape of wound care and medical intervention, highlighting such emotions as revulsion, disgust, and fear. They reveal what is generally overlooked, and rarely examined, in the experiences of medics: the emotions involved in encounters of medical intervention, and the struggle to reconcile the conflicting demands of the medical role.

The emotional responses which Botcharsky illustrates in this passage align her feeling of revulsion with that of horror. In fact, this is 'fear-imbued disgust'.[3] Although disgust does not always involve fear, and fear does not always contain disgust, the two emotions are very strongly aligned. An encounter with something which induces horror is a threat towards the self, bodily as in contamination or damage, and psychical, as damage to the personal ego, selfhood, and identity – especially when it involves body horror and the literal breakage of bodily boundaries and spilling of interiors. There is particular threat brought on by the turning of the familiar into the unfamiliar: in her account *A Woman's Diary of the War* (1916), Sarah Macnaughtan describes hearing a surgeon saying, '"These are not wounds, they are mush"'[4] – the body in front of them no longer resembles a person whom they can clean up and cure. In order to explore the relationship the medics have with the bodies and body parts that disgust them, I suggest engagement via the lens of the psychoanalytic concept of abjection, where substances or sights which threaten bodily and psychical integrity must be eradicated. On the face of it, this is disgust in action – we do not want that which disgusts to touch us, for fear it endanger or contaminate us. However, the intermingling of disgust and fear also pulls us in slightly different directions: 'It is usually supposed that fear leads to flight and disgust more to a desire to have the offending item removed.'[5] While we may struggle to function under the conditions of fear, we can more realistically survive in relation to that which disgusts. Strangely, we can be drawn towards and captivated by those sights which disturb and disgust: 'Even as the disgusting repels, it rarely does so without also capturing our attention. It imposes itself on us. We find it hard not to sneak a second look or, less voluntarily, we find our eyes doing "double-takes" at the very things that disgust us.'[6] This pull towards

---

[3] William Ian Miller, *The Anatomy of Disgust* (Cambridge, MA and London: Harvard University Press, 1997), 26.

[4] Sarah Macnaughtan, *A Woman's Diary of the War* (London: Thomas Nelson and Sons, 1916), 23.

[5] Miller, *Anatomy*, 25.

[6] Ibid., x.

that which disgusts or repels us is similarly evident in how I come to discuss the concept of the grotesque.

In this chapter, I propose exploring the emotional responses to wounds through a theoretical prism which considers abjection in conversation with the aesthetic grotesque through a nexus of emotions such as repulsion, fear, and disgust. Scholarship exploring abjection in the context of medicine is generally considered along the lines of body horror, mutation and contagion, and anxieties around biomedicine and science. These traits are often exemplified and examined in relation to the Gothic and horror more broadly.[7] It is often considered with outright experiences of fear and threat to life – whether as contagion, contamination, or threat to one's bodily borders. In turn, this comes to interact with images of othering, marginalisation, and revolt against the stranger. Here, however, I focus on how the imperatives of the medical role and landscape influence the medics' relationship between abjection and other conflicting emotions.

Corporeal identity is both constructed and threatened by the presence of the opened body and bodily waste. In *Powers of Horror* (1982), Julia Kristeva explains the instinctual process of abjection, the casting off of that which threatens the subject: 'refuse and corpses show me what I permanently thrust aside in order to live'.[8] The abject is a threat to bodily boundaries and margins, and consequently to subjectivity. Confrontation with the abject is frequent in First World War literature generally, but an epitomising example can be found in *Her Privates We* (1929), Frederic Manning's semi-autobiographical account of his combat experience on the Western Front.[9] Early in the text the protagonist, Bourne, witnesses the obliteration of fellow soldiers and attempts to make sense of, and disentangle himself from, the sights of death and destruction:

> one sees such things; and one suffers vicariously, with the inalienable sympathy of man for man. One forgets quickly. The mind is averted as well as the eyes. It reassures itself after the first despairing cry:
> 'It is I'

---

[7] For example, Frances Pheasant-Kelly, 'Towards a Structure of Feeling: Abjection and Allegories of Disease in Science Fiction "Mutation" Films', *Medical Humanities* 42 (2016): 238–45.

[8] Julia Kristeva, *Powers of Horror*, trans. Leon S. Roudiez (New York: Columbia University Press, 1982), 3.

[9] As discussed in Trudi Tate, *Modernism, History and the First World War* (Manchester: Manchester University Press, 1998), 65–9.

'No, it is not I. I shall not be like that'
And one moves on, leaving the mauled and bloody thing behind.[10]

The crucial detail here is '"It is I" "No, it is not I. I shall not be like that"', which illustrates the instinctive disentanglement from a sight which horrifies and destabilises. In order for the individual to maintain their boundaries, and thus their assured selfhood, they must repudiate the comparison between 'the mauled and bloody thing' and their own body. They cannot afford to 'suffer vicariously' in this environment of crisis and emergency.

Abjection in the context of war presents a complex duality. For the active combatant abjection is a necessary tactic for personal survival and persisting in their duty: the soldier needs to dissociate himself from the fact that he is directly engaged in perpetrating such mutilation and death. Military-medics, however, can only experience a *gesture* towards abjection in order to perform their role of recovery and healing. In this gesture, the medics must make use of abjection, but cannot fully adopt it; in order to persevere in medical procedures they similarly need to 'leave the [. . .] bloody thing behind', but as caregivers they cannot afford to lose sight of the body as human. For the medic, it is important to separate the sights of the wounded from the dead, in order to sustain their connection with a vision of the healthy body, for the purpose of healing and regeneration. If abjection can offer resolution for a soldier, it is more problematic for the medic. The role of the caregiver entails an empathetic response, the 'It is I' element, which is in conflict with the defence of their personal ego. They can allow themselves only an internal gesture towards abjection alongside their caregiving actions, in order to adhere to the professional and ethical imperative to retain the humanity of the wounded.

The medics' experiences of conflicting emotions from confrontation with suppurating wounds are frequently conveyed through the representational mode of the aesthetic grotesque. Images of protrusions typify a confrontation with the grotesque, drawing attention, for example, to distended abdomens, bulging intestines or 'a lump of brain sticking out of [the patient's] forehead'.[11] Protrusion is the eruption of form, and disordering of the body, so that parts of the body are literally out of place. Significantly, however, this is a

---

[10] Frederic Manning, *Her Privates We* (1929; London: Serpent's Tail, 1999), 11.
[11] Kate Luard, *Unknown Warriors: Extracts from the Letters of K.E. Luard, RRC, Nursing Sister in France, 1914–1918* (London: Chatto and Windus, 1930), 70.

movement beyond the uncanny; the aesthetic grotesque enables the representation of the deeper conflicts raised by confronting, visually and haptically, the wounded body. Mikhail Bakhtin's discussion of the grotesque allows us to explore its specifically spatial aspect – especially given his discussions of orifices and fluidity of form – and the effects of the internal/external conflict: in the grotesque we see the bringing together of things which should be kept apart. The Bakhtinian grotesque provides us with the means to understand the fluidity of 'the grotesque body [. . . as] in the act of becoming'.[12] Representations of the grotesque body are not interested in the surface, but look at 'excrescences (sprouts, buds) and orifices, only that which leads beyond the body's limited space or into the body's depths'.[13] Transgression into and outside the border is central to its disconcerting effect. The vulnerability of the body to the grotesque precipitates the abject, marked by the eruption or emission of inner bodily fluids and unknown matter.

In order to explore representations of encounters with wounds, I begin by unravelling the various affective reactions to wounds, considering the significance of abjection and the aesthetic grotesque. While abjection is an instinctive everyday process of casting off that which threatens one's bodily margins and, by extension, one's subjectivity, the grotesque offers us a way to explore certain moments of extremity: focusing on that conflicting feeling of being pulled into while also recoiling from an image. These are therefore concepts which aid our understanding of witnessing the exposed body, by addressing the conflicting emotions involved in confronting such extreme situations. Exploring these concepts in conjunction allows us to uncover a new subset of the grotesque, one that is specifically related to the medical encounter: a 'medical grotesque'. This is more than simply the grotesque within the medical context: it is a particular stance through which medics represent and critique their own roles as caregivers.

Disgust and Abjection

The nature of wounds and injuries inflicted throughout the war presented medics with unprecedented complications, for which no

---

[12] Mikhail Bakhtin, *Rabelais and His World*, trans. Hélène Iswolsky (1964; Bloomington: Indiana University Press, 1984), 317.
[13] Ibid., 317–18.

training could fully prepare them. For many, these were their first encounters with injured bodies, and of bodies undergoing such strain. Confrontation with medical procedures and the collapse of the body yields an array of conflicting emotional responses: disgust; fear; pity; resentment, for example. Lesley Smith, in *Four Years Out of Life* (1931), depicts assisting in an amputation, a trying experience that produces 'a sickening sensation, but there was no opportunity to be sick. I stuffed the leg into the dressing pail beside the other arms and feet and kept my head down as long as I could by pretending to pick up some soiled dressings'.[14] Suppressing sickness or faintness is only part of the necessary inoculation to medical care; medics must also navigate their emotional and psychological reactions to the punctured body, as well as controlling their innate sensibilities towards bodily waste, breakage, and weaknesses.

Bodily fluids and substances stain these texts throughout. At various moments we witness gushing blood, faecal matter, bubbles, foam, pus, and slime. Occasionally the medic expresses their own sense of discomfort, including repulsion and disgust; for example, in *We That Were Young* (1932), Irene Rathbone admits that 'The stench which rustled forth as the last dressings dropped off was just humanly endurable, and only just.'[15] Confrontation with the bodily fluids of others can be an alarming and even threatening experience, but most often it involves disgust. While the affective qualities of disgust serve to protect us, its presence also raises complexity about how and why we feel that way towards the object. Why does that disgust us, and perhaps more importantly, how do we handle that impulse? If we bring this notion to the specificity of the medical context, where emotional response is often overridden with action, then we can see how the medics' sense of disgust is already different to disgust felt ordinarily. What is disgusting for most changes, and contains the potential to no longer be disgusting.

Repulsion through disgust implies its contingency on fear, and it is fear and vulnerability which move the body, especially given that 'Disgust pulls us away from the object, a pulling that feels involuntary, as if our bodies were thinking for us, on behalf of us.'[16] However, if we broaden out different categories of disgust, we can begin to see that there are different degrees of threat, which do not

---

[14] Lesley Smith, *Four Years Out of Life* (London: Philip Allan, 1931), 159.
[15] Irene Rathbone, *We That Were Young* (1932; London: Virago, 1988), 200.
[16] Sara Ahmed, *The Cultural Politics of Emotion* (Edinburgh: Edinburgh University Press, 2014), 84.

always accommodate the caregiving impulse, and indeed, 'disgust [. . .] exists on a spectrum of fear'.[17] In *On Disgust* (originally published as *Der Ekel* in 1929), Aurel Kolnai clarifies the difference between fear and disgust:

> What is disgusting is in principle not threatening, but rather disturbing, even though a mere disturbance by itself, however strong, cannot evoke disgust. A thing which is perceived as disgusting will always be something which is not going to be regarded as important, which is neither to be destroyed, nor something from which one has to flee, but which must rather be put out of the way. [. . .] where fear coerces me principally to retreat from my surroundings, to alter my circumstances or my situation, disgust leads me much more to a cleaning up of my surroundings, to a weeding out of what is disgusting therein.[18]

In this conceptualisation, disgust ensures an active response, lending itself to productivity and maintenance of the body. As an alternative to simply recoiling, the medic learns to prioritise response. In this way disgust works as a form of defence reaction for medics who must persist in their duties. Disgust and fear are certainly entangled, but they can also go their separate ways. If something is presented as disgusting, there is not so much a fundamental need to flee as a need to clear it away. If, however, what disgusts also induces fear, the ego must flee. The bodily substances create disturbances, but these can be addressed and resolved within the terms of the innate reaction of disgust. As bodily substances become familiar, the compulsion of fear is more or less thrown off. Therefore, it is evident that reactions to the leaking body are not wholly negative or useless; and as discussed in Chapter 1, strong reactions to outside stimuli can also have a diagnostic function.

Such distinct psychological responses and bodily reactions reveal the instinctual process of abjection. For Kristeva, borders are fundamental for successful abjection.[19] The presence of a corpse 'is death infecting life',[20] due to its 'paradox of sameness and difference',[21] wherein it is simultaneously unfamiliar as an object and familiar

---

[17] Rina Arya, 'Abjection Interrogated: Uncovering the Relation Between Abjection and Disgust', *Journal of Extreme Anthropology* 1, no. 1 (2017): 57.
[18] Aurel Kolnai, *On Disgust*, ed. Barry Smith and Carolyn Korsmeyer (Chicago and La Salle: Open Court, 2004), 41–2.
[19] Kristeva, *Powers*, 3.
[20] Ibid., 4.
[21] Tate, *Modernism*, 71.

as resembling the subject.[22] Abjection is a defence against such moments, 'wherein each man resembles his own corpse'.[23] A dividing border between the living and the dead must be psychologically marked for the witness, so that they can maintain the boundaries of the self and ask, '"*Where* am I?" instead of "*Who* am I?"'[24] It is only through the assertion of a border that abjection can successfully be achieved. The corpse is just one end of the spectrum of abjection; as these texts illustrate, abjection occurs in the medical sphere in the presence of not only 'a corpse' but also the exposed body, mutilated or dying, and so requires some re-evaluation in this context.

Trudi Tate elaborates on abjection in relation to the First World War, explaining that, especially in combatant texts, 'we find the living defining themselves in relation to the dead, and celebrating their difference. Yet at the same time, the soldier's sense of his bodily identity is threatened by the mere presence of a corpse.'[25] The corpse is central to Kristeva's theory, becoming 'the most sickening of wastes [...] a border that has encroached upon everything'.[26] The presence of corpses was an especially disturbing aspect of war in the trenches, where limited transport, recovery, and burial services meant that bodies were interred into the parapet fortifications, inevitably resurfacing to the distress of the remaining soldiers. With a 'vast cemetery'[27] of bodies erratically resurfacing, combatants and medics alike needed to develop psychological defences through strategies of abjection.

The nature of the wounds meant that viscera spilled from transgressed boundaries, sometimes with the complete breakdown of bodily integrity, so that 'mangled flesh and blood mixed with mud, sandbags and timber', and the 'remains of one man had to be collected and put in a sack for interment'.[28] Yet, this pervasive experience of the abject must be explored further in relation to the specifically medical context, where the body and body parts are not necessarily 'discarded' in the same way. We need to reconsider

---

[22] Justin Edwards, *Grotesque* (London and New York: Routledge, 2013), 6.
[23] Georges Duhamel, *The New Book of Martyrs*, trans. Florence Simmonds (New York: George H. Doran, 1918), 14.
[24] Kristeva, *Powers*, 8.
[25] Tate, *Modernism*, 68.
[26] Kristeva, *Powers*, 3.
[27] William St. Clair, *The Road to St. Julien: The Letters of a Stretcher-Bearer from the Great War*, ed. John St. Clair (Barnsley: Pen & Sword Books, 2004), 32.
[28] J. H. Newton, *A Stretcher Bearer's Diary: Three Years in France with the 21st Division* (1931; London: Arthur H. Stockwell, 2009), 421, 124. Kindle.

the ways in which 'waste' is both discarded and retained, and the consequence that the psychological mechanism of abjection is not entirely available for the medic. In some ways, body parts are more easily discarded; for example, faced with an amputation, the medic recognises that discarding the infected limb gives the patient a chance at survival. The amputated limb can be discarded, literally and psychologically, so that the empathetic response of the caregiver to the patient can persist.

Kristeva explains:

> The corpse (or cadaver: *cadere*, to fall), that which has irremediably come a cropper, is cesspool, and death; it upsets even more violently the one who confronts it as fragile and fallacious chance. A wound with blood and pus, or the sickly, acrid smell of sweat, of decay, does not *signify* death.[29]

What the 'wound with blood and pus' does signify, however, is the *rupture* of the body and the translation of body into waste.[30] Bodily fluids are waste, and are the substances and signs by which we acknowledge the boundaries of our self. In the medical space the demarcation of the clean and unclean becomes increasingly difficult to maintain yet more important than ever. As Elizabeth Gross explains, 'The abject demonstrates the impossibility of clear-cut borders, lines of demarcation, divisions between the clean and the unclean, the proper and the improper, order and disorder.'[31] Blurred cleanliness is specifically identified in Ellen N. La Motte's *The Backwash of War* (1916), when she states, 'we see [patients] in this awful interval between life and death [. . .] Life is clean and death is clean, but this interval between the two is gross, absurd, fantastic.'[32] This interval is messy and threatens the subjectivity of not only the victim but also the witness to the mutilated body. The abject is ever present, ever threatening, in the medical environment. La Motte's identification of this gross interval clarifies the anxiety of facing violated boundaries. The abject exacerbates corporeal vulnerability: 'Death is dignified and life is dignified, but the intervals are awful.

---

[29] Kristeva, *Powers*, 3.
[30] While the presence of blood may not always signify rupture, e.g. menstruation, its presence with pus certainly implies something is wrong with the body.
[31] Elizabeth Gross, 'The Body of Signification', in *Abjection, Melancholia and Love*, ed. John Fletcher and Andrew Benjamin (London and New York: Routledge, 1990), 89.
[32] Ellen N. La Motte, 'The Interval', in *The Backwash of War* (1916; London: Conway, 2014), 86–7.

They are ludicrous, repulsive.'³³ La Motte demonstrates the need for the psychological middle ground of abjection. There is certainty, and an established border, when the patient is dead, but in the 'interval', in the passage between health and death, the impulse to repudiate waste must be overridden by the empathetic drive and the effort to heal. In treating the wounded patient, the medic can only allow themselves a gesture towards abjection, for they must retain a certain immersion in the medical encounter. Abjection, then, is complicated by both the affective power of disgust and the imperatives of the medical context.

Reactions to the human, especially as it changes and overflows, are intrinsically complex. Faced with the wounded body, and internal viscera leaking forth, there is both a threat to subjectivity and repulsion at the sight of matter that is usually kept hidden. The wounded body, with its protrusions, swelling, and distensions, is frequently a grotesque figure, and generates a complex and contradicting affective response. This is especially evident in the tension between fascination and repulsion, similar to the aforementioned allure of that which disgusts, which is most helpfully elucidated by Wilson Yates:

> When we encounter the grotesque, we are caught off guard, we are surprised and shaken, we have a sense of being played with, taunted, judged. It evokes a range of feelings [. . .] uneasiness, fear, repulsion, delight, amusement, often horror and dread, and through its evocative power it appears to us in paradoxical guise – it is and is not of this world – and it elicits from us paradoxical responses.³⁴

The grotesque elicits a complex emotional reaction of uneasiness mixed with intrigue; we cannot look, but we cannot look away. The grotesque has an affinity with abjection, given that both concepts are based on the reaction to bodies and bodily processes, often concerning the bodies of others. But the grotesque goes beyond this, to bring out two significant issues that build on reactions to the open body. First, the grotesque offers a representational strategy, which aids the communication of the experience of facing transgressed bodies. Second, the grotesque holds in balance the tension between the gesture towards abjection and the intensity which is part of its

---

[33] Ibid., 91.
[34] Wilson Yates, 'An Introduction to the Grotesque: Theoretical and Theological Considerations', in *The Grotesque in Art and Literature: Theological Reflections*, ed. James Luther Adams and Wilson Yates (Grand Rapids, MI: W. B. Eerdmans, 1997), 2.

aesthetic quality; its force grabs our imaginative attention while we recoil, so that we struggle to look away. The specifically *aesthetic* grotesque enables a synthetic perspective, which articulates and holds in tension the conflicting emotions of caregiving.

The Aesthetic Grotesque

As these texts illustrate, the wounded body exceeds its boundaries in multiple ways, from bloating or swelling to leakage and rupture. These realities are depicted by the medics through a particular representational stance, in the mode of the aesthetic grotesque. Distortion and incongruity are immediately recognisable features of the aesthetic grotesque, according to Bakhtin's *Rabelais and His World* (1964). While Bakhtin's grotesque is especially concerned with the political and social entanglements of the carnivalesque, I focus here on the discrete human body, drawing on features of the aesthetic grotesque, to explore how it influences the observer of the battle context and the medical environment, and the ways in which it provides a conceptual formulation for the incongruous, unfamiliar, and distorted figure.

When a familiar or typical form is altered, with 'distortions, exaggeration, a fusion of incompatible parts in such a fashion that it confronts us as strange and disordered, as a world turned upside down',[35] we are facing an example of the aesthetic grotesque in action. Specifically, applications of the grotesque are dominated by a distortion of what is human. For example, Bagnold offers this description of one of her patients:

> Ryan, the man with his nose gone, was lying high on five or six pillows, slung in his position by tapes and webbing passed under his arms and attached to the bedposts. He lay with his profile to me – only he has no profile, as we know a man's. Like an ape, he has only his bumpy forehead and his protruding lips – the nose, the left eye, gone.[36]

The comparison to 'an ape' evokes a seemingly savage image: not only is the figure distorted, but it is no longer human. In losing his facial profile, he has lost what initially distinguishes one man from another: he has lost his identity. Bagnold's emphasis on his 'bumpy

---

[35] Ibid.
[36] Bagnold, *Without Dates*, 14.

forehead and his protruding lips' further evokes physiognomy, reducing identity to somatic shape, while comparing a patient to an 'ape' or a 'monkey'[37] expresses 'a post-Darwinian angst'.[38] One of the features of the aesthetic grotesque is an intensified blurring between human and animal, which is in turn experienced as a threat to human subjectivity.

As well as distortion and protrusion, the grotesque is especially characterised by orifices. Bakhtin notes various orifices: the mouth, the anus, where 'the confines between bodies and between the body and the world are overcome'.[39] The emphasis on 'gaping jaws', and orifices generally, offers 'the most vivid expression of the body as not impenetrable but open'.[40] The soldiers' wounds are often orifices: 'great, red, bleeding cavit[ies]',[41] 'holes as big as your fist',[42] which expose the internal body in grotesque confrontation. One particularly unsettling example speaks of a patient with 'a great opening in his side, a kind of fetid mouth, through which the will to live seemed to evaporate'.[43] The 'fetid mouth' is vivid; rot seems to take over the body, so that his soma is devoured from the inside out. The evaporation of his 'will to live' typifies this overcoming of the boundary between body and world, suggesting that the soul is escaping through the 'great opening', as a kind of imperceptible vapour.

Bakhtin foregrounds specific attention to the orific mouth, which 'dominates all else', especially when it is open: 'it is the open gate leading downward into the bodily underworld. The gaping mouth is related to the image of swallowing, this most ancient symbol of death and destruction.'[44] Significantly, we often see descriptions of the 'mouths of wounds', a common anatomical descriptor for openings on the body, such as Mary Borden's description of 'the yawning mouths of his wounds',[45] in *The Forbidden Zone* (1929). 'Yawning' wounds seems to be a stock expression which can be traced back to

---

[37] Elizabeth Walker Black, *Hospital Heroes* (New York: Charles Scribner's Sons, 1919), 149.
[38] Terry Phillips, 'A Study in Grotesques', *Gothic Studies* 7 (2005): 43.
[39] Bakhtin, *Rabelais*, 317.
[40] Ibid., 339.
[41] William Boyd, *With a Field Ambulance at Ypres* (Toronto: Musson, 1916), 26.
[42] Mary Borden, 'Moonlight', in *The Forbidden Zone* (1929; London: Hesperus Press, 2008), 43.
[43] Duhamel, *Martyrs*, 46.
[44] Bakhtin, *Rabelais*, 317, 325.
[45] Borden, 'Conspiracy', in *Forbidden*, 80.

Bede and Edmund Spenser.[46] The 'yawn' suggests a particular movement of the mouth that is an involuntary action of exposure and opening. But the mouth is also an emblem of communication and channel of breath, intimately related to the spirit, soul, and essence of being human. This is what makes it so amenable to the grotesque and the way the aesthetic grotesque holds in tension the negotiation between what is and is not human.

While the open mouth typifies the grotesque image, these narratives more often represent a denial of the grotesque mouth. Rather than an open void suggestive of devouring, the mouths of the wounded are 'fixed'. To an extent, there is a literal reason for this, associated with the prevalence of tetanus in the wounded – 'commonly known as "lockjaw" because, as the infection invaded the muscles of the jaw, it caused them to contract, pulling the mouth into an uncontrollable rictus grin'.[47] This phenomenon is evoked, for example, in the description of a soldier 'with quite definite spasms, his jaw tight shut and looking like a horrible wooden image with that same fixed grin they all get';[48] or references to a 'ghastly tetanic grin';[49] or the way 'contracted muscles held his mouth in an unchanging smile'.[50] The clenched, gripped, and fixed mouth is no longer a distinct orifice. There is exceptional consciousness of this in a scene from Bagnold:

> the foot of the bed near me began to catch my attention: the toe beneath the sheets became more and more agitated, then the toes of the other foot, beating a frenzied tattoo beneath the coverings. I looked up.
> Facing me a pair of blue eyes were bulging above an open mouth, the nostrils were quivering . . .
> 'My jaws want to close.'[51]

---

[46] Bede, *The Old English Version of Bede's Ecclesiastical History of the English People*, trans. Thomas Miller (Cambridge, ON: In Parentheses Publications, 1999), 144; Edmund Spenser, *The Faerie Queene*, Book I, Canto XI, 35, in *The Faerie Queene Books I to III*, ed. Douglas Brooks-Davies (1609; London and Vermont: Everyman Classic, 1987), 148.

[47] Christine Hallett, *Veiled Warriors: Allied Nurses of the First World War* (Oxford: Oxford University Press, 2014), 82.

[48] Harold Dearden, *Medicine and Duty* (1928; Ilminster: Richard Dennis, 2014), 13.

[49] Smith, *Four Years*, 140.

[50] Botcharsky and Pier, *They Knew*, 12.

[51] Bagnold, *Without Dates*, 120–1.

The patient fears the symptoms of tetanus that he has witnessed in other patients; his actions are possibly psychosomatic, but the scene centralises recognition of the fear of involuntary movement – or lack of movement. Fear of the abyssal orific mouth is nothing compared with the overwhelming fear of losing control over one's own body; 'As [tetanus] progressed, the muscles of the back would contract, resulting in a dramatic and excruciatingly painful arching of the body.'[52] This sudden contraction of muscles is illustrated in Smith's patient's 'bad tetanic spasm when his body, racked by an unseen torturer, lifted slowly from the bed and became twisted into a rigid hoop',[53] and Botcharsky's patient whose 'head and feet curved backwards, and in his torture his body rose into an arch'.[54] The pose of the patient mirrors the victim undergoing torture on the rack, by which the body is unnaturally twisted. Both examples appeal to the idea of torture, reinforcing the sense that the patient's body movement is not their own. The 'unseen torturer' is the infection which has invaded the body, and usurped personal autonomy.

Rigidity pervades the images of bodies, turning them into objects and revealing the tension between the human and non-human. Instances of the body as object are frequent and significant, taking numerous forms and encompassing effects of defamiliarisation, and themes of objectification and stasis. This is summed up by Rathbone, who, on removing a dressing, witnesses 'a swollen, shrapnel-blasted lump that had lost all resemblance to a human foot'.[55] In losing 'all resemblance' to the human, it becomes something else, Other, and epitomises the grotesque. Such objectification conforms to the recurrent sense of body parts as themselves waste to be discarded: 'Amputated limbs were simply swept or thrown out into the courtyard';[56] 'Sometimes legs and arms wrapped in cloths have to be pushed out of the way. We throw them on the floor – they belong to no one and are of no interest to anyone.'[57] Thoroughly dehumanised once and for all, these body parts have become redundant objects, to be thrust aside.

Otherness is especially evident in images of wood and woodenness, which are used to distinguish the patients from healthy, vital

---

[52] Hallett, *Veiled*, 82.
[53] Smith, *Four Years*, 142.
[54] Botcharsky and Pier, *They Knew*, 11.
[55] Rathbone, *Young*, 199.
[56] Baroness de T'Serclaes, *Flanders and Other Fields* (London: George G. Harrap, 1964), 62.
[57] Borden, 'Moonlight', 41.

bodies. As well as producing a sense of uncanniness, these images imply motionlessness and redundancy. For example, in a case of trench foot, 'swollen blackish lumps [...] resembled more than anything else a couple of charred blocks of firewood'.[58] It is implied that once they are seen as pieces of wood, they are then treated as such. There is emphasis too on the woodenness of expression, in phrases such as 'looking like a horrible wooden image',[59] 'his own wooden visage laboured under the stress of all kinds of feelings',[60] and 'harshly carven face',[61] which reinforces the implication that the patients are stiff and unnatural, their character rigidified, and have become non-human.

This ambiguous status with respect to humanity is compounded by multiple references to dolls and dummy figures, images with strong connections to the Freudian uncanny. In *Testament of Youth* (1933), for example, Vera Brittain describes a recently deceased patient as resembling a 'wax doll'.[62] Although the bodily form remains, the human and subject are evacuated, leaving an inanimate object. As part of his analysis of the uncanny, Freud draws out 'the impressions made on us by waxwork figures, ingeniously constructed dolls and automata' which, according to E. Jentsch, Freud adds, induce '"doubt as to whether an apparently animate object really is alive and, conversely, whether a lifeless object might not perhaps be animate"'.[63] What is most uncanny in Brittain's description is that the figure which had been animated is suddenly without animation. It is the sudden shift from movement to stasis which is most jarring. The scene is reminiscent of Siegfried Sassoon's *Memoirs of an Infantry Officer* (1930), when he encounters a dead soldier whose 'face was grey and waxen, with a stiff little moustache; he looked like a ghastly doll, grotesque and undignified'.[64] Further examples emphasise the uncanny, jolting movement of dolls: in Rathbone's novel, '[t]he ghastly broken doll – half-waxen, half-human – stumbled its way in

---

[58] Rathbone, *Young*, 290.
[59] Dearden, *Duty*, 13.
[60] Georges Duhamel, *The New Book of Martyrs*, trans. Florence Simmonds (New York: George H. Doran Company, 1918), 79.
[61] Smith, *Four Years*, 58.
[62] Vera Brittain, *Testament of Youth* (1933; London: Penguin Books, 2005), 379.
[63] Sigmund Freud, *The Uncanny*, trans. David McLintock (1919; London: Penguin Classics, 2003), 135.
[64] Siegfried Sassoon, *Memoirs of an Infantry Officer* (1930; London: Faber and Faber, 1997), 51–2.

and out of Joan's dreams',[65] provoked by hearing the popular song 'A Broken Doll'. In such examples the doll's movement, 'lolling'[66] and stumbling, though unnatural and stilted, contradicts its normal classification as inanimate object.

There is curious specificity to these descriptions of *wax* dolls, given their legacy as simulacra and ex-votos:

> Wax [...] epitomizes a type of verisimilitude that does not merely portray or illustrate the image of the living but reproduces it, 'doubles' it [...] Wax has long been associated with the skin – and can resemble human flesh to a degree unsurpassed by any other media.[67]

Furthermore, Elizabeth Kowaleski Wallace explains that 'wax objects not only imitate or copy, but they are thought *to substitute for human agency*, or in effect to enact human want'.[68] Victorian mourning dolls exemplify this, used as substituting figures, especially by parents grieving for the loss of a child, often disturbingly imbued with human qualities by the attachment of human hair, intensifying the degree of simulacrum. When the patients' bodies become like a 'wax doll', then, they are associated with replication, as if having been subject to a sudden 'changeling' replacement of the human with an object. The materiality of the wax also has many connotations, especially if considered in relation to Sartrean 'viscousness', as an 'unbalanced material that threatens human subjectivity and haunts consciousness'.[69] In this sense the viscosity of wax resists actual and conceptual stability or solidity. Wax figures also often functioned as *modelli* for larger statues and sculptures, as a stage in the progression of figurative representations and simulacra, suggesting an idea of the wax doll patient as on his way to funereal sculpture. The gradation between materials and states is apparent in one of Kate Luard's patients, whose 'total silence and absolute stillness and

---

[65] Rathbone, *Young*, 238.
[66] Sassoon, *Memoirs*, 51.
[67] Roberta Panzanelli, 'Compelling Presence: Wax Effigies in Renaissance Florence', in *Ephemeral Bodies: Wax Sculpture and the Human Figure* (Los Angeles: Getty Research Institute, 2008), 31.
[68] Elizabeth Kowaleski Wallace, 'Recycling the Sacred: The Wax Votive Object and the Eighteenth-Century Wax Baby Doll', in *The Afterlife of Used Things: Recycling in the Long Eighteenth Century*, ed. Ariane Fennetaux (London: Routledge, 2014), 155. Also see Georges Didi-Huberman, 'Viscosities and Survivals', in *Ephemeral Bodies: Wax Sculpture and the Human Figure*, 154–69.
[69] Kowaleski Wallace, 'Recycling', 155.

unconsciousness have already given him the marble statue look'.[70] The soldier 'has been peacefully dying all day',[71] but this passage suggests that the appearance of death has preceded the actual loss of life. The patient has transitioned from the human to the object, even while remaining alive. As with the wax images, the connotation of death is equivocal, and further obfuscates the human/non-human dichotomy.

The doll is a macabre caricature of the human, especially when it becomes a puppet. In an evocative scene, Smith describes how 'burned and sightless eyes made all the faces of the patients look like a ghastly row of masks, and the utter silence completed the illusion of being surrounded by inhuman puppets'.[72] The patients become sinister presences: both 'inhuman' and manipulated, they are objects beyond pathos and become threatening. But the idea of the 'puppet' can inspire a further complex reaction to, and negotiation with, the wounded human form. In *The New Book of Martyrs* (1918), French doctor Georges Duhamel depicts how treatment morphs part of his patient into a puppet:

> He [the patient] lifts up the sheet, and I see the apparatus in which we have placed the stump of his leg. It makes a kind of big white doll, which he takes in both hands with a laugh, and to which he has given the playful name of 'Mariette'.[73]

The playfulness of '"Mariette"' is presumably in part its closeness to 'marionette'. The puppet suggests manipulated movement, which is precisely what is happening to the body as it is supported by the apparatus. Marionette is also the diminutive of the soldier's name, Marie, thus becoming a playful nickname for his amputation. This is a particular movement beyond the uncanny to the grotesque; the movement of the 'doll' is both manipulated and a distorted depiction of the human. The amputation/puppet becomes a miniaturised self, a puppet strung on the tendons of the human body, and consequently imbued with the contradictory force of the grotesque: amusing yet repulsive. It is strange, but it is more than just the familiar turning against us: the marionette is an aesthetic grotesque conceit, which depicts the tension between conflicting emotions that accompanies such reduction of the body to an unnatural vestige of itself.

---

[70] Luard, *Unknown*, 37.
[71] Ibid.
[72] Smith, *Four Years*, 233.
[73] Duhamel, *Martyrs*, 175.

Although externally controlled behaviour is the basis of military life, it is particularly inherent in the experience of pain. Movement driven by pain, and constrained by medical intervention, is vividly conveyed in Bagnold's description of a patient whose

> knees shot out from under him with his restless pain. His right arm was stretched from the bed in a narrow iron frame, reminding me of a hand laid along a harp to play the chords, the fingers with their swollen green flesh extended across the strings; but of this harp his fingers were the slave, not the master.[74]

Although there is no explicit allusion to puppetry, this is an evocative example of involuntary movement. The wounded soldier is a puppet on a string, unconsciously and reluctantly 'playing' and performing for an invisible 'master'. He no longer has control over his own body and movement. He has become the 'slave' to pain and to the medical apparatus, which now determine his actions. Furthermore, the collocation of the 'swollen green' fingers with the musical instrument jarringly represents an uncanny juxtaposition of the brutally distorted body with a refined object of leisure. The 'slave'/'master' dichotomy is a telling allusion to manipulation and obedience, itself a comment on the notion of a docile body. Within the medical realm the soldier moves from being a military-puppet to a puppet constrained by medicine, driven by a force beyond all human control: pain.

One of the most oblique and disturbing ways in which the grotesque is evoked is through the strong prominence of food images, which are a striking representation of the body as Other; in particular, there is an unsettling tendency to describe wounds as pieces of food. The prominence of food metaphors is in part, perhaps, a technique of using the familiar to explain the shape and size of unfamiliar things. Orderly and ambulance driver Edward Toland, in *Aftermath of Battle* (1916), describes how a piece of shrapnel removed from the patient 'was about the size and shape of the cork of an orange marmalade jar',[75] which seems oddly specific and precise. The image of an orange is again recalled with: 'The entire side of his jaw is gone. You could put an orange into his mouth through the cheek.'[76] It seems that the food image is designed to give as exact a depiction of the size and shape of the wound as possible, but it does not

---

[74] Bagnold, *Without Dates*, 26.
[75] Edward Toland, *Aftermath of Battle: With the Red Cross in France* (New York: Macmillan, 1916), 32.
[76] Ibid., 43.

make it less disturbing. In the latter example the orange is imagined as fitting 'through' the hole in the cheek; the location of food in the mouth is not unusual, also correlating with Bakhtin's discussion of the grotesque mouth, and the threat associated with swallowing and devouring. Yet, it is a difficult image, one that disturbs and allies itself with a reflex of disgust. Additionally, we might wonder at the repeated prominence of an 'orange' specifically, which is also referenced by Rathbone: 'The cheek was swollen like a bloated orange.'[77] Here again we see the orange related to the location of the face and mouth. Part of the resonance of the orange perhaps relates to its distinctive skin and fleshy texture. Fruit is also perishable, and will rot; the repeated presence of fruit in the damaged body may carry overtones of the decay of organic matter, which develops into a further recoil in disgust.

Further examples use food items to represent size and shape: 'a piece of shrapnel is sometimes bigger than a hen's egg';[78] 'The opening, a few inches above the wrist, was the shape of the opening in a melon when a single slice has been removed.'[79] Such referents offer a benign analogy for the ways in which bodily integrity has been compromised, especially when it is not the size or shape but the colour of a food which is invoked to describe the strangeness: 'his face is just the colour of cream on a glass of milk',[80] or 'all tendons were cut and the hand chocolate colored'.[81] An even more benign rhetoric operates when the soldiers' wounded bodies are likened to items of food, 'pulled out of the ambulances as loaves of bread are pulled out of the oven';[82] or, in a variation of the same image, 'the sitting cases are going to bed in a big ward having tiers of beds arranged on metal supporting rods. The effect is [. . .] somewhat grotesque for the arrangement reminds one of so many tins of cakes in the cooling room of a bakery.'[83] Wounded men, temporarily housed in a railway shed ahead of evacuation, look to Sarah Macnaughtan 'like nothing so much as shot pheasants laid out in rows after some big shoot in the coverts'.[84] These examples also extend the

---

[77] Rathbone, *Young*, 201.
[78] Boyd, *Ypres*, 64.
[79] Rathbone, *Young*, 240.
[80] Dearden, *Duty*, 28.
[81] Toland, *Aftermath*, 75.
[82] Borden, 'Conspiracy', 79.
[83] Olive Dent, *A Volunteer Nurse on the Western Front* (1917; London: Virgin Books, 2014), 104.
[84] Macnaughtan, *Diary*, 79.

metonymic treatment of the individual, however, and the objectification and indistinguishable anonymity of patients.

Food images offer evocations of disgust, especially when depicted as rotten. Toland offers vivid examples of a hand as 'a slimy green thing, the size of a mop, with the poor fingers like rotten cucumbers', and a wound that 'looked and smelt like rotten fish'.[85] The presence of rot and decay conjures an especially visceral reaction. The idea of rotten food is a fundamental threat to the boundaries of the self, and repugnant to the notion of ingestion. While it may be far preferable to handle rotten food than rotten human flesh, visualising the patient's body in terms of a piece of food is inherently unsettling.

Food is the Other that we ingest and, crucially, which we assimilate. This complicates the concept of abjection: ingestion is the inverse of abjection. Items of food, in these images, become abject, polluting the idea of nourishment and pejorating ingestion. This is most marked with the numerous references to meat, arguably the most disturbing of the food images, which remind us that flesh *is* meat. Toland's patient smelt 'like rotten meat, which it was. Three fingers were gone from the other hand and a piece of flesh missing from the calf of his right leg as big as a mutton chop.'[86] Luard consolidates this theme with the image of a 'leg still in the raw-meat stage',[87] while Smith describes a patient's shoulder, which 'had been scooped out of his body as the oyster is scooped from a chicken'.[88] Rathbone describes 'her arm, now swollen to the dimensions of a nightmare German sausage'.[89] Jane Marcus suggests this is 'a grotesque and phallic German sausage, a phallic enemy inside the woman's body'.[90] However, perhaps what is more important here than the specificity of 'German', which is Otherness, foreignness, and the enemy, is that more crucially, it is meat, and puts an object for consumption *within* the human body.

Furthermore, there is a worrying risk in conflating food and discarded body parts. Vicki Tromanhauser suggests that the proliferation of such meat images emerges due to how 'the pressures of food scarcity and rationing introduced new and unrecognizable meats to

---

[85] Toland, *Aftermath*, 60, 68–9.
[86] Ibid., 74–5.
[87] Luard, *Unknown*, 41.
[88] Smith, *Four Years*, 139–40.
[89] Rathbone, *Young*, 238.
[90] Jane Marcus, 'Afterword: The Nurse's Text: Acting Out an Anaesthetic Aesthetic', in *We That Were Young*, by Irene Rathbone (New York: Feminist Press, 1989), 475.

the wartime palate'.⁹¹ The instability of food sources and the unfamiliarity of the food item cooking in the chef's pot conflates meat and meatiness of the human and animal, in turn reminding us 'that beneath our figurative human dressing we, too, might be consumable goods'.⁹² This is more explicitly illustrated in Borden's account, in 'Blind', of mistaking a body part for animal meat:

> 'Where's that knee of mine? I left it in the saucepan on the window ledge. I had boiled it up for an experiment.'
> 'One of the orderlies must have taken it,' she says, putting her old needle on to boil.
> 'Good God! Did he mistake it?'
> 'Jean, did you take a saucepan you found on the windowsill?'
> 'Yes, sister, I took it. I thought it was for the *casse-croûte*; it looked like a *ragoût* of *mouton*. I have it here.'⁹³

While it is telling that the doctor claims possession of the discarded body part, 'that knee of mine', implying that it no longer belongs to the patient/soldier, more significantly this scene illustrates the disturbing possibility of mistaking human for animal flesh, a knee for a joint of mutton. Underlying this is the suggestion, had nobody realised, of unintentional cannibalism. It is the ultimate realisation of body consuming body, and a microcosmic vision of body destroying body.

The connection between ingestion and medical treatment is taken further with multiple references to utensils. In particular, the prevalence of 'spoon': 'I have never seen so deep a wound, it is exactly as if one had taken a great sharp spoon and scooped a large spoonful out'; or, more subtly, 'his physical appearance improved with every teaspoonful of healthy blood the other fellow pumped into him'.⁹⁴ A 'teaspoonful' is an unusual way to quantify blood, and such descriptions conflate an instrument of medicine with an instrument of the home; and again, it is associated with ingestion and consumption. Images of domesticity and nourishment become associated with medical intrusion, naturalising it with quotidian images of daily routine; but the connotations may also run in the other direction.

The persistent food images offer a paradoxical link with sterility.

---

⁹¹ Vicki Tromanhauser, 'Inside the "Butcher's Shop": Women's Great War Writing and Surgical Meat', in *Literature and Meat Since 1900*, ed. Sean McCorry and John Miller (Cham: Palgrave Macmillan, 2019), 21.
⁹² Ibid., 29.
⁹³ Borden, 'Blind', in *Forbidden*, 100.
⁹⁴ Dearden, *Duty*, 26, 38.

Attention is often drawn to the fact that the kitchen is where instruments are sterilised; logistically, this might be the only place with running water, especially in improvised settings. For example, Borden details her 'kitchen' scene:

> My own kitchen was an arrangement of shelves for saucepans and syringes and needles of different sizes, and cardboard boxes full of ampoules of camphor oil and strychnine and caffeine and morphine, and large ampoules of sterilized salt and water, and dozens of beautiful sharp shining needles were always on the boil.[95]

Connecting food preparation with surgical preparation in this space once again links food with bodies, ingestion with medical intrusion. The conflation of sterility with food and ingestion tends to contaminate the latter.

This grotesque discourse articulates some of the horror of medical care, uncovering the perceived threat of the open body to its closest observer: the medic, who must touch it. The medics witness the body not only at its most vulnerable but at its most unknown, eliciting ungraspable emotions and reactions. As represented in these narratives, the wounded body is Othered in order to draw out the details of medical care, and to express the psychological pressure experienced by the caregiver. The shock of the war context, the bodies, and what bodies can survive are most evocatively resonant throughout these representations; the resources of the grotesque enable the medics to depict the unimaginable scenes before them, in an unprecedented war, with unprecedented casualties, with due recognition of the inevitable conflict of perspectives between medic and patient. The medic must recognise the human beneath the inhuman, yet the challenge of coping with the ambiguously human is exacerbated by the modes and means of medical intervention itself.

The aesthetic grotesque is a particular representational mode that these texts employ to express their authors' encounters with broken and transgressing bodies. This mode of representation opens up a means by which we can articulate our interactions with bodies, and how they can be Othered or assimilated, by turns, and enables the exploration and critique of encountering wounded bodies. In reading medics' personal narratives, the reader is positioned as a witness to retrospective efforts to represent medical treatment and caregiving. We expect to see wounds and wound care, through the softening mediation of the medic; the horror and disgust that accompanies the

---

[95] Borden, 'Blind', 97–8.

medical treatment is assimilated by the medic, so it becomes difficult to articulate and communicate that to a reader. The medic-as-writer adopts the literary mode of the aesthetic grotesque in order to communicate the tensions of the medics' position as they treat their patients and witness pain and suffering. The mode of the aesthetic grotesque allows the medic to offer a view of the wounded which communicates the essence of the experience. It is not an unmediated perspective, precisely because they are employing a specific aesthetic; but it does allow for the reader to align with the position of the medic. The deliberate pursuit of a grotesque aesthetic throughout their writings serves to illuminate their conflicting emotions and reactions to transgressing bodies. But most specifically, this mode of representation allows us to uncover the tangled psychological and emotional demands accompanying medical witnessing and medical care.

A Medical Grotesque

In order to provide proper medical intervention, the medic must intrude and interfere. They must pierce the skin, or augment the human form, breaking the body's boundaries further, all the while dissolving the distinction between inside and outside. Considering this, I wish to advance the idea of a 'medical grotesque', as a subgenre of the grotesque. The wounded body, with its transgressed boundaries, becomes the site of this specific kind of grotesque, in which the body is extended or intruded upon, and its boundaries further violated by the medical touch. Crucially though, this is not a social or ideological concept but an aesthetic one. These reflections do not comment on the social, political, or personal implications of (dis)ability or deformity, which are explored through Disability Studies. Instead, I wish to employ this concept as a route to understanding the ways in which the tensions in medical encounters are represented. The medical grotesque is a particular case of the aesthetic stance of the grotesque, which serves, for these writers, to accommodate the conflicted nature of medical intervention.

The foundation of the medical grotesque is the uncomfortable visual incongruity created by the meeting of human matter and synthetic, medical materials. At its heart is an inherent conflict between protrusion and intrusion. In the traditional aesthetic grotesque, the soma is ruptured by protrusions and openings; by swelling, bloating, and distension. The medical grotesque, however, forces us to rethink this in terms of the visibility of ruptures caused by the intrusion of medical materials and instruments. In such circumstances, the human body is attached to, and supported and reinforced by, unnatural appendages. Strangeness and Otherness return in the form of various material attachments, such as 'a dozen forceps [...] clipped on to the arteries' of a leg being amputated, 'hanging like a Medusa fringe round the bleeding stump'.[96] Appearing outside of the body, this is a moment of protrusion, overhanging and crossing the bodily margins, but the forceps hanging and becoming attached *add* to the wounds, morphing the sight into something strange and unsettling. Such examples of intervention present the complex medical bind of cruelty and care, and corrupt the integrity of the somatic form with the interference of material structures not only connected to but *put into* the body.

The use of medical tubing offers numerous vivid impressions of such grotesquery: 'The man [...] has no nostrils; they were blown away, and he breathes through two pieces of red rubber tubing: it gave a more horrible look to his face than I have ever seen.'[97] These medical materials produce vivid instances of grotesque distortion from intrusion: 'A large area of raw flesh lay revealed, with two pieces of rubber tubing embedded in it for drainage purposes.'[98] The embedded tubes pierce the bodily boundary, and alter the surface and depths of the body. With the advent of the Carrel-Dakin method, a pivotal moment in advanced wound care, attention is especially drawn to tubes running in and out of the wounded bodies. Dakin's solution was fed through the Carrel tubes, which were

> divided into maybe as many as five different nozzles [...] packed into various parts of the wound. They were kept in place with bandages; and then a clamp was fixed onto the biggest rubber tube so that the right quantity dripped through the wound.[99]

The method required the repeated insertion and reinsertion of tubing to cleanse the wound, so the body was regularly interfered with and intruded upon.

Demonstrations of medical suspension apparatuses, such as pulleys, strings, straps, and slings, reinforce the impression of

---

[96] Smith, *Four Years*, 158.
[97] Bagnold, *Without Dates*, 7.
[98] Rathbone, *Young*, 196–7.
[99] Rebecca West, *War Nurse: The True Story of a Woman Who Lived, Loved and Suffered on the Western Front* (New York: Cosmopolitan Books, 1930), 60–2.

distortion, representing the body as held subject to multiple forces: 'He was laid up with a shell fracture of his left leg and right arm and was swung in a maze of pulley ropes and weights.'[100] Although such suspension and 'traction' was designed to heal and inhibit deformity,[101] deformity is precisely the visual impression initially communicated: 'it gave a more horrible look [...] than I have ever seen'.[102] The method produces a strange spectacle, as the pioneering surgeon Fred Albee explains in *A Surgeon's Fight to Rebuild Men* (1943):

> The first thing that met my eyes on visiting the wards [...] was an array of wooden beams and frames, reaching from each bed part way to the ceiling, with weights and pulleys of every description. It was like stepping into a building under construction. Suspended in this forest of soft pine were hundreds of arms and legs, broken by gunshot wounds, or otherwise.[103]

The array of medical apparatuses initially obscures any perception of the human figures. The ward becomes a space of curious contrasts: simultaneously 'a building under construction' and a 'forest'. The dominance of wood echoes and accentuates the fixedness of the reinforced, suspended bodies. The inclusion of 'soft pine' complicates the image, however, suggesting some malleability in the bodies and implements. The forest metaphor also evokes a contrasting image of nature unaffected by artificial interventions, which opposes the scene of bodies destroyed and patched back together by human hands. Such an analogy to forests is also made by James Robb Church, in *The Doctor's Part* (1918):

> The wards devoted entirely to the fracture cases were a forest of uprights and cross-pieces traversed in all directions by cords running through pulleys and at the ends of the cords dangled sandbags and weights like some queer fruit in this conventional grove.[104]

Church focuses on the apparatuses, making no mention of the body parts, though we can still envisage how limbs are strung up in this

---

[100] James Robb Church, *The Doctor's Part* (New York: D. Appleton, 1918), 93.
[101] Christine Hallett, *Containing Trauma: Nursing Work in the First World War* (Manchester: Manchester University Press, 2009), 44.
[102] Bagnold, *Without Dates*, 7.
[103] Fred H. Albee, *A Surgeon's Fight to Rebuild Men* (New York: E. P. Dutton, 1943), 116.
[104] Church, *Part*, 84.

forest. The 'queer fruit' is reminiscent of the aforementioned connection between wounds and food, but the emphasis is on the pulleys and uprights that contradict the natural image. Such unsettling analogies are further developed by Rathbone, who states, 'Almost every other bed was raised into a tunnel-like shape by a protective cage under the bed-clothes, or else looked gallows-like with some strange arrangement of wood and cord supporting the shattered arm of its occupant.'[105] The 'gallows-like' simile aligns the wooden structure with the dual meaning of 'hanging': suspension and execution.

We cannot fail to see that such examples of medical interference are edged with the uncanny, specifically in relation to the intersection of body and object. Intervention is aid, but although it has the long-term goal of healing, it may take the form of violent intrusion. Toland refers to a particularly brutal style of intervention by drawing attention to the use of nails: 'Two spikes or nails were driven through the leg; one through the bone of the femur and the other through the joint of the knee, on each side of the fracture', which is the 'best way of supporting a fractured limb'.[106] Toland makes the strangeness of the sight explicit: 'It does not seem to hurt the patients, but it looks very queer to see the head of an ordinary nail sticking out of the flesh with a string tied to it.'[107] The intervention with the sharp object seems altogether wrong; the nail is simultaneously associated with building construction, or even, if we think of Christ nailed to the cross, becomes itself a complex image of pain and sacrifice. The specificity of the nail, considered perhaps more familiar in a domestic or labour setting, is transformed in the anomalous context of the medical sphere.

In all of these cases the bodies undergo a distortion, which is a central motif of the medical grotesque. The medical apparatus modifies the physical form by not only altering but *adding to* the body. As with protrusions, where the body forces itself outwards, expanding the body's surface, here too the body encroaches outwards. But here the situation is more complex, since these artificial extensions and inhuman apparatuses are simultaneously manifestations of medical intervention. These are bodies extended by augmentation, and the something added elicits strong reactions of discomfort:

---

[105] Rathbone, *Young*, 203.
[106] Toland, *Aftermath*, 148, 76.
[107] Ibid., 76.

it is not the mere imperfection of life in itself, but rather *the life in the wrong place* that is perhaps founded therein – the precipitous slope of life in its plasticity – which evokes disgust. It seems indeed above all the intensified (not simply 'mechanized') activity of life which is disgusting in its exaggerated operation, insofar as it exceeds the limits of the real, or as it were quasi-'personal', purposeful organic unity.[108]

The wound, or injury, is exaggerated. The medical apparatus draws attention to the point where life has been interfered with and highlights 'life in the wrong place': an extra-corporeality.[109] The apparatus, serving to counteract the lack, augments the modern body.[110]

The medical grotesque is a representational strategy which illuminates the complex layers of medical care, particularly the crisis of medical intervention. These particular narratives address two manifestations of a medical grotesque: one through the clinical gaze, and the other through representations of medical violence. In order to fully form an idea of the medical grotesque, especially in relation to medical intrusion and its potential violence, we need to understand 'the clinical gaze', and how it features in these texts and the contemporary medical context. By rethinking the clinical gaze through the medical grotesque, we can acquire a more informed understanding of the complexities of caregiving and begin to disentangle the layers of brutality and violence, and the apparent carelessness of the medic, so gaining a more profound understanding of the complexities of the medic's position.

The Clinical Gaze

The concept of 'the clinical gaze' refers to the professional perspective of medics, though it is typically more associated with doctors than nurses, and assumes that medics view patients with very specific attitudes. Its connotations are often negative, especially in current-day medical discussions; yet there are elements of it which are positive for the patient as well as the practitioner. It is more than just dehumanising the patient; it is also a means of treating, caring, and healing.

---

[108] Kolnai, *Disgust*, 62 (italics in original).
[109] Tim Armstrong, *Modernism, Technology and the Body* (Cambridge: Cambridge University Press, 1998), 80.
[110] These themes could be explored further in relation to prosthesis, mechanisation, and technology, even gesturing towards the post-human, but that is beyond the scope of this book.

In order to adequately appreciate the role of the 'gaze', we must understand it as both literal and metaphorical, as Johanna Shapiro encourages. The clinical gaze is both a tool of observation and data-collecting and a source of 'broader, more intangible dimensions of interaction and relationship in ways of great importance to both patient and doctor'.[111] Michel Foucault's concept, outlined in *The Birth of the Clinic* (1963), arises from the eighteenth-century approach to medicine, when pathological anatomy expanded doctors' knowledge and skills. The doctor's knowledge was able to literally penetrate the patient's body: 'The medical gaze must therefore travel along a path that had not so far been opened to it: vertically from the symptomatic surface to the tissual surface; in depth, plunging from the manifest to the hidden; and in both directions.'[112] Medical knowledge moved from a purely passive, detached observation to a more hands-on approach, which allowed doctors to 'gaze' inside the confines of the body.

Sight persists as a familiar metaphor for knowledge, especially in the medical context. This is enigmatically suggested when Duhamel speaks of the patient's being 'enfolded by the blue radiance of the Master's gaze',[113] implying that the doctor can see beyond the confines of the body. The image of 'blue radiance' connotes an outward gaze, which is powerful and awe-inspiring. The doctor as 'Master' is not only evocative of authority and expertise but likened to a theological or mythical figure. The 'man' and 'Master' is 'white-bearded', 'white-haired', giving an impression of wisdom but also of being wizened and aged: 'The white-bearded man considers them in silence, turning in his hand the cunning knife.'[114] Duhamel places curious emphasis on the doctor's eyes, confirming the significance of their gaze: 'we look at [the infected leg] anxiously, and the white-haired Master fixes two small light-blue eyes upon it, eyes accustomed to appraise the things of life, yet, for the moment, hesitant'.[115] The doctor's skilled sight epitomises his medical authority, the key parts of which are his store of knowledge and his deliberation on a course of action, or sometimes of inaction: 'Every morning, the good head doctor stared at the swollen flesh with his little

---

[111] Johanna Shapiro, '(Re)Examining the Clinical Gaze Through the Prism of Literature', *Families, Systems & Health* 20, no. 2 (2002): 161.

[112] Michel Foucault, *The Birth of the Clinic*, trans. A. M. Sheridan (1963; Abingdon: Routledge, 2005), 166.

[113] Duhamel, *Martyrs*, 14.

[114] Ibid., 14.

[115] Ibid., 27.

round discoloured eyes and said: "Come, we must just wait till tomorrow."'[116] The power of the gaze reinforces an authoritative and assured skill, which manifests itself as mastery. Borden, similarly, likens the surgeon to a wizard, implying the influence of magic: 'I thought of the chief surgeon, the wizard working like lightning through the night, and all the others wielding their flashing knives against the invisible enemy'.[117] The power of the surgeon is trusted as a benevolent force.

Detached observation is an inherent element of the medic's role, and the medical space. Borden explains, 'Day after day he [the patient] lies there and we watch him. All day and all night he is watched.'[118] This is especially telling precisely due to the switch between active and passive verbs. This pairing of 'watch' and 'is watched' emphasises that the observation is constant, not merely a matter of agency but an ongoing state; its epigrammatic repetition implies that nothing will go unnoticed. The medic must attend to what the body can and cannot tell them; hence, 'signs' pervade these descriptions: 'I scan the surface of the floor where the men are spread like a carpet, for signs, for my special secret signals of death.'[119]

Adequate care hinges on knowledge and, despite the accumulated codification of knowledge over the last century, there is always more to learn. Duhamel depicts a scene of (presumed) autopsy:

> Well! I came for a certain purpose. I came to learn certain things at last that your body can tell me now.
>
> I open the case. As before, I cut the dressings with the shining scissors. And I was just about to say to you, as before: 'If I hurt you, call out.'[120]

The idea that the body will 'tell me now' establishes the idea of the body as a semiotic system, bearing information that will add to medical knowledge; hence, Duhamel's desire 'to learn certain things' through dissection, and finally receive answers. Yet, the way that the body will speak now offers knowledge that could not be gained when the patient was living; the contrast between what can be verbally expressed and what can be elicited from signs in the body

---

[116] Ibid., 58.
[117] Borden, 'Blind', 97.
[118] Borden, 'Conspiracy', 81.
[119] Ibid., 101.
[120] Duhamel, *Martyrs*, 94.

is poignantly double-edged: the will to know is detached from the effort to save this patient, and is rather an acquisition of knowledge to be accumulated in the medical 'granary'.[121] Like many medical memoirs, these texts demonstrate a yearning to solve a puzzle or mystery: 'Lying there propped on his pillow [. . .] he is all the centre of my thoughts; I am preoccupied with the mystery that is in his lungs.'[122] Louisa May Alcott's *Hospital Sketches* (1863), representing her American Civil War nursing experiences, gives a similar impression: 'There was an uncanny sort of fascination in watching [the surgeon] as he peered and probed into the mechanism of those wonderful bodies, whose mysteries he understood so well. The more intricate the wound, the better he liked it.'[123] Alcott captures the fascination of the medic, to whom exploring and solving these mysteries is as much a reaffirming activity as saving the dying. We see this intrigue on multiple occasions in Rathbone's text, where there is 'fascination in watching the way the wound grew less dirty-yellow and more bright-red beneath the cleansing stream' and 'in seeing the new pink skin forming beneath'.[124] Even in her own wound 'Joan took a professional interest [. . .] and was amazed at the quantity of yellow pus which poured forth',[125] not recoiling but captivated by the wound and the process of healing.

The complex system of medical care demands efficiency, so that medics are rarely able to spend much time with their patients, or provide long-term care, and consequently often seem impersonal or detached. Bagnold relates specific instances of this patient experience: 'Corrigan was angry all day; the idea that "a bloomin' woman should come an' shove something into me systim" was too much for him. But he forgets himself: there are no individualists now: his "system" belongs to us.'[126] Bagnold puns on 'system', as bodily and bureaucratic, an observation which is similarly expressed, with levity, when 'Sister said, laughing to Smiff the other day, "Your leg is mine" "Wrong again; it's the Governmint's!" said Smiff.'[127] Bagnold depicts these patients as fully aware of their own place in the medical

---

[121] Rick Rylance, 'The Theatre and the Granary: Observations on Nineteenth-Century Medical Narratives', *Literature and Medicine* 25, no. 2 (2006): 260.
[122] Bagnold, *Without Dates*, 78.
[123] Louisa May Alcott, *Hospital Sketches* (Boston: James Redpath, 1863), 23–4, Kindle.
[124] Rathbone, *Young*, 197, 290.
[125] Ibid., 240.
[126] Bagnold, *Without Dates*, 99.
[127] Ibid., 99–100.

system, in which the military and the government continue to have a larger claim on the soldier's wounded body.

As one consequence of this system, bodies are metonymised according to their complaint: 'There's a knee for you, doctor, and three elbows. In five minutes I'll send in the lung'; '"I've got three knees, two spines, five abdomens, twelve heads. Here's a lung case."'[128] Pragmatically they are distributed to specific wards according to their wound, but the impersonal effects are implicitly critiqued in a further example from Borden's sketch 'Moonlight': 'The moon is just above the abdominal ward. Next to it is the hut given up to gas gangrene, and next to that are the Heads. The Knees are on the other side, and the Elbows and the fractured Things.'[129] It is an example of spatial dismemberment, brought about by the hierarchising and triaging of wounds, which seems legitimate until Borden's list descends into the vagueness of 'fractured Things'. They are reduced to what Arthur Kleinman terms 'an anonymous medical euphemism':[130] removing the complex emotional, social, and moral implications of their wounds, and reducing them yet again to objects.

The inevitability of reducing the wounded to their complaint is profoundly depicted by Bagnold's patient who 'looked down at the almost unrecognizable twelve inches which we call "Rees's wound," [...] "'Tisn' no more me arm," he said at length, "than ..." he paused for a simile. "'Tisn' me arm, it's me wound," he finally explained.'[131] His arm *becomes* his wound. Not only is he physically restricted by his wounded arm, he is defined by it. The wound becomes a synecdoche, in which a patient's part speaks for their whole. Even physically, the wound takes over: 'This leg, infected to the very marrow, seems to be slowly devouring the man to whom it belongs',[132] and soon the man no longer exists. There is significant variation in how often the patients are identified by name, rather than by their patient number, or more metonymically by their wound, as in 'jaw case'. Nurses more often refer to patients' names: Bagnold, for example, refers to 'Ryan', 'Rees', 'Dad', and 'Corrigan', whereas in contrast, Harold Dearden typically introduces the patient

---

[128] Borden, 'In the Operating Room', in *Forbidden*, 86; Borden, 'Blind', 100.
[129] Borden, 'Moonlight', 43.
[130] Arthur Kleinman, *Writing on the Margins* (Berkeley: University of California Press, 1995), 115.
[131] Bagnold, *Without Dates*, 132.
[132] Duhamel, *Martyrs*, 27.

impersonally: 'a very interesting case today. A man had his arm very badly shattered.'[133]

Professional detachment and the imputation of professional insensitivity is encapsulated in Borden's 'Conspiracy'. Borden illustrates the conspiratorial power of the medics over the wounded body: 'It is all carefully arranged. Everything is arranged.'[134] Order and management are reinforced not only by the repetition of 'arranged' throughout, but also by the immediate framing of the wounded body as prone and passive:

> This is the place where he is to be mended. We lift him on to a table. We peel off his clothes [. . .] We handle his clothes that are stiff with blood. We cut off his shirt with large scissors. We stare at the obscene sight of his innocent wounds. He allows us to do this. He is helpless to stop us. We wash off the dry blood round the edges of his wounds. He suffers us to do as we like with him.[135]

The persistent repetition of 'we' plus active, present tense verb makes it clear the body is passive and the hands of the medics are active and forceful. It is framed as a conspiracy of medicine and medical professionals against the body: 'We confer together over his body and he hears us. We discuss his different parts in terms that he does not understand, but he listens while we make calculations with his heart beats and the pumping breath of his lungs.'[136] The medical system isolates the patient, who is marginalised even by the medical jargon of the medics' discussion. Like Smiff's leg, the patient's body is no longer their own. Agency transfers to the caregiver, who takes over the body.

Importantly, there are no exceptions: 'He is only one among thousands. They are all the same.'[137] Equally anonymous, and equally submissive, these are clear examples of docile bodies in the medical realm. The docile body of the military system, though altered, remains: 'a body is docile that may be subjected, used, transformed and improved'.[138] The docility evident in these passages is further consolidated, and the patients' discipline and obedience compounded, with their passive acceptance of treatment: not only

---

[133] Dearden, *Duty*, 38.
[134] Borden, 'Conspiracy', 79.
[135] Ibid., 79–80.
[136] Ibid., 80.
[137] Ibid., 81.
[138] Michel Foucault, *Discipline and Punish*, trans. Alan Sheridan (London: Penguin Books, 1977), 136.

must they 'bare' themselves, without complaint, they must allow the power of the medic to transfer and run through their bodies, to the point where 'They all let us do with them what we like.'[139]

For the most part the clinical gaze has a dehumanising effect. As Shapiro succinctly explains:

> The effect of the gaze was to turn the patient into the Other, someone (or something) completely different and separate from the examiner. At its worst, the gaze evolved into a form of symbolic medical violence against patients, a powering-over that reduced and demeaned their humanity.[140]

Although the 'gaze' aids that differentiation of self and Other, its essence can add to the brutalisation of the medical space. Yet, Borden's example is more complex than this, given her self-awareness: her satiric tone demonstrates the self-reflexive nature of the narrative, which is evident in many of these examples. Borden, among others, recognises the tension between cruelty and care. Thus we can identify the inherent tension in the 'clinical gaze', in terms of its positive and negative use and purpose, and the consequent ambivalence. The tension is not solely in the clinical gaze itself but also in how these mediated accounts represent the gaze. In these examples, the representation of the gaze is particularly negative, which enables the medic to critique their own role as caregiver. This is especially manifest in the self-reflexive style of these medical accounts, which often draw self-critical attention to moments of perceived violence.

Medical Violence

'When one shoots at a man it makes a hole, and the doctor must make seven others.'[141] Bagnold adeptly points out that in order to perform healing sometimes further damage must take place. We must remember that in this context medical treatments, even invasive ones, sometimes had to be performed without appropriate, or even any, anaesthesia. For the medics concerned, the 'symbolic medical violence' is profoundly real, and they depict it through self-reflexive images of violence. The violent scenes they narrate express their own discomfort with their duties, as well as opening up difficult issues

---

[139] Borden, 'Conspiracy', 81.
[140] Shapiro, '(Re)Examining', 163.
[141] Bagnold, *Without Dates*, 103.

concerning the complex layers of caregiving and torturing affective terrain.

Bagnold distinctively articulates her awareness of how necessary medical procedures, especially invasive ones, require someone – the nurses – to remove and repeat the dressings, inevitably inflicting further pain. When the surgeon packs the wound, the nurse must go inside and retrieve it: 'It was all very fine for the theatre people to fill his shoulder chock full of pluggings while he lay unconscious on the table; they had packed it as you might stuff linen into a bag: it was another matter to get it out.'[142] On retrieving the dressing, 'Six inches deep, the gauze stuck, crackling under the pull of the forceps, blood and pus leaping forward [...] when one hole was emptied there was another, five in all.'[143] Bagnold conveys her regretful resignation to the inevitability that the patients must continue to experience pain: she makes it clear that it is necessary to intrude, and to reintrude, but this does not make the job any easier to perform.

Similarly, in *'Sister': The War Diary of a Nurse* (1927), Helen Dore Boylston repeatedly illustrates how difficult it is to avoid further hurt: 'it was impossible to take the dried and stiffened bandages off carefully. The only way was to snatch them off with one desperate yank.'[144] Later on, during a period of particularly 'heavy dressings',[145] she relates the trouble she has with the dressing for her patient 'with a frightful arm; elbow joint smashed, and the whole arm stiff and swollen, and full of gas gangrene':

> In getting off the dressing I *had* to move it some, and though I was careful as I could be, I could hear the bones crunching and grating inside. Then I had to pull off hard, dry sponges, and haul out yards of packing that kept catching on the splintered bone [...] Once, accidentally touching a bare nerve-end with my forceps, I hurt him terribly.[146]

Clearly, Boylston regrets and resents what she has to do, and what she must persist with even though she is evidently causing more pain. Effective provision of medical care necessitates causing more discomfort; the removal of clothing, bandages, and dressings is not

---

[142] Ibid., 140–1.
[143] Ibid.
[144] Helen Dore Boylston, *'Sister': The War Diary of a Nurse* (New York: Ives Washburn, 1927), 64.
[145] Ibid., 148.
[146] Ibid., 149.

tangential to the pain of the wound or injury but adds to the pain event. Nor do moments of surgery or intrusive procedure, even if successful, undo the experiences of suffering. In *Containing Trauma* (2009), Christine Hallett argues that the often used 'phrase "one can't help hurting them horribly" summarises the central dilemma of nursing work: in order to provide ultimate relief, pain-inducing processes had to be somehow endured by both patient and "carer"'.[147] This is often felt by the nurses, but it is also experienced across other medical roles.

To an extent, the 'callousness of hospital work'[148] is crystallised in certain representations of the doctor figure, who is characterised as a 'brute', an 'assassin', and a 'cruel man'.[149] Duhamel's depiction of the doctor is especially haunting and menacing, setting him up as a villain figure:

> Dr. Boussin probed the wound, and felt the cracked bone. He was an old surgeon who had his own ideas about courage and pain. He made up his mind.
> 'I am in a hurry; you are a man. There is just a little something to be done to you. Kneel down there and don't stir.'
> A few minutes later, Gautreau was on his knees, holding on to the leg of the table. His head was covered with blood-stained bandages, and Dr. Boussin, chisel in hand, was tapping on his skull with the help of a little mallet, like a sculptor. Gautreau exclaimed:
> 'Monsieur Bassin, Monsieur Bassin, you're hurting me' ... 'Monsieur Bassin, I tell you you're killing me ... you're driving nails into my head, it's a shame' ... 'it's all over now' said the surgeon, laying down his instruments.[150]

Presumably, this is an example of trepanation, a precursor to the modern day craniotomy, but the manner of treatment appears outdated and wholly archaic. The doctor ignores the cries and pleas from the patient, instead preoccupied with 'driving nails into' the head of the conscious man. The absence of anaesthesia makes this most astonishing; yet the judgement is muted, for this is a doctor whose experience, we assume, has influenced 'his own ideas about courage and pain'. The villain/victim dichotomies are further depicted by an orderly in Ana Carden-Coyne's *The Politics of Wounds* (2014):

---

[147] Hallett, *Containing*, 103.
[148] Ibid., 102.
[149] Duhamel, *Martyrs*, 81, 59.
[150] Ibid., 84–6.

> Private E. Northend, writing under the pseudonym Castorius Iodinus describes 'The Dispensary' as a place where an orderly witnesses 'innocent victims cruelly maltreated', and is forced to assist in 'bloodthirsty deeds and acts of violence' [...] The orderly imitates the medical discourse: 'It Won't Hurt – to which both the professional and amateur masters of the knife were addicted.' The orderly was so used to hearing it he almost lost his 'humane instinct'. As the Major 'bores a cavity into the patient's neck' he 'repeatedly assures his victim in a suave tone that "It won't hurt", but condescends to add that "it will be a little uncomfortable".'[151]

The language of violence pervades the orderly's story, with terms, such as 'bloodthirsty', more typically associated with battle. Iodinus' use of 'professional and amateur masters of the knife' establishes the damning irony of their routine disregard for the pain they inflict.

Details such as nails embedded in hanging flesh present powerful visual images of violence, but these and other methods must be contextualised in order to recognise their relation to care. Such violent interventions were intrinsic to the rapid progress being made in reconstructive surgery, for example. It is impossible to separate the bodily violence of such interventions from their reconstructive purposes:

> They borrow pieces of rib and bits of shin-bone and make new noses of them; they twist and pull and coax adjacent tissue until it covers the gaps and they bridge in vacant areas by skin grafts until finally the unfortunate wretch comes forth somewhere in the shape that God made him.[152]

While Church is describing legitimate acts of somatic reconstruction, of a sort that became fundamental to recovery and rehabilitation, he does so with the language of force and violence. The body is manipulated, twisted, pulled, and coaxed into an approximate new version of itself. The implication of 'borrow pieces of rib' is representative of Adam's rib, suggesting life created from another. It would be remiss not to recognise an allusion to Mary Shelley's *Frankenstein* (1818) in Church's passage, which echoes some of the pioneering novel's ideas: '[Adam] had come forth from the hands of God a perfect creature, happy and prosperous, guarded by the especial care of his Creator [...] but I was wretched, helpless, and

---

[151] Ana Carden-Coyne, *The Politics of Wounds: Military Patients and Medical Power in the First World War* (Oxford: Oxford University Press, 2014), 295.
[152] Church, *Part*, 74–5.

alone.'¹⁵³ The work of God the Creator is set beside that of men acting the part of God, and Church recognises in these mutilated soldiers a version of Frankenstein's 'creature', whose 'yellow skin scarcely covered the work of muscles and arteries beneath';¹⁵⁴ the wounded soldiers' skin is stretched and coaxed to cover up 'the gaps', echoing the crude botchery of Frankenstein's work.

Church is not alone in alluding to *Frankenstein*. In *A Green Tent in Flanders* (1917), Maud Mortimer describes the 'procession of bandaged heads so obsessing us with the mysterious horror of disfiguration. Since 1914, Frankenstein['s creature] himself would be little more than one of a great family of shelterless spirits crouching behind newly hand-made faces.'¹⁵⁵ Being so obsessed with the 'horror of disfiguration', Mortimer's allusion to a novel centred on a disfigured scientific creation is unsurprising. The meaning behind such a vivid description is left ambiguous, particularly what these 'newly hand-made faces' actually are. They might be facial reconstructions, but given her focus on wounded soldiers, it may be the injuries that are 'new', implying that it is the wounds which have created these 'newly hand-made faces'. Furthermore, it seems Mortimer makes that common error of conflating Victor Frankenstein with his 'creature'; although, of course, only the 'creature' is a scientific fabrication, disfigured and 'shelterless', and comparable to the wounded soldiers, who have had 'all their intimate personal values of touch with the outer world brutalized and shifted'.¹⁵⁶ Both ambiguities, however, as well as the invocation of the 'Modern Prometheus', speak to the ambivalence of the medical grotesque, and express the entangled ethics of medical intervention and the remaking of bodies.

Church synthesises the paradox of intrusive medical care as 'construction versus destruction',¹⁵⁷ also central to Shelley's novel, and foregrounded in the context of warfare. To an extent any depiction of medical ethics will inevitably evoke *Frankenstein*, but the allusions here open up disturbing questions about the ethics of bodily repair and recreation. Borden pictures the passive body subject to medical activity, in ways that tie healing to discovery and experimentation:

---

[153] Mary Shelley, *Frankenstein* (1818; London: Penguin Popular Classics, 1994), 125.
[154] Ibid., 55.
[155] Maud Mortimer, *A Green Tent in Flanders* (New York: Doubleday, Page, 1917), 184.
[156] Ibid.
[157] Church, *Part*, 75.

> We conspire against his right to die. We experiment with his bones, his muscles, his sinews, his blood. We dig into the yawning mouths of his wounds. Helpless openings, they let us into the secret places of his body. We plunge deep into his body. We make discoveries within his body. To the shame of the havoc of his limbs we add the insult of our curiosity and the curse of our purpose, the purpose to remake him. [...] He lays himself out. He bares himself to our knives. His mind is annihilated. He pours out his blood, unconscious. His red blood is spilled and pours over the table onto the floor while he sleeps.[158]

The wounded soldier gives himself up, opening himself to strangers, who 'conspire against' him, enforcing care. There is a seemingly sacrificial element, when his 'blood is spilled', gesturing towards the familiar rhetoric of war, of nations sacrificing their sons. Borden develops an image of sinister medical experimentation 'with his bones, his muscles, his sinews, his blood'; her language evokes ideas of (imperial) exploration, making 'discoveries' of 'secret places' never before seen or touched. Medical experimentation is brought together not only with discovery but also with colonisation, the appropriation of territory against the will of the dominated patient.

Imagery of territorial invasion is continuous with the multiple modes of intrusion described in these accounts, emphasised through the evocative verbs: 'digging', 'probing', 'push', and 'insert'. These are extremely vivid physical actions, especially when they are penetrating not only human skin but tissues, muscle, and bone. Toland, for example, comments on how 'Joll got about a teaspoonful of splintered bone out of his [patient's] brain [...] How he can go digging around in the brain the way he does without killing the patients, seems marvellous.'[159] Aside from offering another uncanny quantification, with 'a teaspoonful of splintered bone', Toland here emphasises the thin line between effective treatment and irreparable harm in the moment of intrusion. La Motte, similarly, describes a case of rapidly developing gas gangrene in the thigh, which must be removed by deep incision:

> The *Medécin Chef* took a curette, a little scoop, and scooped away the dead flesh, the dead muscles, the dead nerves, the dead blood-vessels. And so many blood-vessels being dead, being scooped away by that sharp curette, how could the blood circulate in the top half of that flaccid thigh? It couldn't. Afterwards, into the deep, yawning

---

[158] Borden, 'Conspiracy', 80.
[159] Toland, *Aftermath*, 39.

wound, they put many compresses of gauze, soaked in the carbolic acid, which acid burned deep into the germs of the gas gangrene, and killed them, and killed much good tissue besides.[160]

Both Toland and La Motte express surprise and awe at how the body can endure such unnatural intrusion. La Motte's observation that killing off the infection also 'killed much good tissue' is a commonplace of the unavoidable collateral damage of medical care. Such bodily invasion becomes even more intense, however, when an instrument will not suffice: there are numerous examples where the medics have to physically place their hands inside the wounded body: 'a great jet of blood shot out across the floor and I had to catch hold of the artery in the wound with my fingers and hang on'.[161] In some cases, 'Human pressure was the only hope.'[162] Bodily invasion is brought to a new level with the physical infiltration of the medic's hands into the anatomy of the patient.

These images of medical violence, and of the medic as antagonistic, are hyperbolic, expressing the disturbing tone of the medical grotesque. The medical grotesque is a vehicle for self-conscious reflection on the dilemma of medical violence, which derives from the unsettling medical necessity to enter the body, to intrude and apply force and pressure inside, and so seems allied with the traumatic invasion of the wound itself. The extent of self-conscious reflection on such moments testifies to the experience as a fundamental paradox of caregiving. These representations allow us to recognise and explore the burden of care, in particular caregivers' sense of responsibility and the pressures of decision making. Albee insists that 'The complete trust of a patient is an overwhelming reminder of the surgeon's responsibility. The patient [...] waits helplessly for the surgeon to do what he will with him; placing his life, with serene confidence, in the hands of another person.'[163] The responsibility bears not only on their practice but also on their decision making in situations where a medic will have to 'meditate deeply, and make a decision as to the sacrifice which would ensure life', taking it upon themselves to 'weigh a man's whole existence, then act, with method and audacity'.[164] Medics are placed in a position of power, of both salvation and destruction, and the burden sits

---

[160] La Motte, 'Alone', in *Backwash*, 52.
[161] Dearden, *Duty*, 38.
[162] Rathbone, *Young*, 235.
[163] Albee, *Rebuild*, 57.
[164] Duhamel, *Martyrs*, 112.

heavily on their shoulders throughout the war, and for a long time afterwards.

By drawing out these concerns, the medic-writers are commenting on the wider responsibility and stress of caregiving, especially in such a demanding setting. They foreground the moments of medical intrusion, or perceived violence, in order to illuminate the emotional and psychological toll, on both patient and caregiver, which pervades all aspects of medical care. These representations do offer some gestures of dramatic irony; as readers we are well aware that these medical procedures are for the patient's benefit, with the sole aim of healing, even if manifested as power exerted over the 'docile', passive, wounded soldier. The care is also contrarily manifest in confessions that there are patients 'whom we fear to touch':[165] the reluctance to treat and to touch suggests that care can include elements of revulsion and fear.

It is a constant wonder that the medics are able to dissociate themselves from the extreme actions of medical intrusion. Yet, the drive and purpose of such actions is illustrated in the strategies of divided selfhood that make them possible: 'The soul must withdraw, for this is not its hour. Now the knife must divide the flesh, and lay the ravage bare, and do its work completely.'[166] While 'the knife' takes on the role of a weapon, the medic and the instrument seem to be separated. There is an ambiguous suggestion that because 'the soul must withdraw', the medic's body becomes itself an instrument. Along with the literal medical instrument as a distancing device, it is the instrument which enacts the violence and does the 'work completely'. The 'soul' is aligned with the shared human sensibilities of medic and reader, while 'knife' is aligned with the skills and responsibilities of the medical profession. This prompts questions about the medic's consciousness and awareness: how they are situated, psychologically as well as physically, in such an act. With the withdrawal of their 'soul', the role of the medic as a decision maker takes on new complications, and we come to ponder how the medic remains in both mind and body.

The opposition between 'soul' and 'knife' conveys the double bind of the medical profession: to care and heal, and maintain empathy, while inevitably causing further pain and distress. Duhamel offers a particularly telling moment of self-awareness about his actions, evident in the visceral, reciprocal nature of his emotional response:

[165] Ibid., 198.
[166] Ibid., 14.

things become very trying. I feel at once that whatever I do, Gregoire will suffer. I uncover the wound in his thigh, and he screams. I wash the wound carefully, and he screams. I probe the wound, from which I remove small particles of bone, very gently, and he utters unimaginable yells. I see his tongue trembling in his open mouth. His hands tremble in the hands that hold them. I have an impression that every fibre of his body trembles, that the raw flesh of the wound trembles and retracts. In spite of my determination, this misery affects me, and I wonder whether I too shall begin to tremble sympathetically.[167]

Duhamel elaborates on the situation of the self-aware medic, complicit in the protraction of pain and suffering. There is an endemic psychological impact from this emotional and ethical struggle over having to inflict further pain. The corpographic concept, outlined in Chapter 1, is complicated in relation to the sympathy between bodies: the corpographic and the empathetic body become sympathetically entwined. Duhamel and his patients are 'both tremulous, you from the effort to bear your pain, I sometimes from having inflicted it':[168] what they share is complex, both experiencing the wounded soldier's pain, but each carrying a different burden.

It is not surprising then that there are patients whom the medics 'fear to touch'. There is a crisis of care concerning the ethics of intrusion, most especially in the compromised circumstances of military-medical care. The medics are up against the contradiction latent in the Hippocratic Oath, to 'do no harm'. As caregivers, the tension they experience between care and even mere contact demands functional and psychological compromise. Among the traumas of war, this is specific to the medical role. The tension is a function of institutional as well as personal circumstances, but consistently experienced by medics as an internal contradiction. The 'medical grotesque' is the articulation of that contradiction, and serves to elicit the reader's own affective and ethical engagement: to put us too in the position of sympathetic trembling.

Through an acknowledgement and understanding of the medical grotesque, we can gain a greater understanding of the role of the caregiver. The medic cannot be reduced to a figure of power and exertion of force but is rather undertaking a complex negotiation between empathy and detachment. Confrontation with the wounded body elicits an array of conflicting emotional responses which are difficult to rationalise. With these complex emotions underpinning

[167] Ibid., 170.
[168] Ibid., 93.

and shaping their narratives, these writers develop a medical discourse that interrogates the position of the medical witness not only in relation to the patients but also to the wounds, and crucially to their own, and others', acts of medical care. The 'medical grotesque' is not just a trope or image but a discourse by which medical personnel can both represent and critique their roles as caregivers.

Chapter 4

Countering: Representing Coping Strategies

While performing the various medical tasks, there is little room for pause and reflection: the work must be done, no matter how hard it is for the medic. The medics must manage themselves psychologically and emotionally, by developing coping strategies to counter the distress and strains of war. These coping mechanisms are hard to identify, especially in the moment they are taking place. Often, it is only through reflection, and by articulating the experience of the moment itself, that the discrete ways in which the medics cope can be identified. The selection of medics' memoirs discussed throughout this book depict a particular kind of coping that relies on psychological negotiation between different planes of consciousness, and is conveyed through certain representational choices. These narratives present the bodily experience of caregiving *in parallel with* the emotional and psychological experience of coping, offering a challenge to ways of seeing and the politics of perception.

By considering emotional and psychological spaces, this chapter explores the medics' coping strategies in the moments of caregiving, and crucially how they are subsequently represented. Coping, in this context, is manifested spatially, with the development of psychological 'counter-sites', wherein the medics' experiences are realised in ways that allow them to move between psychological spaces. Their experiences are placeless: they are not tethered to a single psychological space but are able to move figuratively between the real and imaginary, facilitating psychological countering in the moment of emotional crisis and afterwards. In Chapter 2, I explored the simultaneous identities of spaces, arguing that there are both literal and psychological/figurative palimpsests, so that spaces are not only what they appear on the surface but are made up of layers, from the past and from the mind's conscious and unconscious superimpositions. Here, I develop a complement to this argument, exploring the idea of 'other spaces': discrete emotional, psychological, imaginative spaces, which are experienced in parallel. Rather than exploring the layered, complementary identities of one space and place, here I discuss the simultaneous yet divergent psychological spaces in a single place. While the palimpsest offers a sense of convergent space, these 'other spaces' offer divergence and differentiation, which produce the 'counter-sites'.

This chapter is concerned with how the medics represent such coping mechanisms and reflect on how they coped in the exact moments of caregiving and traumatic experience. Although written after the event (sometimes later that day, sometimes months or years later), the experiences represented concern the immediate emotional impact during acts of caregiving. They are representations of perceived coping strategies; perceived, because full knowledge of their own mental state is difficult to achieve. These representations consist of both recollections of the moment and retrospective reflections on how they coped. The focus in this chapter is on how the memoirs represent actual first-hand moments of caregiving; while Chapter 5 will discuss the potential difficulties of relating distressing or traumatic experiences, here I treat the difficulties of representation as unproblematic in order to focus on the writers' reflections on the represented experience.

This sense of movement to a 'counter-site' also contains a vestige of suspension. In an affective line of thought, Sianne Ngai's concept of 'restricted' or 'suspended agency'[1] can assist in how we consider the medics' affect. In the countering of trauma or negative or harmful emotions (fear; hopelessness; despair), I suggest that these writings offer insight into the handling of emotions. In those moments of caregiving (in which I include: performing procedures; washing patients; watching over wards), the emotional landscape is subordinated – there is not time to think or assess how one is feeling. The work is being done. Not only is affective agency suspended, the medics' emotions are forced to stultify: they might feel anger at the damage done to the broken bodies of young men in their care, but to whom or what can they address that anger? Their anger must become care, compassion, and commitment to delaying the pain and death of their patients and themselves. It is possible to see, however,

---

[1] Sianne Ngai, *Ugly Feelings* (Cambridge, MA: Harvard University Press, 2005), 1–37.

in the representation of such coping mechanisms, and the complex layers of narrative depiction, that a sense of agency is restored in the retrospective retelling of these moments.

While there is significant focus in trauma studies on the temporal relations between an experience and its retelling, these medical narratives represent a particularly spatial, as opposed to temporal, set of relations between experience and response. Cathy Caruth explains that, in established trauma scholarship, 'The history that a flashback tells [. . .] is a history that literally *has no place*, neither in the past, in which it was not fully experienced, nor in the present, in which its precise images and enactments are not fully understood.'[2] In this statement, Caruth foregrounds the temporal dislocation not only between experience and flashback but also between experience and its retrospective retelling, in which context the detail of 'no place' warrants further attention. In these medics' narratives, the event as it happens is realised yet placeless: the psychological response is a placelessness, or rather, a 'movement' of the psyche to counter-sites, between planes of consciousness. The individual's psyche is placeless in that, unlike the body, it can relocate: it can alter its perspective, and by shifting between the real and imaginary, negotiate with experience by moving beyond its boundaries to counter-sites, which are 'other' to the immediate situation. The concept of placelessness that I employ here provides a way to negotiate the psychological aspect of counter-sites by thinking about how the immediacy of the traumatic moment is represented. This is not 'placelessness' in Edward Casey's sense of 'The emotional symptoms of placelessness – homesickness, disorientation, depression, desolation [. . .] a sense of unbearable emptiness.'[3] Instead, this is not loss but gain. This particular kind of 'placelessness' is the sense of not being wholly tethered to a certain psychological space, hence the ability to 'move' to an imaginative space. And it seems logical to suggest that these experiences as they happen, having 'no place', might present themselves not as a flashback after the event but as a psychological negotiation of spatiality. This is not to say that the spaces are entirely distinct and separate, but that the invocation of imaginative realms and spaces functions as a way of coping with the experiences. By exploring the

---

[2] Cathy Caruth, 'Recapturing the Past: Introduction', in *Trauma: Explorations in Memory* (Baltimore: Johns Hopkins University Press, 1995), 153 (italics in original).

[3] Edward Casey, *Getting Back into Place: Toward a Renewed Understanding of the Place-World* (Bloomington: Indiana University Press, 1993), x.

perception of psychological place, and especially the sense of moving between spaces within the narratives, we can gauge how the traumatic onslaught and affective terrain is experienced, perceived, and ultimately, expressed. The medics' narratives emphasise the spatial negotiation between experience and psychological response in the immediate present. The psychological response, then, makes use of the ungrounded shifting between sites that placelessness affords. By virtue of being 'other', these sites become 'counter-sites' and provide the occasion for countering and coping.

In order to fully understand the idea of countering and counter-sites, this chapter appropriates Michel Foucault's sociological concept of the heterotopia, as explained in 'Of Other Spaces: Utopias and Heterotopias' (1986), and adapts it to a psychological context. The heterotopia is the development and emergence of another space; seemingly abnormal, it is in fact alternative: the history of the term 'heterotopia' even has relevance to this subject, as it derives from medical discourse, referring to the growth of a particular kind of tissue in an abnormal place. The counter-site offers the possibility of difference and alterity. As a psychological counter-site 'the heterotopia is capable of juxtaposing in a single real place several spaces, several sites that are in themselves incompatible',[4] which, to an extent, accounts for coincident reality and unreality, where conflicting perceptions are experienced in parallel. Unlike the simultaneous, palimpsestic space, which is convergent, and in which identities are layered on one another in the same conceptual space, the counter-sites are divergent: multiple psychological spaces are located in the same place. The convergence of palimpsestic sites tends to draw the layers together, but in the divergence of the counter-sites there is a continuing differentiation and increasing incompatibility. When the medic appears to reside in an alternative space to either the war or the place of caregiving, there emerges the creation and articulation of an alternative imaginative, and thus narrative, terrain. Building on this, I outline how we can make radiographic, or X-ray, readings of these narratives, as a way to see the coincident parallel sites and see their differences.

The representations of these counter-sites, then, must articulate multiple narrative planes, revealing the bodily action, as it might be viewed by others, as well as the psychological terrain only accessible by the medic. To an extent, this is the central challenge of life

---

[4] Michel Foucault, 'Of Other Spaces: Utopias and Heterotopias', trans. Jay Miskowiec, *Diacritics* 16, no. 1 (1986): 25.

writing; in articulating events and one's own experiences of those events, there are necessarily two selves at play: the self as subject and the self as object. As Susanna Egan explains, 'autobiographers have always wrestled with the split between subject and object, between writing and written selves, seeing the very act of autobiography as present "reflection" upon the past'.[5] Arguably, this is intensified when we consider the conception of 'the self' in relation to trauma, with the immediate association of a split self. In these life writing examples, the psychologically split self seems to meet the split self of autobiographical writing. Yet, it is not entirely helpful to consider the individuals' psychological state as splitting, and thus as dividing. Instead, the idea of 'splitting' in the context of narrative representation of psychological states requires a deeper level of consideration. Perhaps it is most helpful to think, in line with Nancy Miller, that it is as much about 'doubling *out* as split within'.[6] This line of thought helps us to think of the ways in which the medics move 'out' to 'other spaces', and how they acquire different viewpoints and perspectives by moving between these different spaces.

In order to explore how different angles of perception help to articulate the complexities of coping and countering, this discussion adopts and extends Margaret Higonnet's discussion of 'the multiplication of angles of perception' in nursing accounts,[7] which considers different ways of seeing through the medium of technologies of sight and representation. Higonnet hints at a radiographic conception of narrative strands when she introduces the idea of the 'double image', an idea which derives from Marie Curie, who 'laid out the importance of X-rays for the surgeon who sought to locate shrapnel or broken bone. The successful tactic, she explained, was the "double image" – two X-rays taken at different angles.'[8] I build on the idea of the X-ray, in order to see how coping strategies are perceived and represented. In the triangulation of narrative angles, the caregivers' actions are juxtaposed with their navigations of the psychological terrain. Three angles are presented through the correlation of the two planes: the bodily action, the psychological experience, and the representational approach. Through the triangulation

---

[5] Susanna Egan, *Mirror Talk: Genres of Crisis in Contemporary Autobiography* (Chapel Hill and London: University of North Carolina Press, 1999), 11.
[6] Nancy K. Miller, 'Facts, Pacts, Acts', *Profession* (1992): 13 (italics in original).
[7] Margaret Higonnet, 'Cubist Vision in Nursing Accounts', in *First World War Nursing: New Perspectives*, ed. Alison S. Fell and Christine E. Hallett (New York: Routledge, 2013), 157.
[8] Higonnet, 'Cubist Vision', 156.

of the different narrative planes, the representational effect conveys both of the parallel spaces. The 'multiplication of angles of perception' is represented through a triangulation of narrative angles.[9] The triangulation is in the writing, and at times also in the reading, of these texts.

Attention to these narratives quickly reveals a complex negotiation between what feels real and what does not. To many, the war experience, in which they are directly part of the action, is experienced as unreal: a strange dream, or numbed immersion in the work. Contrastingly, and often conflictingly, some of these same medics consider that it is the civilian life which is unreal, characterised by the unengaged and detached perspective of onlookers who are estranged from the full force and effects of the war. Consequently, the medics are entangled within opposing states of meaning and feeling. As they do their duty, performing caregiving tasks and undertaking traumatic work, they are presented as conscious of different senses of reality. The real and the unreal are not spaces but reversible evaluations of the spaces of the war environment and the civilian environment. Each of these functions as a counter-site to the other, with the third space being the unresolved relation between the two. In the third space, we can see the effort towards representation of these conflicting states. The real and the unreal are antithetical evaluations of the same experience, but one of these supplies refuge or escape and thus becomes the counter-site to the other. This fundamental detail can be seen through discussion of two particular symbols of the heterotopia: the theatre and the mirror.

The countering relationship between the real and unreal allows the medic to shift between perspectives, and is commonly represented through tropes of theatricality. Yet, the gesture towards the theatrical does not refer to the medics' performing certain roles; it is not that they are following a script and temporarily playing their parts. The theatrical has a long-standing connection to warfare, demonstrated by Paul Fussell, who argues that 'the most obvious reason why "theatre" and modern war seem so compatible is that modern wars are fought by conscripted armies, whose members

---

[9] Importantly, 'narrative angles' should not be confused or conflated with Gérard Genette's distinctions of 'narrative perspective', relating to mood and focalisation, or 'narrative levels', relating to narrative voice, in *Narrative Discourse: An Essay in Method*, trans. Jane E. Lewin (1972; Ithaca, NY: Cornell University Press, 1983).

know they are only temporarily playing their ill-learned parts'.[10] In particular, Fussell discusses the relationship between theatre and psychology: 'Seeing warfare as theatre provides a psychic escape for the participant: with a sufficient sense of theatre, he can perform his duties without implicating his "real" self and without impairing his innermost conviction that the world is still a rational place.'[11] Although Fussell speaks only for male combatants, this can apply to combatants and medics alike. Indeed, both men and women, in combatant and non-combatant positions, experience a 'psychic escape' through the imaginative and figurative adoption of theatricality, although it is not as simple as pretending and performing. The tropes of theatricality become a means of representing how multiple realities can be experienced simultaneously, and how an alternative space can be a site of refuge. Fussell's comment aligns itself with general understandings of mental illness and dissociation, but what has been less discussed is his idea that 'seeing warfare as theatre' is a 'psychic escape'. The relation of coping strategies with the theatrical goes beyond the idea of simply playing a role or performing. Instead, there is a series of layers within this theatrical image: the basic real/unreal opposition between the stage and the auditorium, and the stage which is inhabited by the participants as both actor and character. To see warfare in terms of the theatrical, and thus a space in which multiple imaginary and conscious levels exist, is to identify a figurative movement that represents how the individual copes.

The idea of 'escape' suggests a movement towards protection, but at the same time such movement alters perspectives and ways of seeing. The shift in perspective is key here, which is enlarged on by references to a divided selfhood in relation to different mediums of seeing. A particular facet of Foucault's discussion of 'other spaces' focuses on the mirror, which provides the occasion for the utopia and heterotopia to exist in the same place, where 'there might be a sort of mixed, joint experience':

> The mirror is, after all, a utopia, since it is a placeless place. In the mirror, I see myself there where I am not, in an unreal, virtual space that opens up behind the surface; I am over there, there where I am not, a sort of shadow that gives my own visibility to myself, that enables me to see myself there where I am absent: such is the utopia of the mirror. But it is also a heterotopia in so far as the mirror does

---

[10] Paul Fussell, *The Great War and Modern Memory* (New York: Oxford University Press, 1975), 191.
[11] Ibid., 192.

exist in reality, where it exerts a sort of counteraction on the position that I occupy.[12]

Seeing oneself in the mirror is the ultimate case of being in more than one place at the same time, or at least being *seen* to be in more than one place, and it thus offers a way for the subject to figuratively move to another site, and so enables countering to take place. The mirror is a boundary between reality and unreality, as well as between here and there. Foucault's mirror aids the exploration and representation of psychological counter-sites, and is essential for the discussion in this chapter. In one's reflection there is a dual perspective: seeing oneself in the mirror, and seeing oneself looking in that mirror; there is the self as subject looking in the mirror, and the self as object *in* the mirror. They are not split between these two figures but instead doubled outwards, so that there are multiple visual perspectives. The mirror offers the ultimate 'counteraction': while the image in the mirror is unreal, the counteraction between the two perspectives of the self that it exerts is experienced as psychologically real. Consideration of Foucault's depiction of the mirror perspective therefore provides a useful means by which to build on the trope of theatricality and explore sight and perspective, recognising the significance of traversable boundaries allowing access to the counter-site.

This chapter focuses on the imaginative spaces to which these individuals move themselves in order to 'avoid' the instantaneous moments of the traumatic experience or harmful emotions. In turn, it illustrates the suspension of affective agency within the moment, which is reclaimed in the retelling. It uncovers their negotiations and navigations of the thresholds between the real and imaginary, the physical and psychological, the concrete and abstract. The narratives represent a very particular amplification of sight, challenging not only its most direct senses but also, in terms of perspective and viewpoint, the technological and artistic complexities of representing experience. If we literally look at something in a different way, perhaps we can see more. If we apply a literary radiography to these narratives, we can see the experience, the perceptions of experience, and the representations of those experiences in a new light.

---

[12] Foucault, 'Of Other Spaces', 24.

Experiencing the Unreal

In performing their tasks and going about their necessary roles, the medics experience various states of unreality. The presentation of reality and unreality is inconsistent and conflicting, not just across the different texts but also within them, as is the relation between experiential and conceptual aspects of the 'unreal'. The idea of the 'unreal', especially in this context, is in itself difficult to define: at different times it can be manifest as something unbelievable or unfathomable; as something intangible and ungraspable; or as fantasy or illusion. It is difficult to gauge entirely the ways in which an 'unreality' is experienced, but it does become clear that the difference between the real and the unreal is what allows the development of counter-sites, and specifically facilitates representations of multiple narrative angles.

In *Hospital Heroes* (1919), Elizabeth Walker Black, when describing the hospital surroundings, observes how a sense of the unreal meets with the real: 'It seemed unreal, like a stage-setting with ruins on every side [. . .] From a distance the long, monotonous roll of artillery, like surf beating on the seashore, made it all too real.'[13] War gives the appearance of unreality, particularly with the latent sense of artifice and pretence; yet the unreal is in direct confrontation with the real. It seems that if war can continue to appear unreal, perhaps its extraordinariness and implausibility, with the ethereal 'stage-setting', can continue to be a comfort. At the same time, all sense of imaginative escape is countered by the realisation that it is 'all too real' and can no longer be ignored. The 'real' is forced into Black's consciousness to remind her that what she is experiencing is genuine, and there cannot be a literal escape to the realm of the unreal. The opposition between these simultaneous experiences of the real and unreal demonstrates the inherent psychological tension in these perceptions.

The complexity of experiencing the real and the unreal is developed in Black's later equation of her experience with a nightmare: 'I was too tired to worry about the poor dying blessés or the danger. The feeling of it all being a dreadful nightmare from which we must waken acted as a narcotic. It seemed too unreal and too unnatural to last.'[14] Once again there is a conflict in what 'real' means: the

---

[13] Elizabeth Walker Black, *Hospital Heroes* (New York: Charles Scribner's Sons, 1919), 86.
[14] Ibid., 206.

nightmare is experienced as unreal, with a particularly negative connotation, which is 'too unnatural to last'. In this case, the sense of unreality is not simply a respite and refuge from the painful truth, for there is an inherent contradiction in this image, especially between the 'nightmare' and the 'narcotic'. The horrific nature of the experience is conveyed in the idea of the 'nightmare', yet, like the image of 'narcotic', there is a sense that this is comforting because it is unreal. It is a nightmare, a manifestation of the psyche's anxieties in the subconscious, and therefore not what is really going on. At the same time, the 'narcotic', as a painkiller, is presumably numbing: she is experiencing the nightmare with the effect of the narcotic. We are led to understand that the expectation that one will wake from the nightmare *is* the narcotic. If this 'dreadful nightmare' is edged with the awareness that it will end, then in some way it enables a counter-site. It 'seemed' unreal, but in the confusion of this reality with unreality it is possible to see the psychological tension of a flight towards some better, if unreal, idea of reality.

The pull towards something different, whether from the real to the unreal or the unreal to the real, is founded on the sense of separation and possible refuge. Movement between the real and the unreal is what affords protection, by enabling the psychological process of countering. In *Four Years Out of Life* (1931), Lesley Smith also plays with different senses of reality in her description of preparing medical instruments:

> The light rain-washed air made everything seem remote and tenuous. Even the ominous rumble of the guns was far away and unreal, and it was possible to forget that it had any connection with our sinister preparation of dressings and instruments. The cheerfully mundane scrubbing brush and hot soapy water were supremely real and comforting, and I sang as I scrubbed and forgot the war.[15]

For Smith, the 'real' is what is tangible, and here and now. Experiencing the 'ominous rumble' as unreal allows her to separate herself from its implications. The very physicality and tangibility of the 'scrubbing brush' enables a realness which allows her to forget what is going on 'far away'. Though she states that she was able 'to forget the war', of course she is still participating and fulfilling her role by the very fact that she is working for the war effort. Such activity and occupation seems to ensure a break from reflecting too much on the war, to the point where her sense of place is erased by

---

[15] Lesley Smith, *Four Years Out of Life* (London: Philip Allan, 1931), 47–8.

repetitive action, and the act of 'mundane scrubbing' becomes both a countering action and gateway to a counter-site.

This countering action is similarly evident on a number of occasions where 'Laying trays soothes the activity of the body, and the mind works softly';[16] or, as Black further states, 'One can only endure war when one is not thinking. At the front there is no time to worry and wonder where the shells are falling, no time to think, just a lot of work that must be done quickly.'[17] In *A Surgeon's Fight to Rebuild Men* (1943), Fred Albee asserts that 'activity was a psychological necessity',[18] suggesting that occupation provided a necessary distraction or outlet. He further muses:

> Perhaps it is as well that a surgeon in a military hospital is too overworked to have to think. To use all the skill and ingenuity you possess to heal a shattered body so that it may be useful again to stop more bullets, does not bear thinking of. And in the military hospitals of France there was not time for thought.[19]

The repeated assertion that 'there is no time' is almost incantatory. In fact, as Black suggests, 'The arduous task of doing so many things at once over and over again, and being in several rooms at the same time, acted as a panacea at this time of danger and anxiety. It was stiff, dirty work, not sympathetic.'[20] The inclusion of 'panacea' suggests such actions provide the function of a prescribed treatment or occupational therapy, but not by separation; instead, she is fully immersed, too caught up in the close-up urgency of the immediate demands upon her to step back and see it whole. The absence of time to think is also an absence of time to feel: their affective agency is restricted. Shutting off the opportunity to feel is evident in the main, but we also see how those emotions must play out somewhere and so do so in the counter-site and the impulse to move to a counter-site. Emphasising the necessity to be 'in several rooms at the same time' appears unwittingly to confirm the figurative notion that the psyche can be doubled and reside in different places simultaneously. Within these comments on the necessity of activity, a link between time and space is established: while there is no *time* for thought, perhaps there

---

[16] Enid Bagnold, *A Diary Without Dates* (London: William Heinemann, 1918), 5.
[17] Black, *Heroes*, 198.
[18] Fred H. Albee, *A Surgeon's Fight to Rebuild Men* (New York: E. P. Dutton, 1943), 119.
[19] Ibid.
[20] Black, *Heroes*, 215.

can be space for escape – removal and refuge in the created, alternative counter-site.

The dichotomy of the real and unreal leads to the development of more than one place and state of mind, held relatively simultaneously. But, crucially, one of these spaces provides a sense of escape or comfort: for many of the medics, being fully occupied by useful work allows them to psychologically move away from what is all too painful and unnaturally real. The shift between the real and unreal enables 'something like counter-sites, a kind of effectively enacted utopia in which the real sites, all the other real sites that can be found within the culture, are simultaneously represented, contested, and inverted'.[21] The counter-site which the psyche can 'move' towards is conceived as a potential utopic space: one that can offer a complete inversion of the traumatic reality of the present. The unreal enables the development of other spaces, specifically spaces which can take on a character, persona, and atmosphere designed to protect the individual's psyche. These alternative imagined spaces help to account for the recurrent representations of the hospital/medical space as performative and theatrical. The trope of the performative and theatrical resonates for these writers precisely because it resists being reduced to an idea of a single imaginative site. The power of the theatrical image actually relies on a duality of space, the demarcation of stage from auditorium, and so emblematises the overlap and shift between spaces.

Theatrical Perspectives

A strong thread throughout the medics' narratives is their awareness of the performativity not only of their roles but also of the spaces they inhabit, depicted by imagery of pretence, contingency, and illusion. There is repeated recognition of the illusory status of warfare, and of their medical role within it. For example, Smith describes how

> The clear frosty air of an early September morning made the whole hospital theatrically unreal, the tents swam in a luminous haze and the sounds of bugles and the hum of the ambulances came faint and far away to the night bunk.[22]

---

[21] Foucault, 'Of Other Spaces', 24.
[22] Smith, *Four Years*, 155–6.

'Theatrically unreal', the space takes on an ethereal glow, and remoteness from the flurry of activity further away. The hospital site has a theatrical atmosphere and appearance, according to Smith's further description of the hospital 'lit up by a theatrical row of footlights'.[23] Lit up, under the spotlight, attention and focus is centred on the medical space, which becomes the stage.

Men and women in the medical space accordingly take on theatrical roles, from actors to stage-hands. In *Ambulancing on the French Front* (1918), ambulance driver Edward Coyle describes himself as 'a sort of scene-shifter in the wings of the greatest tragedy ever staged'.[24] If the 'battlefield' is the stage, then the ambulance drivers are the crew moving scenery and actors about, and waiting 'in the wings'. Simultaneously they represent stage-hands to the medical ward as the stage, facilitating the roles played out in this adopted space. The ward as stage aligns with the suggestion made by Maud Mortimer in *A Green Tent in Flanders* (1917), when she explains that the *Médecin Chef* 'is one of our most characteristic silhouettes, for he keeps an eye on every trifle and is never for long off our stage'.[25] The 'characteristic silhouette' adopts a shadow theatre conceit: in the course of her narrative Mortimer titles chapters 'Shadow Pictures' and 'Shadow Pictures Again', in which she introduces the key players of the hospital ward on 'our stage'. The hospital ward becomes the stage on which the doctors' shadow picture is performed. In taking on the associations of performance, the space distances itself from the hospital as the site of pain and death, instead enacting an alternative, constructed identity. The concept of the stage corroborates the idea of the placeless psyche, given that the stage can adapt to take on the character of anything, and is not anchored to a singular, imaginative site.

The theatrical space allows for the coexistence and overlap of different sites of association. Crucially, Foucault included the theatre, and by extension cinema and other sites of performance, as a facet of the heterotopic model:

> The heterotopia is capable of juxtaposing in a single real place several spaces, several sites that are in themselves incompatible. Thus it is that the theater brings onto the rectangle of the stage, one after

---

[23] Ibid., 74.
[24] Edward R. Coyle, *Ambulancing on the French Front* (New York: Britton, 1918), 15.
[25] Maud Mortimer, *A Green Tent in Flanders* (New York: Doubleday, Page, 1917), 78.

the other, a whole series of places that are foreign to one another; thus it is that the cinema is a very odd rectangular room, at the end of which, on a two-dimensional screen, one sees the projection of a three-dimensional space.[26]

Theatre, 'in a single real place', brings together diverse and wide-ranging associated spaces, consequently allowing for the parallel exploration of other psychological and emotional spaces. As Joanne Tompkins's *Theatre's Heterotopias* (2014) demonstrates, 'the use of space in theatre facilitates all types of illusions so that a character can occupy more than one reality, time, or place without questioning the bounds of theatrical possibility'.[27] If the individual is able to occupy more than one place, then, like the mirror, it 'gives my own visibility to myself, that enables me to see myself there where I am absent'.[28] Theatre as heterotopia allows us to recognise the coinciding and coexisting possibility of imaginative states, while enabling an individual to 'occupy more than one reality'.

The medical space as the stage is emphasised and complicated by analogies of the staff and patients as actors, which reinforce the suggestion that these medics are performing these temporary roles, and thus are torn between different manifestations of their personality and characters. In Mortimer's narrative we see how 'the chief actors in these moving scenes are so absorbed that they dress and undress for their parts in public'.[29] Characteristic of Mortimer's style, the direct meaning behind this scene is obscure: it is unclear who the 'chief actors' are, but it seems these are the medics. The extended metaphor of performance continues with the pun on 'dress and undress', conflating the wearing of costumes with the medical dressings of wounds.

Yet, behind the exterior surface of acting is the inherent tension of selfhood. The medics feel that they are taking on a certain role, and are therefore performing, but this directly assumes there is a part of themselves which is subverted or repressed, especially in terms of emotions. Consequently, their actions are negotiating a conflicted selfhood. Olive Dent, in *A Volunteer Nurse on the Western Front* (1917), enigmatically describes the difficulty of reconciling the divided, often conflicting, selves, by explicitly describing nurses as actresses:

[26] Foucault, 'Of Other Spaces', 25.
[27] Joanne Tompkins, *Theatre's Heterotopias: Performance and the Cultural Politics of Space* (London: Palgrave Macmillan, 2014), 9.
[28] Foucault, 'Of Other Spaces', 24.
[29] Mortimer, *Tent*, 182.

> It is our privilege, pleasure and pride to dispel that fear [of hospitals],
> – a pride which actually grows to a conceit. It is very feminine to
> enjoy rising above expectations, and to hear stumbling expressions of
> gratitude after a dressing [. . .] It is a form of vanity of which we are
> not ashamed, indeed, we revel in it. We try as hard to gain compliments as any actress ever works to 'get over' the footlights.[30]

What marks this passage as unusual is the leap from 'privilege' and 'pride' to 'conceit', and its overt link with theatrical performance. 'To "get over" the footlights' suggests that as an actress, she is striving to play the role convincingly. Yet, it also suggests the desire for her role as a nurse to be affirmed. Dent's image conveys a double self, a woman working as a nurse and simultaneously a woman playing the role of the nurse with conviction.[31] 'Getting over' develops a spatial analogy, suggesting movement from one area to another: from the stage into the audience. The simile with the acting profession, and specifically the effort 'to gain compliments', on the one hand suggests the provision of exceptional care, but on the other hand it is an attempt by the nurse to enhance the performance or her own status. References to 'conceit' and 'vanity' imply self-interestedness but are also a sign of striving to rescue a sense of self within the role as a nurse. In focusing so intently on this effort to maintain an air of fictionality, they are distracting themselves from the horror and distress of what they witness. Self-interest becomes a psychological need for affirmation; both that the nurse has a vital role and that she as an individual still exists.

The act of performance is not only for their own benefit, but is often for the benefit of others, which exacerbates the sense that they are existing in a dual position, pulled in two directions. Nurses, in particular, acknowledge the 'tactful artifice' they must adopt while treating patients, so that they do not alarm the wounded with the extent of their injuries – suggesting it is better to pretend than to let their faces betray their true reactions. By this standard, performance and pretence is inevitable and necessary in the medical care context, evoked with the recurrent image of the mask, as Black explains:

---

[30] Olive Dent, *A Volunteer Nurse on the Western Front* (1917; London: Virgin Books, 2014), 34.

[31] Additionally, with the enjoyment and thrill of 'rising above expectations', there is a dialogue with the wider and complex context of gender expectations and stereotypes. It is likely that Dent's comments are knowingly ironic: she does not seek to represent the women working in this war environment as shallow or two-dimensional figures, but highlights the psychology of working in this environment.

> During the harrowing moments when the doctors were doing most painful dressings, I tried to wear a mask of cheerfulness as I gave the doctor compress after compress to cover a large expanse of mangled flesh, or poured ether or 'mencière' on the wound. I did not want them to see in my face how serious and horrible it was.[32]

Not only does the metaphorical 'mask' become a protective shield for the medic but Black foregrounds it as a mechanism for the benefit of the patients. The 'act' is a conscious and deliberate performance. Not only does the mask hide, it also performs. Specifically, this creates a separation between guise and reality, and enables the individual to move beyond themselves, to consider explicitly how they look and act. Enid Bagnold's *A Diary Without Dates* (1918) offers a similar example, questioning, 'Whether to wear, or not to wear, a mask towards one's world? For there is so much that is not ripe to show – change and uncertainty . . .'.[33] Bagnold highlights her self-consciousness of the performance she must undertake. Her comment takes the form of an antithetical device, echoing Hamlet's 'To be or not to be' soliloquy. Unlike Hamlet, however, 'being' and living is swapped for the trope of the mask, which acts as an analogy for identity as well as agency. Like Black, Bagnold implies that there are things she must conceal from onlookers – patients, other staff, visitors. There are expressions on one's face, reactions to sights and events, which must be kept hidden beneath a mask of pretence. It is necessary to maintain a neutral expression that does not distress, for 'nobody must appear, for a moment, to be seeing beneath the surface, to be envisaging the tragedy, and not the comedy, of wounds'.[34] The 'comedy' is the pretence being imposed on the scene, where the patients are spectators to the medics. It is part of the medics' duty to ensure the pretence is maintained, but this requires in some way suppression of their true feelings, and denial of a certain aspect of the self.

Late on in her narrative, Black implies the mixed and contradictory feelings of being, and being seen as, this actress performing. She explains how in the hospital,

> There were gangrene cases and a 'trépané,' and the work was the hardest and most disagreeable I had ever done. But it was so necessary I liked it better than the canteen, where I felt like a

---

[32] Black, *Heroes*, 79.
[33] Bagnold, *Without Dates*, 76.
[34] Irene Rathbone, *We That Were Young* (1932; London: Virago, 1988), 152–3.

moving-picture actress as I ran wildly about among heavy wagons with my veil floating in the wind and cigarettes dropping from my overflowing hands.[35]

In cutting the figure of 'a moving-picture actress', Black fulfils an aesthetic or superficial role in the canteen, unlike in the hospital, where she is actively doing what is 'so necessary'. In the canteen she is an object of the male gaze, but in the hospital the male gaze is curtailed by serious injury. This is reinforced by her acknowledgement that she preferred her work in the hospital, because 'In the hospital I was treated with respect.'[36] Thus it seems that the figure of the nurse-as-actress is held in tension; it is not assured that maintaining illusions or performing is always effective for the medic. This draws out the concept of artifice, especially that which is involved in performing and acting.

Crucially, theatre is not so much the means of coping as it is the means of representing the process of coping. As further examples will support, the authors of these representations depict the hospitals and medics through an 'autoscopic' gaze: they are able to see themselves from an alternative perspective, partly through narrative formation but also through the innate techniques of self-protection. The nature of parallel psychological spaces is conveyed through particular narrative techniques, which emphasise the ways in which self-reflection and shifting perspective can encourage the emergence of the counter-sites.

An Alteration in Perspective

The overriding feature across all of these theatrical examples, and what most often complicates the analogies and imagery, is the focus on vision and perspective. Sight is a fundamental trope throughout these texts, becoming a vital thread in the relationship between perception and representation. As previously discussed, in the context of war sight has lost its reliability and privilege at the pinnacle of the hierarchy of the senses, but further exploration establishes how the visual continues to be fundamental to representation. Foucault's mirror especially demonstrates the significance of the shift in perspective, where the mirror encourages a dual perspective and shifts

---

[35] Black, *Heroes*, 203.
[36] Ibid.

perspective to oneself and one's situation. Perspective is affected not only by the vantage point (the relation between what is viewed and where it is viewed from) but also by different modes and technologies of seeing (how the object is perceived and represented).

One of Irene Rathbone's most evocative statements in *We That Were Young* (1932), regarding coping strategies, draws on the image of the 'safety-curtain' as a means of not only separating but also altering perspective:

> Every night during the first week Joan dreamt about the wounds, saw them floating before her eyes, almost had the stench of them in her nostrils. It was inevitable this should be so, for, during the day, sensibilities had to be hardened, quivering disgust controlled, and head and hand kept steady for the sake of the sufferers themselves. With unconscious wisdom she let down a sort of safety-curtain between her mind and the sights before her, keeping them at bay, preventing their full significance from penetrating. If she had not done so she would have been useless.[37]

Rathbone's imagery generates the impression of an acquired technique of survival. We are given a brief insight into the fragility of the nurse, and how she might maintain an ability to perform duties. At the beginning of her service, the 'full significance' of what she sees had manifest itself in her dreams, which she must quickly counter:

> The nights were reactions from this discipline, and the safety-curtain no longer functioning the horror rushed in on her in the shape of dreams.
>
> But after the first week she no longer even dreamed. She had adjusted herself inwardly and outwardly to the conditions in which her life must now be lived – conditions which, if they could not be accepted as normal, would mean her defeat.[38]

As she goes on to explain, in unconscious moments initially the curtain fails at night, but her mind learns to use it. The metaphor of the 'safety-curtain' is very much a figurative physical barrier, designed to prevent access from one area to another. The specific inclusion of 'safety' also reinforces this self-protective coping strategy and its effect on her personal psyche. Such a comment is a clear indication of the productivity and necessity of this coping strategy, especially the way the divide can enable the demarcation of a

---

[37] Rathbone, *Young*, 195.
[38] Ibid.

heterotopic counter-site. Most significantly the 'curtain' generates change, so that her inward psychology can be manipulated to allow for an outward display of coping. This change is not performance, however, because the image of the 'safety-curtain' places her as an onlooker to events. The conditions become normalised, and the coping strategy follows, so that she maintains a distance from the 'sights before her'. It is a conditioning and inuring to the environment through self-protective instincts.

Furthermore, the 'safety-curtain' analogy is overtly theatrical. In one of the few close analyses of Rathbone's novel, Jane Marcus underplays Rathbone's use of the 'safety-curtain' metaphor, explaining:

> It is a standard characteristic of women's World War I novels to figure the war as scenes of drama, a way, one thinks, of imagining an end to suffering. The war is a theatre, and the response to the ideological call for female self-sacrifice is sketched as role-playing – acting (as in war work), a *temporary* role for the duration of the war. Rathbone's novel participates in this rhetoric of the theatre of war. In fact, she articulates her own anaesthetic aesthetic of the Nurse's Text in the metaphor of the theatre by describing Joan's V.A.D. nursing [...] as requiring her to let down a 'safety curtain' of the mind in order to perform her duties.[39]

Indeed we can see that 'war is a theatre', and the nurses can be considered as 'role-playing', much like Fussell's argument, but there is far more to be read into Rathbone's adoption of the theatrical curtain image. Marcus's suggestion that Rathbone adopts the 'metaphor of the theatre' does not account for the effect of the 'safety-curtain', and consequently the way in which its presence alters perspective. The curtain creates a division and barrier, but further consideration shows that it is not a distancing mechanism but a separating one; one which opens up the opportunity to form a psychological counter-site. With the curtain, the medic moves from one psychological sphere to another. In an act which is without literal movement, she resides in a *remade*, even fictional, space, which consequently enables her to dissociate and alter the view she has of herself and her role in the wider action. The introduction of the curtain alters the space into a theatrical one, but it is not as straightforward as implying that Joan is the one onstage; in fact, the ambiguity about whether she is on

---

[39] Jane Marcus, 'Afterword: The Nurse's Text: Acting Out an Anaesthetic Aesthetic', in *We That Were Young*, by Irene Rathbone (New York: Feminist Press, 1989), 480–1 (italics in original).

the stage or in the audience marks a self-division. The emphasis on 'sights' seems to place her in a spectatorial position, given that she is looking on, with images of the wounds 'floating before her eyes'. Her key concern is 'let[ting] down a sort of safety-curtain between her mind and the sights before her', with the implication that this is a divide between her eyesight and her mind's interpretation of those sights. After all, it is difficult to unsee, so it is better to not see at all. Yet, in this need to cope and keep on being useful, she is inherently a part of what is taking place. We can thus read this as the nurse as both actress and spectator. She is presented as a figure who switches between the roles of spectator and performer, a shift in perspective which enables an autoscopic view and allows for the viewing of one's own life.

Rathbone offers a particular conception of viewpoints which accounts for altered perspective in specific relation to the theatrical, but the shift is further elucidated by considering mediated vision. The significance of perspective is emphasised through the different modes of looking and devices for seeing, which are more explicitly explored in Black's metaphor of opera-glasses. The performer is now also a spectator: 'One cannot be homesick when looking back is like seeing a view through the wrong end of opera-glasses, so small and insignificant.'[40] The opera-glass metaphor explicitly relates to technologies of seeing and, most importantly, to a mode of seeing which alters perspective. The 'wrong end of opera-glasses' provides an altered perspective, and we are encouraged to question where Black is situated in this scene. One impression suggests she is using the opera-glasses the wrong way round, and therefore 'seeing a view through the wrong end of opera-glasses'. Yet, by putting the opera-glasses back into their theatrical context, there is also the sense of her being on the wrong side of those glasses: she is not in the audience but on the stage as a performer looking out into the auditorium, seeing the audience as 'small and insignificant'. Once again, it is ambiguous where the medic is situated, an effect which is intensified by the triangulated narrative angles, which actively challenge ways and representations of seeing.

As well as introducing the images of the actress and the stage, Black consciously invokes technologies of seeing with indirect implications for her own representational strategies, for example when she refers to a kinematoscope or kinetoscope: 'Our life seemed unreal, like a series of moving pictures turned very fast over and

---

[40] Black, *Heroes*, 17.

over again.'[41] She employs 'moving pictures' as a metaphor which draws out further, multiple readings of perspective. In one sense we conclude that they are becoming actors, performing duties and roles which are far removed from the normality and 'reality' of their former lives. Yet, again we can see the ambiguity of the performer/spectator perspective, making us question whether they are watching 'a series of moving pictures' and thus distanced from the actions of this unreal life, or are self-aware of their place as performers and participants. The inference is that they view themselves as if on a film reel, beginning to resemble other selves. Almost like Foucault's mirror, they are seeing themselves in an unreal virtuality, while remaining in a bodily singularity.

Black's use of the film metaphors continues, with increasing reference to the artifice of the film medium:

> When we did have time for a short walk, it was like stepping into an illustrated Sunday paper or into a *Pathé Weekly* of 'Somewhere in France.' Behind us on the road and ahead of us were millions of men in blue, almost the same height. It seemed unreal, like a stage-setting with ruins on every side, and yet we were actually in it, marching along with men who would soon be in the first-line trenches.[42]

The specificity of the *Pathé Weekly* image evokes stepping into a newsreel, one shown at the cinema. The footage in these newsreels was sometimes genuine, and sometimes staged,[43] but whether censored or not, Black suggests she has stepped into a mediated vision of the environment, which determines a specific perspective, with clean, unharmed soldiers on their way to the trenches. This image, then, presents a remade, sanitised space. Given this sense of the heterotopic space, the repetition of 'in' and 'into' and the sense of being within cements the overlapping of alternative orderings, though perhaps this is one of few instances with a distinct boundary – given that they step 'into', crossing this invisible threshold, off- and onstage.

References to the 'pictures' and film imagery occur with remarkable frequency in Black's narrative, moving beyond media journalism

---

[41] Ibid., 219–20.

[42] Ibid., 86.

[43] An extensive collection of First World War *Pathé* film reels survives, but the details remain unclear, due to missing dates and locations. In many cases it is not even clear if they are conveying real action or are staged. See 'History of British Pathé', British Pathé, https://www.britishpathe.com/blog/history/.

to art and film production. In order to satisfactorily capture the atmosphere of her accommodation and surroundings, she adopts explicit analogies with the film-making world:

> The interior of our barracks looked like a series of stage-settings for moving pictures, the incongruous sights one sees at the Universal City in California being the only approach to the impression we gave, each one busily occupied with something that had no connection with what went on beside her.[44]

The articulation of this metaphor and extended image captures a complex illustration of her representational strategy. The sentence construction emulates a derealising *ekstasis*, as she moves from seemingly within the space, where it looks like 'stage-settings', to observing her and her fellow nurses, who seem to emulate the incongruity of film lots. This is a metaleptic moment, where the self as object momentarily merges with the self as subject; at one moment she is in the space being described, and then she moves outwards and comments on how the scene looks from the perspective of an onlooker, through the eyes of others. The repetition of that phrase 'like a series of stage-settings' (across her narrative) is taken further with the very specific evocation of Hollywood – Universal City – and reiterates her consciousness for the artifice of film. The reference to 'Universal City in California' is oddly specific, suggesting a personal experience of the location.[45] The space is unreal, and captures in part the earlier discussion in Chapter 2 on the incongruity of overlapping spaces. 'Universal City in California' evokes a strong image of the film lot, with multiple locations set up close together – we can almost imagine, for example, the scenery for a western saloon set alongside the exterior of some grand palace: 'something that had no connection with what went on beside'. Studio lots are also reused spaces (with palimpsestic layers), consciously reused and remade over time, to which Black knowingly alludes. The film set is the ultimate creative site where imagination and creativity are literally, visually enacted on spaces and sites. Like the theatrical stage, the film lot allows for multiple realities to exist, which intensifies the issues of reality and illusion within the film medium.

---

[44] Black, *Heroes*, 176.
[45] The pervasiveness of the film images in Black's narrative suggests, to me, some personal connection to the film world, and possibly first-hand experience of Hollywood. Unfortunately, I have not been able to find out any biographical details for Elizabeth Walker Black.

The images of altered perspective, especially through different visual technologies, also affect the management of medical sights. Mediated viewpoints, whether by technologies or movement, are significant in relation to the encounter with sights that are shocking and potentially traumatising. The need to change what or how one sees is crucial to techniques of coping and emotional endurance, and is mirrored in the different narrative angles with which these writers challenge perception. In a similar way to Rathbone's dividing metaphor of the 'safety-curtain', Vera Brittain, in *Testament of Youth* (1933), installs the image of a shutter as fundamental to seeing and not-seeing traumatising sights:

> As for the wounds, I was growing accustomed to them; most of us, at that stage, possessed a kind of psychological shutter which we firmly closed down upon our recollection of the daily agony whenever there was time to think. We never dreamed that, in the years of renewed sensitiveness after the War, the convenient shutter would simply refuse to operate, or even allow us to romanticise – as I who tried to write poetry romanticised in 1917 – the everlasting dirt and gruesomeness.[46]

The 'psychological shutter' enables the medics to separate themselves from the trials of the day. Yet, Brittain acknowledges that this barrier fails in retrospect, at a temporal distance, and that she was surprised by her 'renewed sensitiveness'. Brittain and her colleagues 'never dreamed that' the shutter would fail, oblivious to the as yet unknowable psychological cost of what they experience: they assume that if they had been able to cope at the time, then surely they would continue to cope with the memories of the events. Carol Acton and Jane Potter suggest that

> Brittain employs 'sight' as a metaphor to draw attention to the tension between the psychological necessity of dissociation in the immediate term, and the post-trauma inability to shut out intrusive memories of the wounded and the dead, a feature of traumatic witness.[47]

To us, this is the inevitable return of the repressed emotion, especially once the vigilance of the moment has lapsed. But 'sight' also reveals

---

[46] Vera Brittain, *Testament of Youth* (1933; London: Penguin Books, 2005), 384. Brittain's narrative style is discussed in Chapter 5.

[47] Carol Acton and Jane Potter, *Working in a World of Hurt: Trauma and Resilience in the Narratives of Medical Personnel in Warzones* (Manchester: Manchester University Press, 2015), 35.

more about the direct moment of trauma, wherein Brittain and her colleagues adopt the shutter mechanism to alter their perspective and limit what they see. Again, we must explore the effect of mediation through technology: although Brittain is not explicit about the technological allusion, the 'shutter' at this historical point onwards is increasingly connected with technologies of seeing, as distinct from its more traditional association as a barrier.

Further technologies of seeing are evoked when Mortimer conjures a poignant camera metaphor, to describe the beginning of her hospital service:

> The Directress gives me a few details and touches on the psychology of the hospital very lightly, for she is going to take me for a first round of the wards. While I wait for her a shutter snaps in my mind and I see again, ominously vivid, the salon ornaments and the railway station at Paris.[48]

The 'shutter' in the mind implies a division between images. It suggests that at this transitional moment of entering the hospital and beginning her work here, she experiences a momentary self-questioning hesitation – the last chance to renege on her support, and a last look back at Paris. It is ambiguous if she is viewing or taking pictures, but the shutter snapping amounts to the imaginative transportation back to the time in which she formed the memory, or took the picture. It is a momentary replacement of the scene before her with images of another space, one which is further from the Front, more domestic, and more sanitary: to 'see again' a space of safety, luxury, and sanctuary. This does not seem to be a conscious or voluntary action, however: the 'shutter snaps' in her mind with no suggestion that she actively chooses to alter the scene before her eyes, implying she has little choice over what she views. Mortimer's use of imagery here is a powerful precursor to Christopher Isherwood's 'I am a camera with its shutter open, quite passive, recording, not thinking [...] Some day, all this will have to be developed, carefully printed, fixed.'[49] Mortimer's shutter is not open, however: the 'shutter snaps', abruptly opening and closing, to convey the immediacy of the moment and the momentary image of somewhere else. Mortimer's mind as a camera actively takes pictures and views them, in instant development. Whereas Isherwood offers the vantage of

---

[48] Mortimer, *Tent*, 60.
[49] Christopher Isherwood, *Goodbye to Berlin* (1939; New York: New Directions Books, 2012), 3.

retrospection when he views his images with his continuous record of experience, Mortimer seeks to represent the immediate challenge of fixing experience as it happens.

Controlling what is and is not seen is not only the subject matter of these narratives but is also realised through the rhetorical style. The performative dimension of writing functions simultaneously to show the coping strategy of altering perspective and to raise the issue of how to convey the subjectivity of viewing, as well as reclaim a sense of affective agency. The effect is one of rhetorical confrontation, the subject and manner of which foregrounds motifs of sight and perspective. In her discussion of 'Cubist Vision in Nursing Accounts' (2013), Higonnet extols the influence of vision, sight, and perspective on these writers, primarily focusing on Mary Borden's *The Forbidden Zone* (1929) and Ellen N. La Motte's *The Backwash of War* (1916).[50] Higonnet, with what she terms 'cubist vision', explores the images of sight and vision in nursing narratives, and gestures towards its significance at this particular time of artistic and literary experimentation, signalling the importance of the 'multiplication of perceptions'.[51] Higonnet's discussion bridges the gap between artistic vision and ideas of perception inclined towards clinical sight. In order to read these medical narratives while simultaneously recognising the medical point of view, Higonnet employs the idea of the, aforementioned, 'double image' of the X-ray, which results in the amplification of knowledge through the penetration of the clinical gaze, while also revealing the value of open, as opposed to narrow, vision. Part of Higonnet's invocation of the X-ray challenges preconceived notions of seeing and representation, which she situates contextually with cubism and emerging technologies. While the divergent angles of the X-ray aid visual interpretation, she argues that 'the divergent angles often underscore a rupture in the familiar conception of "the real," rather than bring together perspectives to join in an illusion of coherence'.[52] The new technique, while illuminating and true to life, creates a rupture in abstract perspective. A new level of perspective, and thus perception, is opened up. Narratives such as La Motte's and Borden's revert to cubist technique as a way of conveying the alteration and multiplication of perceptual angles, through 'narrative experiments with voice, with the splitting of characters, and with a dialectic exchange of gazes

---

[50] Higonnet, 'Cubist Vision'.
[51] Ibid., 157.
[52] Ibid., 159.

between nurse-narrator and soldier-patient'.[53] Furthermore, '[i]n classic examples of irony, the nurse-narrator may offer two very different images of the same person [...] she may ironically split the narrative voice itself',[54] which becomes an example of concurrent narrative angles. The 'cubist vision' employed by these nurse-writers aims to challenge narrative viewpoints, and in doing so critique the politics of perception.

The narrative style which Mortimer employs, and experiments with to powerful effect, is in many ways reminiscent of La Motte's and Borden's narrative styles. It is significant that not only did Borden and La Motte work together but Mortimer also worked at L'Hôpital Chirurgical Mobile No. I at Rousbrugge, Belgium, at the same time. Mortimer's memoir, in a more formal prose style, seems to emulate the techniques of representation used by Borden and La Motte. While Christine Hallett and Alice Kelly have pointed out that they worked together, and that there is some commonality of events and styles in their work, there has been little explicit critical reading of Mortimer's text.[55] The focus often falls on La Motte's influence on Borden, but there seems to be no discussion of their influences on Mortimer, although there is certainly a way in which Mortimer's work too can be understood in terms of a 'cubist vision'.

Observation is central to Borden's *The Forbidden Zone*, as Hazel Hutchinson argues. In particular, the subjective focus in Borden's narrative technique, and

> use of a high-wire aerial perspective, looking down, birdlike, from a great height on a war-torn nation, a technique that simultaneously places the artist in a privileged, almost godlike vantage point, [...] also creates an obscuring and distorting distance between speaker and subject, and between speaker and reader.[56]

The 'cubist' and distinctive style is evident in how Borden's 'distortion of perspective [...] manifests itself in clipped sentences and sentence fragments and nonstandard punctuation patterns'.[57] By

[53] Ibid., 157.
[54] Ibid.
[55] Christine Hallett, *Nurse Writers of the Great War* (Manchester: Manchester University Press, 2016), 76; Alice Kelly, *Commemorative Modernisms: Women Writers, Death and the First World War* (Edinburgh: Edinburgh University Press, 2020), 54.
[56] Hazel Hutchinson, 'The Theater of Pain: Observing Mary Borden in *The Forbidden Zone*', in *First World War Nursing: New Perspectives*, 144.
[57] Hutchinson, 'Theater of Pain', 144.

comparison, Mortimer's style excludes much of this technique; but that is not to say that their respective representational effects are vastly different. While Borden uses clipped fragments, Mortimer's prose is more clear and coherent, yet it similarly conveys a distorted perspective and a kind of fragmentation. It is easy, given Borden's highly conscious fragmentary techniques, to consider such fragmentation only in terms of broken, standalone scenes, but Mortimer's more traditional prose style depicts similar fragmentation in terms of perspective, with the jarring clash of multiple images and unclear pronouns creating a similar kind of obfuscation. Such distortion shifts towards the perspectival qualities of cubism. Distorted and fragmented vision demonstrates a gesture towards objective, analytical detachment while simultaneously foregrounding the subjective contingency that is central to perspective. A shift towards the 'basic principle of triangulation',[58] in the 'double image', as Higonnet explains, exemplifies the way these medics multiply and alter their gaze.

Such ideas can be considered in a particular scene from Mortimer's narrative, which employs unusual techniques of representation, seeming to zoom in and out on different details:

> And the night nurse often needs such simple cheer. While on her rounds she glides through darkened ward after darkened ward. Death – mysterious, spasmodic breathing-out of life which our instinct so curiously shrinks from – is here, is there, is everywhere. The beautifying touch of his obliterating finger disarms her fear. It is not so with pain, in whose wry, haunted environment is neither life nor death, but a grimly barriered and bounded No Man's Land where the bravest lose their bearings. No intimacy lessens her horror of his presence. He alone seems the great reality, and life no more than a drop of water, detained and magnified for a moment out of relativity, then slipping eagerly from under his distorting lens back into the churning current.[59]

In the curious and obscure perspective of this passage we see pain as a 'No Man's Land', which is worse than death and haunts the night nurse. Pain is an in-between state in which life and health is reduced to the margins. Although the pronouns are ambiguous, it seems that it is 'pain' that 'alone seems the great reality', and it is pain's 'lens' under which life in total is reduced to 'no more than a drop of water'.

---

[58] Higonnet, 'Cubist Vision', 156.
[59] Mortimer, *Tent*, 167–8.

Life itself is only briefly distinguished from the 'churning current' by pain's grotesque magnification, and slipping from its scrutiny into the obscurity of death is a release. This particular manifestation of vision is domineering, implying that the act of looking or not looking is directly implicated in the experience of pain and relief. Mortimer determines the perspective of the scene, controlling what is seen and how it is seen. The passage itself is like a microscope, and Mortimer controls the magnifying dial: an authorial hand directs the image, changing and morphing the object of focus for emphasis, producing a striking angle of vision. Mortimer's rhetorical style is not that of a detached observer, offering a realist impression of the scene, but instead works to emulate the nurse's subjective immersion in the experience, so that the reader too is involved. Mortimer cultivates a way of seeing that is based on repeatedly adjusting and altering the view; veering between empathy and metaphysics, magnifying and blurring, to challenge ways of perceiving. In such ways, these medic-writers challenge easy assumptions by consciously exploring perspectives that do not always correlate with their own, personal viewpoint. The results force the reader to confront difficult sights, without the option to look away.

Technologies and devices for seeing, and how they are used, have the power to alter perspective. The preoccupation with sight in these narratives reinforces the importance of viewing in this context; not merely as a diagnostic tool, or in navigating one's environment, but reflexively, for how the medics see themselves – and thus how they relate, connect to, and disconnect themselves from these spaces. Given the substantial turn to technologically mediated vision in both military and medical contexts, it is no surprise that representation gravitates towards visual technologies and modes in order to elucidate subjective impressions. Altering perspective creates an imaginative space, and thus reinforces the counter-site. In such ways the medics bring new attention to the value of looking on things as they happen, and at themselves, from different angles.

The medics' coping strategies are representational functions, informing not just the subject matter but also the narrative approach. There is self-consciousness in their representational devices, which is itself a reflection on their own experience of developing coping strategies. These narrative approaches strive to communicate coping and the act of attempting to cope. Their aim is to unsettle the onlooker from a narrow perspective, presenting challenges to perspective itself in order to recognise different points of view. The strategy of the double image X-ray works in this way: while revealing multidimensionality, it also uncovers a negative space. The X-ray not only offers penetrating vision, it also highlights what has previously been hidden: traversing the boundary of the skin from multiple angles, it is also a model for seeing beneath the psychological epidermis. It allows us to see the whole, from multiple perspectives, and to negotiate the boundaries between different imaginative spaces.

Negotiating Boundaries

The alteration in perspective, which provides for the triangulation of narrative angles, reveals the fact that each of these parallel and concomitant counter-sites must have a traversable boundary. The shift in perspective is made possible by the shift between spaces; by 'moving' between the different sites, by negotiating with the thresholds, the medic is able to cope, and consequently continue to articulate how they perceive coping. Movement across and between is necessary for remaining within the moment and for recognising what is needed in order to carry on.

The imaginative and alternative spaces discussed so far offer a figurative sense of refuge, but we can also recognise a particularly physicalised sense of separation and movement. Physical and embodied metaphors not only reify the experience but also move towards figuratively externalising how the events are experienced. Rathbone describes being instructed 'to develop a sort of shell',[60] a relatively standard idea of a defence mechanism, where the 'shell' provides a protective layer that allows the individual to continue functioning. Yet, in developing this protective coating, another, enclosed space is formed within the shell, into which to withdraw, with the function of protection. In *Poetics of Space* (1958), Gaston Bachelard focuses on the shell object in relation to the connotations of home and protection:

> whenever life seeks to shelter, protect, cover or hide itself, the imagination sympathizes with the being that inhabits the protected space. The imagination experiences protection in all its nuances of security, from life in the most material of shells, to more subtle concealment through imitation of surface.[61]

---

[60] Rathbone, *Young*, 287.
[61] Gaston Bachelard, *The Poetics of Space*, trans. Maria Jolas (1958; Boston: Beacon Press, 1994), 132.

The shell, especially in this instance, provides an imaginative space of refuge, where an individual actively seeks to 'shelter', 'protect', 'cover', and 'hide' themselves from a potential threat. Specifically, the shell casing initiates a boundary, but one which is traversable, with the implication of an escapist space. The safe space of refuge enables the imagination to work to protect the psyche. In light of Bachelard's comment, Rathbone's 'shell' comes to symbolise the continuity between the literal and figurative shells. The effect of withdrawal may be achieved by the appearance of its opposite: the self may seem to *be* the shell, all on the surface, rather than hidden beneath it. This 'imitation of surface' suggests a psychological camouflaging against the backdrop of war: on the surface the medic is wholly within the exact space and moment, but beneath they are elsewhere. In developing a shell around themselves, Rathbone and these other medics can achieve a move towards shelter and protection. The shell represents both a carapace and refuge: there is clearly the semblance of protective barrier, but there is also the figurative space of withdrawal, which is what is at the heart of these coping strategies.

While the shell is consistent with earlier examples of the shutter and curtain as a barrier, it is by no means the only image through which such complex notions of protection and withdrawal are conveyed. In fact, the invoked images are often conflicting and antithetical, illustrating the subjective nature of their experiences. Having been called back home, Mortimer reflects on her time nursing compared with her pre-war life:

> Through a maze of conflicting emotions I look back along the days. Civilian life seems as far from me as a skin sloughed off. After my breezy corner of a green shack, in this tiny world of keen living, how self-centred, and cluttered with artificial values that other life will seem.[62]

This acknowledged dissociation is represented as embodied: 'a skin sloughed off'. With the shedding of one's skin, different facets of the person may emerge, with the implication that they become a different person. Shedding one's skin seems entirely counter to a more usual idea of coping that develops a stronger barrier between oneself and external threats, such as a thick(er) or second skin. Instead, Mortimer identifies that her skin has been 'sloughed off', suggesting vulnerability, especially given that 'to lose one's skin is to lose the

---

[62] Mortimer, *Tent*, 239.

boundaries of the self, to lose the cohesion of the pieces that make it up, to lose the feeling of identity'.⁶³ Yet, this loss of a particular identity is not wholly negative, suggesting instead that, due to age and experience, Mortimer has outgrown this particular part of her identity. The image turns on a contrast between the inauthentic and the authentic selves, similar to the idea of the 'real thing'. It is particularly unusual that a shell-less, skinless vulnerability should be valorised in this way, but it suggests a kind of coping with, or rationalising of, traumatic experience. This seems initially contrary to the masks of performance we have previously seen, where the application of more and more layers seems to protect the self underneath, while simultaneously providing an epidermic pseudo-self. The shedding of skin is an antithesis to the shell analogy: as a protective carapace and the opening up of a refuge space the shell enables protection and separation, but like the 'skin sloughed off' it is separate and external to the tangibility of the physical body. With the shedding of the skin there is a sense of rejection, distancing the self and the psyche from a hard shell or exterior, so that movement in and between is possible.

We can recognise such an idea if we return to Foucault's mirror and consider how the duality of vision and perspective can relocate the self, particularly in relation to what is going on around:

> From the standpoint of the mirror I discover my absence from the place where I am since I see myself over there. Starting from this gaze that is, as it were, directed toward me, from the ground of this virtual space that is on the other side of the glass, I come back toward myself; I begin again to direct my eyes toward myself and to reconstitute myself there where I am.⁶⁴

The alteration of perspective not only reveals but enables the movement between embodying the self and seeing the self. Specifically, it is 'com[ing] back toward myself' which enables the individual to reground the self, while also maintaining an autoscopic view of oneself, providing for a movement between multiple consciousnesses.

Borden's 'Blind' is a particularly strong example through which to explore this movement between consciousnesses, which can be more fully appreciated through a radiographic reading of the scene. In this 'fragment', Borden offers a dual perspective of herself, drawing specific attention to the experiential dimension of her psychological terrain. Borden's narrative voice delivers a scene in which she is

---

⁶³ Didier Anzieu, *Psychic Envelopes* (London: Karnac Books, 1990), 6.
⁶⁴ Foucault, 'Of Other Spaces', 24.

detached from her ordinary perceptual apparatus in her experience of the world. The depiction of her psychological state allows us to have a kind of X-ray vision of her psychological experience within the physical medical space, which reveals a heterotopic counter-site concurrent with the medical space. The scene is peppered with dream references, establishing an 'unreality' that marks the division between her psyche and her body. As a heterotopic counter-site, the dreamscape is a mechanism of resistance; the figure of the nurse is busy working, mechanically performing duties, and it is through the multiple dreamlike references that we can realise her sense of separation from reality and consciousness. The allusions to blindness throughout refer not only to the blind patient but to her own defensive psychological blindness to what is immediately before her.

The hospital ward, and the atmosphere within, is described as: 'this curious dream-place', 'all, you see, like a dream', 'must have been in a trance, or under some horrid spell', 'as if in a dream', 'this nightmare'.[65] She is fulfilling her duties in an automatic manner, through a hypnotic somnambulism:

> It didn't do to think. I didn't as a rule, but the boy's very young voice had startled me. It had come through to me as a real voice will sound sometimes through a dream, almost waking you, but now it had stopped, and the dream was thick round me again.[66]

She functions only if she is engulfed by this dream mist: 'I see it all through a mist. It is misty but eternal. It is a scene in eternity, in some strange dream-hell.'[67] The events of the medical hut conspire to interrupt her 'strange heaving dream', but it is not until 'a new faraway hollow voice' calls, '"Sister! My sister! Where are you?"'[68] that she is shaken out of her trance. It is a distant voice which 'sounds so faraway, so hollow and so sweet [. . .] like a bell high up in the mountains. [. . .] A lost voice. The voice of a lost man, wandering in the mountains, in the night.'[69] It is the voice of her blind patient, whom she had left alone while attending to others:

> 'I thought I had been abandoned here, all alone,' he said softly in his faraway voice.

---

[65] Mary Borden, 'Blind', in *The Forbidden Zone* (1929; London: Hesperus Press, 2008), 92, 95, 99, 99, 102.
[66] Ibid., 92.
[67] Ibid., 101–2.
[68] Ibid., 102.
[69] Ibid.

> I seemed to awake then. I looked round me and began to tremble, as one would tremble if one woke with one's head over the edge of the precipice. I saw the wounded packed round us, hemming us in [...] The blind man didn't know. He thought he was alone, out in the dark. That was the precipice, that reality.[70]

There is an explicit divide between reality and unreality: her dream-like state is a 'trance' separating her from the 'reality' of the ward; a trance that she maintains as a means of self-protection. Significantly, this divide between real and unreal, and thus between different consciousnesses, is marked by 'the edge of a precipice'. Coming to 'the edge of the precipice' is a moment of abrupt consciousness, and awakening. The episode illustrates her heterotopic counter-site, which we see in tandem with the reality of the crowded hut, full of wounded and dying men, with not enough staff or resources to treat them. Coming out of this somnambulism she is overwhelmed by the harsh reality of pain and distress around her: 'My body rattled and jerked like a machine out of order. I was awake now, and I seemed to be breaking to pieces.'[71] Seeing anew, waking from this induced hypnotism, she is vulnerable; yet alongside this vivid representation of psychological impact of the experience is an implicit acknowledgement that effective medical care cannot be mechanic and detached. In order to provide care and give empathy, the carer must be present in both body and mind.

Borden's development of her trance-like dream state alongside the very real fact of medical care enables a radiographic reading of the caregiving experience. The radiographic reading mimics the triangulation in the actual X-ray process by taking the psychological, figurative, and literary in conjunction. The fragment draws on highly modernist techniques, the 'cubist vision' she uses throughout the text, to represent multiple, overlapping yet divergent planes of existence. She depicts multiple spaces: her own traumatically dissociated dream state; her lucid awakening to the pain and death all around; her awareness of the blind man's horror of being 'alone, out in the dark', and of his unawareness of the antithetical horror around him. In my proposed literary radiography, it is not a case of seeing what is not there, of reading between the lines, but of seeing the reality simultaneously with the unreality: the dreamscape, imagination alongside the actuality of the wounded men. The scene presents the

---

[70] Ibid., 103.
[71] Ibid.

perceptual experience of the real environment, while also providing a direct evocation of the psychological interior.

We can see a similar idea at play, on a smaller scale, in Helen Dore Boylston's *'Sister': The War Diary of a Nurse* (1927) when she explains:

> As the hours went by we ceased to think. Our hands moved automatically. We were hardly conscious of the shuffling of feet and the steady drip-drip of wounds bleeding from surface vessels, torn open when Ruth took off the dressing. I remember hearing a soft thump now and then. I suppose somebody fainted. But there was no time to look up. We were needed elsewhere for stretcher cases at that very moment. After a while Topsey had to give it up, and went away very white. She was sick before we started, anyway.[72]

In a similar fashion to the earlier example of 'no time to think', Boylston and her colleagues are too caught up in the work to pay attention to the full array of events going on around them, nor are they emotionally available to reflect on their actions. Their affect is suspended. We see the concomitance of the inability to think or feel, 'ceased to think', 'hardly conscious', alongside the reality of the wounds, bleeding and dripping. There are things happening not so much in the background as almost in a far-off place, with vague recollections, 'I remember hearing', vague awareness for what is going on around, 'I suppose somebody fainted'. The tale culminates with an awakening:

> We're through now, just as the dawn is coming. I don't know whether I'm sleepy or not, but when I close my eyes the bandages go on rolling and winding and staining crimson. The blur of faces is still there in the sputtery light, and I can hear the ceaseless shuffle of feet. So I'm writing in this until it goes away and I can sleep.[73]

We can see how once she stops working, she slowly awakens from a trance-like, somnambulist state, where reality begins to seep in or come into focus in her mind. There is an intersection of exhaustion, trauma, and the need to write. Movements still seem far off, but her consciousness is coming around to the details of her environment, and the weariness of her body.

---

[72] Helen Dore Boylston, *'Sister': The War Diary of a Nurse* (New York: Ives Washburn, 1927), 65.

[73] Ibid.

The dreamlike state acts as a psychological equivalent to an X-ray. Visually penetrating the epidermis, the X-ray reveals what lies beneath: the negative space that the naked eye cannot distinguish is illuminated, to be viewed at the same time as the whole. In this instance, the heterotopia is the negative space that is a part of the individual and their body as a whole. Through a figurative, radiographic reading of the situated individual we are able to appreciate the relationship between the tangible body and psychological geographies. In an X-ray, the image reveals the minutiae of bodily boundaries: we see where the bone lies in relation to the skin and the muscle; we see the inner architecture of the body and its network of connections. The depth perception and understanding of three-dimensional space is achieved by the combined effect of different radiographic angles, in a kind of stereoscopic vision. Angles of viewing triangulate the image in order to see the whole: we see the body and what is going on within the body. A single radiographic image reveals what is in the body in two dimensions, which when combined with another angle reveals a depth and further multidimensionality. In the psychological X-ray, though non-pictorial, we can see how the heterotopic counter-site relates to the individual in the moment. The boundary between the conscious and unconscious becomes fluid and traversable, enabling the shift between the real and unreal, the real and the countered.

The translation of the heterotopia into the psychological terrain, as this chapter has explored, extends from a concept of functioning as protection to one functioning as illumination, which refocuses the eye on the real space. One of the key principles of Foucault's heterotopias is that 'they have a function in relation to all the space that remains', and this is the most significant part of the role of the heterotopia in this context of trauma and resilience. But furthermore:

> This function unfolds between two extreme poles. Either their role is to create a space of illusion that exposes every real space, all the sites inside of which human life is partitioned, as still more illusory [...] Or else, on the contrary, their role is to create a space that is other, another real space, as perfect, as meticulous, as well arranged as ours is messy, ill constructed, and jumbled. This latter type would be the heterotopia, not of illusion, but of compensation.[74]

All counter-sites are heterotopias, and all heterotopias have the power to contest and invert: some as illusory, some as compensatory.

---

[74] Foucault, 'Of Other Spaces', 27.

The heterotopia of illusion is evident in the examples of theatricality, while the heterotopias of compensation can be seen in the unreality of civilian life, although both can feel the same and be experienced as imaginary. The counter-sites that we see are neither definitively 'illusion that exposes every real space', nor 'a space that is other [...] perfect [...] meticulous', but we can recognise traces of both of these types of heterotopias. Through Borden's example, and the application of an X-ray aesthetic, we can appreciate a rhetorical mode that draws attention to the human and emotional concern for the wounded, while simultaneously illuminating the subjective experiential dimension of difficult caregiving.

The psychological heterotopia becomes a means for the countering of trauma and risk to the psyche. The divisions and barriers between the medics' consciousnesses do not connote separation and distancing but instead enable a movement between psychological sites. The medic is able to renegotiate their situation by exploring the psychological terrain and recognising the permeability of boundaries, as the alteration in perspective affords. While the emergence of counter-sites may be symptomatic of traumatic experience, these are also coping strategies, providing, in the idea of the movement across boundaries, for the possibility that medics can remain functional within such traumatic environments. Refocusing on the boundaries embedded within the negative space reveals what goes on at the edges and intersections of psychological geographies. By exploring representations of heterotopic counter-sites we can recognise the influence of trauma, beyond its retrospective description, as having concurrent psychological and representational impact. The counter-site is the negative space surrounding the subject, but in order to read the subject and their experience, we need to see the whole and explore psychological geographies through the multiplication of angles of perception.

Chapter 5

Surfaces: Articulating Pain and Trauma

On first reading a text we see what is being said, and privilege what is being shown to us. We sweep across the representational surface of the text, meandering through the textual spaces, understanding and interpreting what is said. But we need to not only read what is on the surface but read the text *as* a surface, and begin to identify the inferential depths of textual space. For this chapter I wish to introduce a spatial image of these texts as representational surfaces, and explore the features of that surface. By considering the representational textual surface, we can draw analogies with and gain insight into the more specific presentation of emotional surfaces. As a consequence of their roles, medics' emotions are restricted. This constraint often manifests itself through a flattening of affect in their actions, in their representation of events, and in the form of representation itself. Gaps start to appear on the surface, indicative of the emotions they are unable to feel or unable to express. Yet, there is self-consciousness in the ways the texts do and do not address certain things. Thus, this reading of the texts allows us to take into account representational strategies and choices, including intentional or crafted forms of textual space that work with gaps and ruptures: forms of flattening, fragmentation, and silence on the textual surface.

There are inevitably things left unsaid in the expression of challenging and painful experiences, either because they cannot be appropriately articulated or because they are too difficult to share. Something left unsaid manifests as a gap or rupture in the representational surface, and this gap draws our attention to the absence. In the words of Emily Dickinson's haunting poem, 'Pain – has an Element of Blank – / It cannot recollect / When it begun – or if there were / A time when it was not –'.[1] Dickinson presents the idea of pain as destructive of self-knowledge, thus leaving a gap in self-representation. Once pain overcomes, consciousness can atrophy beyond reason, threatening and harming one's ability to know, to 'recollect', and to communicate. The 'blank' is a gap not only of knowledge but of articulation itself. The space created by this shattering of selfhood is anxiety-inducing and threatening: if we cannot know, then how can we explain and communicate? The 'blank' produces a crisis of representation in which expression falters in the attempt to communicate suffering, pain, and trauma.

But the gaps are not always straightforwardly indicative of, or determined by, pain. Instead, the gaps and ruptures in the surface of the text are also employed as representational strategies which can illuminate the inadequacies of the means of expression in communicating difficult experiences. Like Dickinson, these medics also highlight the inexpressibility of the pain and suffering that they witness, and vicariously experience, through representational strategies and rhetorical choices. As Kathlyn Conway explains, in writing narratives of trauma, pain, or illness, 'some writers use narrative itself not just to represent the gap but to bridge it'.[2] These textual gaps must be looked at not only with an eye to the representational content they omit but also for their own significant form. This chapter focuses on gaps in the surfaces of personal accounts, as well as the conscious and unconscious shaping of these gaps. By reading these texts as representational surfaces, we can explore how gaps in representation are themselves features of the representation.

An initial consideration of these textual ruptures might read them as symptomatic of trauma and unassimilated experience. Established trauma theory suggests that such gaps are often symptoms of traumatic experiences; that they are evidence of repressed memories, or are the consequence of an inability to contain experience in language. When we initially think about trauma narratives, and trauma studies more generally, we tend to think of gaps, of what is missing, and of fragmented discourse – but doing so in a superficial way risks missing the nuances of representation. Shoshana Felman, in her discussion of trauma narratives, explains that trauma testimonies are

---

[1] Emily Dickinson, 'Pain – has an Element of Blank –', in *Emily Dickinson: The Complete Poems*, ed. Thomas H. Johnson (London: Faber and Faber, 1970), 323.

[2] Kathlyn Conway, *Beyond Words: Illness and the Limits of Expression* (Albuquerque: University of New Mexico Press, 2013), 110.

composed of bits and pieces of a memory that has been overwhelmed by occurrences that have not settled into understanding or remembrance, acts that cannot be constructed as knowledge nor assimilated into full cognition, events in fragmented excess of our frames of reference.[3]

This identification of 'bits and pieces' is familiar ground in trauma discussions, also taken up by Arthur Frank in his discussion of illness narratives, who explains that 'these bits and pieces are all that an "overwhelmed" consciousness can deal with'.[4] However, such readings of these primary texts disregard intentionality and the complexities of the multifaceted responsibility of the witnessing caregiver. A vital part of reading and listening to testimonies of trauma and suffering 'is not only to listen for the event, but to hear in the testimony the survivor's departure from it';[5] we need to be alert to the moment of departure, the deviation in the retelling of details, and hence listen out for the communicative force of gaps.

Crucially, we need to pay closer attention to the kinds of departure and silences apparent within these 'bits and pieces' of broken narratives. In discussions of trauma specific to the First World War, critics often quote Walter Benjamin: 'Was it not noticeable at the end of the war that men returned from the battlefield grown silent – not richer, but poorer in communicable experience?'[6] The upheaval of the conflict certainly reverberated across the political and cultural landscape, but it also damaged the confidence and stability of individual articulation. However, Benjamin's point is not confined to the symptomatic silence of veterans. In his subsequent discussion he links his perception that 'the communicability of experience is decreasing' to a decline in storytelling, relating the silence to larger concerns about modern information culture.[7] Yet, silences can be resources for new modes of storytelling if we consider more closely the potential eloquence of moments of silence, instead of just their

---

[3] Shoshana Felman, 'Education and Crisis, or the Vicissitudes of Teaching', in *Testimony: Crisis of Witnessing in Literature, Psychoanalysis, and History*, ed. Shoshana Felman and Dori Laub (New York and Abingdon: Routledge, 1992), 5.
[4] Arthur Frank, *The Wounded Storyteller: Body, Illness, and Ethics* (1995; Chicago: University of Chicago Press, 2013), 139.
[5] Cathy Caruth, 'Trauma and Experience: Introduction', in *Trauma: Explorations in Memory* (Baltimore: Johns Hopkins University Press, 1995), 10.
[6] Walter Benjamin, 'The Storyteller: Reflections on the Works of Nikolai Leskov', in *The Novel: An Anthology of Criticism and Theory 1900–2000*, ed. Dorothy J. Hale (Malden, MA: Blackwell, 2006), 362.
[7] Ibid., 364.

presentation as absence or omission. The communicative gaps explored in this chapter suggest that insight can be born of silence, and of the articulation of silences. Moments of silence can be creative responses to the crisis of representation and the problems of communicating modern experience, even as they exhibit the ruptures and absences in representation. Silence is not always mere absence, nor is it simply mimetic of traumatic symptoms; the silence may be a crafted, shaped feature of representation. Benjamin tells us that storytelling is dying out in the twentieth century, but in fact there are new modes and attitudes to storytelling emerging in response to an overload of information and experience. The sources I explore here demonstrate the survival of storytelling, if we listen and read differently in attending to these new and evolving forms of articulation.

The crisis of representation that these sources confront is influenced by the struggle to offer an authentic representation and to articulate the suffering. Part of it is an inability to 'do justice' to the full weight of the experience and the context of pain and trauma. Pain, Elaine Scarry tells us, 'is language-destroying'.[8] When we suffer we struggle to find the words with which to explain it – we experience the 'blank' – or falter in the narrative of what hurts and how it feels, and this extends to the person witnessing the pain of others. Scarry's formative work, *The Body in Pain* (1985), suggests that putting pain into words is all but impossible: 'Physical pain does not simply resist language but actively destroys it, bringing about an immediate reversion to a state anterior to language, to the sounds and cries a human being makes before language is learned.'[9] However, Joanna Bourke, in *The Story of Pain* (2014), challenges this claim:

> Scarry has fallen into the trap of treating metaphoric ways of conceiving of suffering (pain bites and stabs; it dominates and subdues; it is monstrous) as descriptions of an actual entity. Of course, pain is routinely treated metaphorically and turned into an independent entity within a person, but, for Scarry, these metaphors are literalized. 'Pain', rather than a person-in-pain, is given agency. This is an ontological fallacy.[10]

While pain destroys language in a sense, because it challenges one's ability to articulate and because of an absence of language for pain,

---

[8] Elaine Scarry, *The Body in Pain* (New York: Oxford University Press, 1985), 19.
[9] Ibid., 4.
[10] Joanna Bourke, *The Story of Pain* (Oxford: Oxford University Press, 2014), 5.

these constraints also provide for new and evolving ways in which we can talk about pain and suffering. As Bourke demonstrates, once we consider the voice of the person-in-pain, we can understand more about pain itself. But I wish to extend this, at one remove, and consider the communication of pain by the person-witnessing-pain. The narratives explored throughout this book come not from the person-in-pain but the witness-to-pain, who in turn experiences secondary and vicarious suffering, and whose specific perspective on pain and suffering is informed by caregiving. The witness shares in the need to communicate and articulate, and is thus also involved in the experience of pain. By exploring the testimonies of the witness-to-pain, we can both complicate and disentangle our understanding of the experience of pain, as well as the realities of empathy and witnessing. Such exploration of the pain experience assists us, to borrow Susan Sontag's phrase, in 'regarding the pain of others'.[11]

Such witness testimonies are also driven by a need to understand what is being witnessed. The frontline doctor Harold Dearden, in his introduction to *Medicine and Duty* (1928), explains his rationale for writing a diary while in service. He explains that 'one's mind was receiving a ceaseless flood of new impressions of so vivid and tumultuous a character as imperatively to demand expression, and one wrote to oneself, as it were, for no other purpose than to make that expression possible'.[12] Dearden experiences a human instinct to externalise impressions, not to escape them but to seek some coherence and order. 'Expression' is necessary when inundated by events, scenes, and emotions. When we are in pain we cry out, moan, and groan – we make a noise, but the crafting of narrative is an effort to make sense of and process these experiences. Dearden seeks to express, and thus process, the emotional impact of experiences; yet given that these are substantially experiences of the pain of others, the demand for expression is in part also on behalf of the other, introducing the entangled role of the medic as observer and witness.

The significant themes of this chapter are epitomised by a remarkable extract from Irene Rathbone's unpublished diary, written in 1918 during a break from nursing work in London, when she worked in a YMCA rest camp in France:

---

[11] Susan Sontag, *Regarding the Pain of Others* (2003; London: Penguin Books, 2004).
[12] Harold Dearden, *Medicine and Duty* (1928; Ilminster: Richard Dennis, 2014), 6.

> I read somewhere lately that it was impossible for a woman to write a really disingenuous diary. I believe this is true. I find myself writing this all the time for somebody else – either an interested girl friend, or myself when 60! As a matter of fact the light humorous tone is the only one I find it possible to adopt in writing a diary. I am too shy to make it really intimate, and I don't write well enough ... How I wish I had the gift, because there are all sorts of things going round and round inside my heart which I would love to relieve myself by expressing – queer longings, passionate and strange, which sometimes, I feel I *must* give vent to or burst! Give a feeling a form and it will cease to hurt. I know, but this is impossible for me, so my diary continues to be a valueless record of outward events and observations. Even as such I find it a great comfort – but it is rather a silly 'me' which is revealed in its pages.[13]

It is possible, indeed probable, that Rathbone's use of 'disingenuous' here is in error (especially given that the diary only exists in handwritten form).[14] The effect is one of contradiction, proliferated by the double negative: she seems to suggest that she cannot write an insincere piece, thus implying she can only write a truthful piece, although she acknowledges that her writing is affected by her anticipation of a specific reader. We might conclude that what she means is not 'disingenuous' but actually 'disinterested': 'it was impossible for a woman to write a really [disinterested] diary'. She cannot extricate herself from what she writes, and there is always an investment in an audience, 'always for someone else' and motivated by some intent. Rathbone acknowledges the anxieties and tensions of expression and representation that result. The 'light [. . .] tone' she identifies is perhaps a consequence of an unconscious coping mechanism, but complicated by a lack of confidence in her own skill in expression – though fortunately this did not prevent her from writing. In fact, Rathbone offers us an example of a 'superficial' account of surface events that gives access to complex emotional experiences: by

---

[13] Irene Rathbone, 'July 1918', in 'Unpublished diaries', in The Private Papers of I B Rathbone, Imperial War Museum Collections, Documents.557.

[14] In her otherwise impressive survey of Rathbone's unpublished diary, Geneviève Brassard, in 'From Private Story to Public History: Irene Rathbone Revises the War in the Thirties', NWSA Journal 15, no. 3 (2003): 43–63, appears to overlook or fail to see this possible error by Rathbone. In discussing this quote, Brassard argues: 'Rathbone crafts her wartime diary with deliberate precision and care, creating a definite persona and adopting a voice she invests with purpose [. . .] This candid self-appraisal foregrounds Rathbone's decision early on to adopt a cheerful façade in order to mask painful feelings to herself and others' (ibid., 47).

dwelling on the typical, ordinary, even quotidian, the inner life and truth can be triggered. Her anxious sense that her diary 'continues to be a valueless record', which questions the quality of the content as well as her ability to express it, is an anxiety shared with many of the writers I discuss here.

Not only does Rathbone worry about the content of her diary, she also gestures towards reflection on its formal qualities: 'give a feeling a form and it will cease to hurt'. There is ambiguity in the use of 'form' here, as expression or containment. Given that the comment emerges while discussing expression, this sense is dominant, but there is also the underlying idea of containment, of throwing her 'feeling' into the activity of her work, in order to make it go away or dilute it – to flatten the *affect* and its effect on her conscious self. Yet, a writer can only 'give a feeling a form' by finding one that feels appropriate. And of course, the form that the expression takes is a matter of what is and is not said. The surface of the text is actively moulded into the form it takes by authorial choices of both kinds.

Form is intrinsically part of articulation itself. In light of this, I wish to undertake an interrogation of 'symptomatic writing' as an overarching model of the first-hand narratives I discuss here. Margaret Higonnet advances the idea of 'symptomatic writing', arguing that 'we may interpret these war memoirs and autobiographical fictions symptomatically'.[15] That is, we can consider the gaps and ruptures in their representational surface as evidencing a kind of 'symptomatic' expression. The claim has obvious plausibility, but it needs unpicking further. These texts are not 'symptomatic' in a superficially clinical sense, or a traumatic reading sense – they are symptomatic in a more nuanced, more complex way. Higonnet gives little in the way of further information about what she means by 'symptomatic writing'; in another article she refers, fleetingly, to 'what I have termed a kind of deliberate "symptomatic writing" of the trauma of nursing', and notes that it is important 'not to confuse such a symptomatic writing with "unwitting" or "unconscious testimony"'.[16] There is some clarification here, and the inclusion of 'deliberate' is significant, but we still need a concept of symptomatic writing in positive terms, since Higonnet only qualifies the idea as *not* being unconscious reportage. This chapter, then, argues for a

---

[15] Margaret R. Higonnet, 'Telling Trauma: Women and World War I', in *Savoirs et littérature*, ed. Jean Bessière (Paris: Presses Sorbonne Nouvelle, 2002), 133.
[16] Margaret R. Higonnet, 'Authenticity and Art in Trauma Narratives of World War I', *Modernism/modernity* 9, no. 1 (2002): 101.

reconsideration of symptomatic writing as the negotiation of a conflict between the craft of narrative articulation and certain barriers to representation inherent in the experiences concerned.

Building on Higonnet's comments, and applying them to the narratives, I first identify how symptomatic writing features as an unintentional manifestation, before going on to highlight and closely explore how these 'symptoms' are also intentional and crafted, arguing that 'these spaces are not "empty"'.[17] The chapter then moves on to explore the challenges and ethics of witnessing, by considering how the medic's role as author is caught up in the duty of providing witness testimony, and so is an attempt to speak not only for themselves but also on behalf of their patients. Finally, I explore directly how representational strategies and rhetorical devices change when authors revisit their earlier writing (contemporaneous diaries or letters), and how this retrospect informs the revisioning of their experience.

Crafting Flatness

Self-protective attempts to avoid or buffer wartime trauma often exhibit a form of numbing, identifiable in the writings of these medics as a flattening of affect. Such flattening is a psychological consequence of both the war and the medical environment. The onslaught of intense confrontation, with visceral wounds, profound suffering, and constant threat, puts a severe strain on the nervous system, so that an instinctual numbing of responses necessarily kicks in, to avoid total collapse. In some ways it is like a saturation point. As Russian voluntary nurse Lidiia Zakharova notes, 'the human mind can perceive no more horrors, as a saturated sponge can soak up no more water'.[18] Like saturated sponges, she suggests, they are unable to deal with any more strain on their nerves or sensibilities; and with this they no longer display emotion, and have no more empathy to offer.

While there are numerous examples representing the numbing of

---

[17] Renata Kokanović and Meredith Stone, 'Listening to What Cannot Be Said: Broken Narratives and the Lived Body', in 'Representing Trauma; Honouring Broken Narratives', special medical humanities issue, *Arts and Humanities in Higher Education* 17, no. 1 (2018): 3.

[18] Lidiia Zakharova, 'Diary of a Red Cross Sister in the Front Lines', in *Lines of Fire: Women Writers of World War I*, trans. Cynthia Simmons, ed. Margaret R. Higonnet (New York: Penguin Plume, 1999), 185.

consciousness while nursing and caring, there are also more subtle examples of a flattening of affect *within* the writing itself, which afford evidence of symptomatic writing in the unintentional sense. We can see a specific execution of this in Arthur Martin's *A Surgeon in Khaki* (1915):

> We examined every wound carefully to see that no bleeding was taking place, and all the fractures were very carefully splintered with firm wooden splints. The men suffered very little pain comparatively, and were remarkably cheerful when they had been dressed and placed on the straw.[19]

Martin's description here avoids much specific detail about the nature of the wounds. The wound is displaced as the focus, while the dressing is foregrounded. Insight into the suffering and pain experienced by the patient is only obliquely suggested, skimming over their pain. The suffering is quickly pushed aside, merely acknowledged in a brief note of record. We can see a different kind of flattening in Ellen N. La Motte's *The Backwash of War* (1916):

> Grammont had a hole in his abdomen, when he entered, about an inch long. After about a month, this hole was scientifically increased to a foot in length, rubber drains stuck out in all directions, and went inwards as well, pretty deep.[20]

La Motte emphasises the wound, outlining the medical procedures, but does not empathise with the patient beyond an observation that the wound has been 'scientifically increased', and without recognition of the pain and suffering experienced by the patient. Nor is there any insight into her own feelings, either as witness or part-instigator of further pain. These examples, narrated in a somewhat detached manner, exhibit an absence of empathy; the apparent coldness is indicative of the detachment induced by the clinical gaze, as explored in Chapter 3, not specifically manifest in the use of jargon but rather in their resort to affectless listing. Both Martin and La Motte, here, adopt a detached and matter-of-fact tone, leading to gaps in the relation of their experience, which are unintentional, symptomatic gaps.

Yet, the distinction between unintentional and intentional manifestations of flatness is more complex than it might initially seem, especially when considered in the light of Jane Marcus's idea of an

---

[19] Arthur A. Martin, *A Surgeon in Khaki* (London: Edward Arnold, 1915), 64.
[20] Ellen N. La Motte, 'A Citation', in *The Backwash of War* (1916; London: Conway, 2014), 169.

'Anaesthetic Aesthetic'. In her discussion of Irene Rathbone's *We That Were Young* (1932), Marcus argues that the novel 'operates under an *aesthetic of anaesthesia*, choosing to numb consciousness rather than to prick the conscience'.[21] One aspect of this anaesthesia is the way Rathbone's novelisation of women's work during the war is infused with sentimentality, which offers a kind of 'numbing' effect. Prefacing the first edition of the novel, Elizabeth Delafield identifies the impact of the novel's manner: 'War-time does, amongst other things, breed sentimentality, for sentimentality is one of the most powerful narcotics in the world.'[22] Yet, the effect of sentimentality is inherently contradictory: it directly concerns high and intense emotion, even as it detracts from the real intensity of the war environment. Indeed it does act as a narcotic, distracting from the vivid intensity of Rathbone's detailed account of wounds and nursing, and to an extent Marcus's evaluation is accurate; but such a reading skims over the key visceral scenes, in which the 'aesthetic of anaesthetic' is more complicated.

Marcus argues that while other writers, such as Borden or La Motte, chose to write 'explosive, angry, fragmented modernist texts', Rathbone chose 'to heal and soothe the wounds of war':

> Rathbone, despite her realistic descriptions of wounded men and the especially graphic scenes of the dressing of wounds, remains detached and disinterested, injecting the reader with a narrative aesthetic meant to function as a soothing anodyne to the reader's memories, rather than to arouse one to social action against war. *Rathbone's writing is an exact mimesis of nursing.*[23]

While there is certainly traction here, Marcus's description nods to Rathbone's 'realistic description of wounded men' and 'graphic scenes of the dressing of wounds' without much interrogation. Marcus's suggestion that Rathbone's writing is mimetic of nursing implies she is also nursing and sedating the reader. Arguably, however, Rathbone's aesthetic, precisely because she exhibits flattened affect, actually piques our attention, our consciences, and our awareness – especially for a modern readership. The mimesis of

---

[21] Jane Marcus, 'Afterword: The Nurse's Text: Acting Out an Anaesthetic Aesthetic', in *We That Were Young*, by Irene Rathbone (New York: Feminist Press, 1989), 477 (italics in original).

[22] Elizabeth M. Delafield, 'Preface', in *We That Were Young*, by Irene Rathbone (New York: Feminist Press, 1989), viii.

[23] Marcus, 'Afterword', 476 (italics in original).

nursing characterises the narratorial perspective, but this coincides with a different communicative impact on the reader. Given that the reader does not inhabit the same medical role as the author, it is the rhetorical force of the writing which abrades the reader's consciousness.

This is where Marcus's interpretation of Rathbone's narrative aesthetic only tells part of the story, and so we need to consider more closely the graphic parts of Rathbone's narrative. In these instances, the flattened affect is by no means a 'soothing anodyne', because it pricks and provokes our attention. We can explore this by taking a closer look at some of these 'especially graphic scenes':

> the large piece of linen which served instead of a bandage round the wound was unpinned, and the packs of cotton-wool removed and laid on the bed to be used again. Beneath these was a piece of green oilskin, and beneath that the thick fomentation, now cold, and soaked in blood and pus. This was lifted off – a sodden pancake from which rose a warm and sickly odour – and dropped into the pail. A large area of raw flesh lay revealed, with two pieces of rubber tubing embedded in it for drainage purposes. Each tube was drawn out with a little glooping noise and dropped into a dish.[24]

In a similar vein to La Motte, Rathbone presents a detailed depiction of wound dressing, listing the treatment and the numerous materials involved. The detail with which she explains the process of treatment displays the familiar detachment of the clinical touch, but the sheer intensity of the exhibited scene is designed to disarm the reader and draw their attention to the grotesque reality. In another example, she describes 'McIvor, the jaw-case, who, when his innumerable and complicated bandages were removed, revealed flat holes plugged with gauze where a nose had been, and pendulous shapeless lips'.[25] The exceptionally visceral images open up a gap between what is said and what is imagined. She presents a shocking image of a face without a nose, but omits explicit comment that such a sight is shocking. The extreme violence of the wounds is diluted, perhaps anaesthetised, but that does not mean it is not present. Rathbone shows us images of bleeding, oozing wounds; deep cuts and holes in the body that would not only unnerve but disgust many readers – even while her manner of exposition is such that her own reaction or judgement is omitted.

[24] Irene Rathbone, *We That Were Young* (1932; London: Virago, 1988), 196–7.
[25] Ibid., 200.

Rathbone omits references to the effects on her emotions and psyche, but her artistic crafting produces such effects. While Marcus suggests that '*Rathbone's writing is an exact mimesis of nursing*', it is my contention that Rathbone's writing is a symptomatic response *re-enacted* in her writing. The writing indeed mimics nursing by exhibiting the indications of flattened affect; however, this is not consequent upon the experience itself but a product of her narrative arrangement. The different perspectives of reader and medic are significant, informing the communicative rhetoric of such texts. Rathbone's writing is a mimesis of nursing in the narratorial perspective, but this coincides with a radically different communicative impact on the reader. Precisely because the reader does not occupy the nursing role inhabited by the author, the impact of such 'mimesis' is different. The impersonal voice of the medic gives us a unique insight into the medical experience, where they endure, cause, and witness suffering. These medic-writers employ the aesthetic of blunted affect precisely to express the conflicting dimensions of medical care. The flattened tone evokes the complex expectations of the medics' role – to perform their duty without emotional attachment; to heal and perform painful procedures without risking their own health – all the while retaining their humanity and empathy.

It is difficult to convey this complexity, and so it is evidence of the power of their writing and craft that such meaning is conveyed. The flatness is crafted, a product of artistic and literary decisions that are also evident in the structure of the narratives. In critiquing the style and form of Borden's *The Forbidden Zone* (1929), one contemporary reviewer asks, 'But what price art?'[26] Presumably the rhetorical question is a criticism of Borden's innovative form – or rather its lack of form. In Borden's text we can see a strong example of artistic choice when it comes to her mode of representation, epitomised by her use of 'fragments', which move the text away from a more traditional notion of narrative towards a stream of impressions. In her preface she explains:

> To those who find these impressions confused, I would say that they are fragments of a great confusion. Any attempt to reduce them to order would require artifice on my part and would falsify them. To those on the other hand who find them unbearably plain, I would say that I have blurred the bare horror of facts and softened the reality

---

[26] *Saturday Review of Literature*, 26 July 1930, 7, qtd in Higonnet, 'Authenticity', 101.

in spite of myself, not because I wished to do so, but because I was incapable of a nearer approach to the truth.[27]

Borden presents a contradiction here, emblematic of the 'great confusion' which this narrative induces. Her writing is conflicted by the ironic tension between artificiality and plainness. Despite the extensiveness of graphic and shocking images in her writing, she has 'softened the reality': her intention was to be plain, but she fell short of the full achievement of that aim. Consequently, we can see that Borden's denial of artifice is ironic: plainness requires a great deal of effort. By contending that 'order would require artifice', she draws our attention to the 'artifice' that goes into her writing, and the space between the fragments.

This connects to the idea of 'making' as a key issue in the articulation of pain and suffering. Scarry explains that 'what is quite literally at stake in the body in pain is the making and unmaking of the world'.[28] I wish to borrow the verb 'making', in conjunction with remaking, to explore the drive to actively create within one's personal accounts. If the person-in-pain regains agency and power through the action and activity of making, the witness-to-pain, in their communication of a second-order suffering, might also be able to process the experience through craft. Consequently, the ways in which they articulate the pain of others and their own suffering must be explored through the recognition that their work is also 'the product of a literary decision'.[29]

Writing of this time is no stranger to experimental forms, as is evident in the different styles adopted in these selected narratives. It is particularly notable that several different texts include scenes written as a play-script. Olive Dent's *A Volunteer Nurse on the Western Front* (1917) includes a script-like component in the chapter entitled 'The Trials of a Home Sister':

SCENE I. *The* Home Sister *interviews the* Cook. *Time 9.30am.*

Home Sister *seated at table in mess. Enter* Corporal.

H.S. Good morning, Corporal.
C. Good morning, Sister.

---

[27] Mary Borden, *The Forbidden Zone* (1929; London: Hesperus Press, 2008), preface.
[28] Scarry, *Body*, 23.
[29] Kali Tal, *Worlds of Hurt: Reading the Literatures of Trauma* (Cambridge: Cambridge University Press, 1996), 116.

H.S. What can you give us for meals to-day?
C. [*dryly*]. Well, it's wot have we got.
H.S. I thought you might manage rissoles. That would be a nice change.
C. Yu-u-s. [*Pause, continuing*]. I don't know wot we'll make them of.[30]

Similarly, we can see this form in Borden's 'In the Operating Room':

3rd Patient: I am thirsty.
1st Surgeon: Cut the dressing, Mademoiselle.
2nd Surgeon: What's his ticket say? Show it to me. What's the X-ray show?
3rd Surgeon: Abdomen. Bad pulse. I wonder now?
[. . .]
A nurse comes in from the corridor. Her apron is splashed with blood.
[. . .]
2nd Surgeon: There, there, don't excite yourself. You've got a nasty leg, very nasty. Smells bad. Mademoiselle, hold his leg up. It's not pretty at all, this leg.
2nd Patient: Ah, doctor, doctor. What are you doing? Aiee-.
2nd Surgeon: Be quiet. Don't move. Don't touch the wound, I tell you. Idiot! Hold his leg. Keep your hands off, you animal. Hold his leg higher. Strap his hands down.[31]

Angela Smith suggests that this results in 'a polysemic narrative that allows other voices to penetrate the text in independent forms'.[32] We can even see an example of this device in Rathbone's contemporaneous diary, which also includes a dramatic scene. The photographs in Figure 5.1 capture how she set out the scene dramatically on the diary page, with the conventions of a theatrical script, complete with stage directions. Such conventions emphasise the text as a surface of expression, but the temporary break from traditional prose also disrupts the surface of the text, so that both author and reader temporarily alter their position. Each of these examples uses the script style only once or twice, while the rest of the text is more or less traditional prose.

---

[30] Olive Dent, *A Volunteer Nurse on the Western Front* (1917; London: Virgin Books, 2014), 77.
[31] Borden, 'In the Operating Room', in *Forbidden*, 85–6.
[32] Angela K. Smith, *The Second Battlefield: Women, Modernism and the First World War* (Manchester: Manchester University Press, 2000), 86.

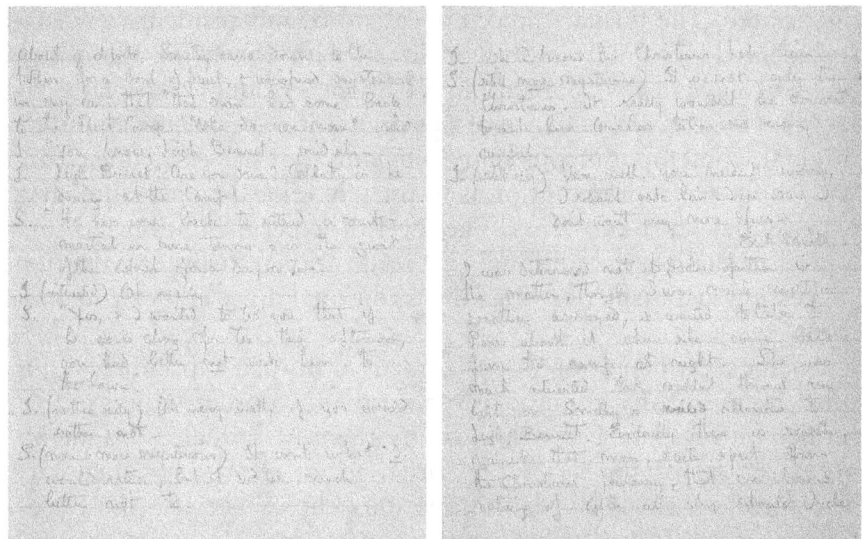

Figure 5.1 Pages from Irene Rathbone's diary, showing a playscript. From The Private Papers of Miss B I Rathbone, Documents.557, IWM Collections. Photos by Imperial War Museum.

These script-style examples experiment with the communication of events. The presence of a theatrical and dramatic form might at first suggest the notion of performance and enactment, but the form is in fact antithetical to performance. Instead, the effect is distancing. Because the authorial voice is altered, the source of the speech, and the silences, also seem different. There is an oblique narratorial detachment, as if the author occupies the same space as the reader: looking on. This narrative style enforces third-person narration, creating an external focalisation which is entirely impersonal. The account is no longer in first-person perspective but switched to encourage the reader to rethink where they and the caregiving witness stand in relation to the suffering. Such detachment in the writing is characteristic not of the role of the nurse but of the authorial/artistic communication: in these very intentional moments of literary craft, the nurse who is writing the represented experience overtly becomes the author who is crafting the reader's experience.

These 'theatrical' scenes show very little commonality on first inspection: while Dent depicts a discussion of meal plans, Borden depicts surgery, and Rathbone discusses an officer coming for tea. Yet, as Borden's operating scene continues, they discuss the possibility of oysters for lunch. So, there is a common theme of food, yet these do not seem to be issues that need to be distanced or dissociated. The formal choice appears to be independent of what is represented, seemingly more concerned with conveying the atmosphere of such an environment. In Rathbone's example especially, the fact that we can see evidence of this dramatic experimentation in the original, contemporaneous diary indicates that her experimentation with modes of representation is intimately related to her immediate experiential sense of events. The level of experimentation indicates a need to challenge traditional and conventional forms of narration, suggesting dissatisfaction with the traditional diary entry or memoir form.

Such experimentation is also evident in Borden's 'fragments', justified because 'Any attempt to reduce them to order would require artifice on my part and would falsify them.'[33] Borden's 'fragments' are a refusal of form, refuting order in an effort at authenticity. The formlessness is Borden's conscious choice because the expectations of traditional narrative are constraining. Her text may not have the coherent form expected of traditional narratives, but it is still crafted. Every word and pause is specifically considered and chosen. For Borden, then, fragmented writing is a craft rather than a symptom of an underlying cause. The fragmentation is a literary articulation of a symptom, presented in such a way as to convey the pervasiveness of the emotional and psychological impact of warfare and suffering, even as it requires consideration and artistic intervention. In actively pushing the boundaries of conventional narrative structures, Borden's communicative intentions are both challenged by and challenging established modes of expression.

In her overt refusal of form, then, there is simultaneously a foregrounding of form as significant. Borden's 'fragments' invoke the idea that conventional narrative must be broken apart, questioned, and challenged in order to reach a kind of expression adequate to her subject. This need to push the boundaries of form in order to find suitable modes of articulation is reminiscent of Virginia Woolf's 'Modern Fiction' (1921), in which she discusses the formal imperatives of modern narration and expression. Woolf tells us that 'life is not a series of gig lamps symmetrically arranged':[34] life is not ordered and arranged, so we cannot, and should not, order and arrange our perceptions of events into a form that compromises the experience. Instead, she says, 'Let us record the atoms as they fall

---

[33] Borden, *Forbidden*, preface.
[34] Virginia Woolf, 'Modern Fiction', in *The Essays of Virginia Woolf Volume 4: 1925–1928*, ed. Andrew McNeillie (London: Hogarth Press, 1984), 160.

upon the mind in the order in which they fall, let us trace the pattern, however disconnected and incoherent in appearance.'[35] Woolf's argument privileges an idea of writing as the mimesis of consciousness; but it is not as straightforward as writing exactly what comes to mind, as the writer moulds the 'atoms' and traces the pattern of the phenomenal experience. If we consider that Borden foregrounds form, then the fragmentation of her narrative is expressive in a more indirect, symptomatic, way. Of course, experimentation with form is never a renunciation of creative intervention: there remains craft in the presentation. Borden's 'fragments of a great confusion' are not just an unmediated record of her experience but can be seen as analogous to a more general confusion: that of the war and of the medical environment, and of their entanglement with each other, of which her fractured account of personal experience is a kind of synecdoche.

Enid Bagnold, in *A Diary Without Dates* (1918), offers an example not quite of fragmented writing but of a narrative shape composed of bits and pieces. Her 'diary' dispenses with dates, disregarding the restrictions of chronology – nor does it have chapter titles, but moves across topics, offering a series of passing observations which may or may not be picked up again later. Bagnold's use of an anecdotal-like form suits her work in a London hospital, where patients often remained for lengthy periods, allowing her to identify patients and occasionally return to them in later discussions. She moves rapidly between thoughts and images, from 'When a woman says she cannot come to lunch it is because she doesn't want to. Let this serve as an axiom to every lover: A woman who refuses lunch refuses everything', to 'The hospital is alive; I feel it like a living being', to 'The hospital is like a dream. I am afraid of waking up and finding it commonplace.'[36] She leaves gaps between thoughts, as well as literally leaving white space on the page. These comments might at first strike the reader as evidence of broken or unfinished thoughts, but they are in fact self-contained individual aperçus within the larger context of an implicit narrative whole.

This is not to suggest that all these texts experiment with form: for some writers traditional form offers an adequate frame for their observations. In his preface, Martin frames his 'attempt [...] to record' in terms that resemble Borden's rationale:

---

[35] Ibid., 161.
[36] Enid Bagnold, *A Diary Without Dates* (London: William Heinemann, 1918), 45.

> In the following pages an attempt is made to record, however imperfectly, some of the scenes, and the impressions formed, during those great days of 1914 [...] The notes in many instances are disconnected, but the things seen presented themselves in a disconnected way, and if they are not all beautifully dovetailed one into another, they are at least given forth somewhat in the way in which I viewed and received them myself.[37]

Martin recognises that experiences do not always lend themselves to a clear narrative: some events must stand alone. Yet, he does not make a formal principle of the fact; and his memoir, like many others in the same vein, he offers chapters with relatively chronological events, shaped into narrative episodes. Though he (apologetically) invokes, like Borden and Bagnold, the resistance of his material to narrative, the sense of disconnectedness is on a different scale. Bagnold's disconnectedness comes from the gaps between observations; Martin does not present scenes as fragmentary or disconnected in themselves, but actually as highly sculpted episodes, presented in tightly woven chapters.

As this example from Martin also demonstrates, even more conventional writers show an awareness of the highly problematic challenge of narrating and articulating their experiences effectively. The anxiety of the form manifests itself in an emphasis on personal truth, particularly in the prefaces or forewords. Bagnold's text opens with: 'I apologize to those I may hurt. Can I soothe them by pleading that one may only write what is true for oneself?'[38] Similarly, Vera Brittain's foreword to *Testament of Youth* (1933) explains:

> I have tried to write the exact truth as I saw and see it about both myself and other people, since a book of this kind has no value unless it is honest ... I have done my best to put on record a personal impression of those incomparable changes which coincided with my first thirty years.[39]

Many of these texts offer a pre-emptive apology for what may be missing, or may not have been a universal or shared war experience. But their focus on personal truth offsets the concern that their accounts may not be immediately recognisable, by affirming the priority of authenticity. The anxious focus on 'trying to find a way' to articulate and report most directly concerns this pursuit of personal

---

[37] Martin, *Khaki*, preface.
[38] Bagnold, *Without Dates*, preface.
[39] Vera Brittain, *Testament of Youth* (1933; London: Penguin Books, 2005), 12–13.

truth, which itself motivates experimentation with different forms of writing.

Nowhere is the anxiety more evident than in Brittain's foreword on the subject of textual form, which relates her growing desire to write her experiences:

> For nearly a decade I have wanted, with a growing sense of urgency, to write something which would show what the whole War and post-war period – roughly, from the years leading up to 1914 until about 1925 – has meant to the men and women of my generation [. . .] Only, I felt, by some such attempt to write history in terms of personal life could I rescue something that might be of value, some element of truth and hope and usefulness, from the smashing up of my own youth by the War.[40]

Brittain pleads eloquently for the value in writing her own experiences, suggesting that one's personal history can provide access to an obscured aspect of generational history. In fact, it is only in the writing of her personal story that she can recover some sense from the war, and provide something 'of value' for others. Her difficulty is with the appropriate form and style for such a 'history'. She goes on to explain her various attempts at it, with their attendant problems. The initial plan for 'a long novel' faltered early in the planning, when she 'found that the people and the events about which I was writing were still too near and too real to be made the subjects of an imaginative, detached reconstruction'.[41] Her second attempt was more mimetic, drawing on her contemporary notes:

> I tried the effect of reproducing parts of the long diary which I kept from 1913 to 1918, with fictitious names substituted for all the real ones out of consideration for the many persons still alive who were mentioned in it with a youthful and sometimes cruel candour. This too was a failure. Apart from the fact that the diary ended too soon to give a complete picture, the fictitious names created a false atmosphere and made the whole thing seem spurious.[42]

Brittain outlines her experimentation with various narrative styles, and the inadequacies of each. She acknowledges that distance is a contributory factor, because the events are 'still too near' for a 'detached reconstruction'. Brittain finds that the intimacy of events

---

[40] Ibid., 10.
[41] Ibid.
[42] Ibid.

is still too much for a fictional narrative – whereas for Rathbone, as this chapter will go on to explore, novelisation seems to enable her expression of the intimate.

Brittain's answer is to strive for as much plainness and simplicity as possible in the retelling of her experience:

> There was only one possible course left – to tell my own fairly typical story as truthfully as I could against the larger background, and take the risk of offending all those who believe that a personal story should be kept private, however great its public significance and however wide its general application. In no other fashion, it seemed, could I carry out my endeavour to put the life of an ordinary individual into its niche in contemporary history, and thus illustrate the influence of world-wide events and movements upon the personal destinies of men and women.[43]

Brittain reaches a decision to articulate, with as little self-consciousness as possible, the authenticity of her experience, an authenticity that lies less in a relation to facts than to a mode of representation. Her 'fairly typical story' privileges an outspoken plainness – with no concealing of identities or semi-fictionalisations to cushion the blunt truth of her experience. Brittain's choice is based on a strong sense of the coherence, and representativeness, of her personal narrative. Her hesitation was about the best means to realise these values, to be as authentic as possible to her memory and her perspective, without diluting the facts and opinions for the sake of public reception.

This sentiment of simplicity is similarly evident in ambulance driver Julien Bryan's preface to *Ambulance 464: Encore des blessés* (1918):

> This book is an attempt to tell something of my own experiences as an ambulance driver with Section Twelve, and, at the same time, to give an idea of what the ambulance service is doing and will have to do probably for some time to come. It is my first book and has not been written without considerable effort, and I might even say sacrifice. Many a time last winter I scribbled in my diary until long after midnight, seated on a stretcher in my ambulance, with two kerosene lamps to give a little light and warmth. I felt that, if necessary, I could revise it in a comparatively short time upon my return home. But the task has not been so easy as I imagined. I have spent many hours during the three months I have been at Princeton trying to put it into shape [. . .] I hope that I have succeeded. If I have, it is because I have

---

[43] Ibid., 10–11.

tried to tell as simply as possible a few of the many things which happened in our section over there.[44]

Like Brittain, Bryan acknowledges the struggle to create his memoir and the time spent 'trying to put it into shape' – suggesting both revision of the text and revisiting of the events themselves. However, the subject itself is far from simple, and he demonstrates that simplicity is something achieved with great effort. While his narrative is partial, telling 'a few of the many things', its truth is representative of the whole of his experience. Bryan would go on to become an influential filmmaker and documentarian, especially in his documentation of the invasion of Poland, life under the Nazis, and the Holocaust. It is poignant that we can look at his writing prior to these events, and perhaps see where his focus on the importance of witnessing emerged. The authenticity that Bryan, Brittain, and these other medic-writers prioritise in their accounts is tied to the duty of witnessing, and the importance and power of the witness's perspective.

Duty as Witness

The struggle to convey experience is entangled with both personal truth and the complex responsibility of the witness. The desire to present an event 'as it really happened' is a part of the overwhelming drive to bear witness amongst these authors, but there is much more to the responsibility of witness testimony, as we can see by focusing on Georges Duhamel's memoir *The New Book of Martyrs* (1918). Initially, Duhamel seems concerned with telling the stories of his patients, wishing to provide a voice for the suffering and those who can no longer tell their own stories – although of course their stories are mediated by his eyes and his pen.

Duhamel writes both *to* and *for* his patients, which is especially evident through his consistent use of second-person address. His writing in part provides a record of what happened for the patients that survived, informing them, and perhaps reassuring them that they were not alone in their suffering; that he was alongside them the whole time. He acknowledges the experience of the patient more poignantly than many others, addressing them and their worries directly:

---

[44] Julien H. Bryan, *Ambulance 464: Encore des blessés* (New York: Macmillan, 1918), vii–viii.

when you come here, there are further sufferings in store for you; and I know with what courage you endure them. The doors of the Chateau close on a new life for you, a life that is also one of perpetual peril and contest. I help you in this contest, and I see how gallantly you wage it.[45]

Duhamel draws our attention to the situation of the soldier who becomes a patient once he enters the medical space. His foregrounded use of second-person address privileges the subjectivity of the patient. But Duhamel also conveys a strong sense that the central function of the medic is to maintain a watchful eye over the patient:

So I will stay and drink in this sinister testimony. And each time that Beal, who has a gaping wound in the stomach, holds out his hands to me with a little smile, I will get up and hold his hands in mine, for he is feverish, and he knows that my hands are always icy.[46]

Not a wrinkle in your faces escapes me. Not one of your pains, not one of the tremors of your lacerated flesh. And I write them all down, just as I note your simple words, your cries, your sighs of hope, as I also note the expression of your faces at the solemn hour when man speaks no more.[47]

In these passages we see the convergence between witnessing and watching for medical signs: watching for developments in the patient's body is a form of medical witnessing, as care depends on identifying such signs. Expressions and sighs are diagnostic signals, but Duhamel's recognition of them simultaneously recognises the patient's personality and subjective experience. The patient's body offers a 'sinister testimony' for which he is the sole witness and scribe. His persistent use of the second-person, speaking as if to his previous, current, and future patients, negotiates with the contrary imperative to universalise the experience and so anonymise the patient. Second-person narration, as a representational strategy, does not necessarily give voice to the soldiers, as the 'you' may be both particular and general. In this way Duhamel's synoptic view of the 'great ordeal' can remain faithful to the individual soldier even as it speaks at a more general level.

[45] Georges Duhamel, *The New Book of Martyrs*, trans. Florence Simmonds (New York: George H. Doran, 1918), 220. The second-person address exists in the original French version, *Vie des Martyrs* (Paris: Mercure de France, 1917); subsequent references are to the English translation.
[46] Ibid., 201–2.
[47] Ibid., 220.

In addressing his narrative to the patients, Duhamel is not only speaking *for* them but also *to* them; giving them back the story of their own experience by providing his witness testimony. In this sense his intended audience is the wounded themselves; he writes not for the benefit of describing the conditions to those who were not there but instead to provide evidence for the victims, reassuring them that their suffering was witnessed. For Duhamel, this is a necessary dimension of his duty, because he believes that medical caregiving is not enough and there is more required of him:

> Not one of your words leaves me unmoved; there is not one of your actions which is not worthy of record. All must contribute to the history of our great ordeal.
> For it is not enough to give oneself up to the sacred duty of succour. It is not enough to apply the beneficent knife to the wound, or to change the dressings skilfully and carefully.[48]

It is also to witness and be there, and to go on to speak. This is his responsibility as a witness to suffering: 'it is not enough to apply the beneficent knife'; he also needs to 'skilfully and carefully' fill in the gaps. It is part of his responsibility as a witness to bridge the gap between the patient and the onlooker at the bedside.

This reading of Duhamel's work stresses the intricate binding between healer and witness in professional duty; but his address to his patients is also a literary conceit, which comes to the fore in the imperative to 'contribute to the history of our great ordeal'. He is determined to speak for, on behalf of, those who suffered.[49] This duty includes bearing witness for those who did not survive: 'our function was not only to tend the living, but also to honour the dead'.[50] As a medic he observes and acts when possible, but his observation is also subsequent witnessing. In this way his account is an attempt at materialising the 'spectre'[51] and writing the victims and events back into existence.

---

[48] Ibid., 220–1.
[49] There are many situations where the prospect of speaking for, on behalf of, others is problematic. In this case, however, the patient cannot speak for himself, or cannot discuss the experience because he was literally unconscious, suffering from delirium, and so on. In some cases, it is a practical source of information transfer, as well as offering an onlooker's point of view.
[50] Duhamel, *Martyrs*, 129.
[51] Patricia Yaeger, 'Consuming Trauma', in *Extremities: Trauma, Testimony and Community*, ed. Nancy K. Miller and Jason Tougaw (Urbana and Chicago: University of Illinois Press, 2002), 40.

Duhamel's writing is an effort to imagine the suffering of his patients, but it is also an account of his own role in the ordeal. He explains, 'For indeed we spent too many days hoping together, enduring together, and if you will allow me to say so, my comrade, suffering together.'[52] In many ways they have indeed suffered together, and it is consequently his responsibility as a survivor to speak of that shared suffering. Duhamel layers his suffering with theirs, foregrounding the sense in which his narrative and all the medical narratives under discussion here are testimonies of a second-order suffering that is vicarious and subsequent. The medics' suffering is a symptom of the patients' suffering, and thus the narratives become another kind of consequential, symptomatic form.

The responsibility of these witnesses is to articulate, but we must realise that this is not a momentary role; it is one that endures:

> The surgeon sees the very seamy side of war. He comes close to the men stricken down in the field, helpless and bleeding and in pain. He stands by them in their dark hours in hospital and by their bedsides when they die.
>
> While the world is hearing the earthquake voice of Victory, he is perhaps kneeling on the straw easing the path to death of a dying man, one of the victors in the fight, or perhaps operating in a mean cottage, surrounded by wounded men waiting their turn on the table.[53]

This is how Martin concludes his memoir, reminding us that his duty and responsibility, as a witness and a healer, continues beyond the end of the war; in fact, it never goes away. Specifically, Martin alludes to the disparities between the political and experiential scales of war, emphasising that the medical role is not defined by political boundaries, so that the medic continues to provide care despite 'the earthquake of Victory'. The medic's role does not concern the wider progress of war but the immediate human emergency before them, which remains the same regardless of declarations of peace or victory. Beyond first-hand engagement with the consequences of war, the medic's responsibility as witness persists further. The medic as witness articulates and contributes to the 'pedagogy of suffering'.[54] It is their professional duty as caregiver, while simultaneously a human instinct, to contribute to the greater understanding of war, pain, and suffering.

---

[52] Duhamel, *Martyrs*, 93.
[53] Martin, *Khaki*, 276–7.
[54] Frank, *Storyteller*, 146.

Beyond the medic's responsibility to the victims, both those who survive and those who do not, there is also the caregiving duty of witness testimony as itself part of the healing process. In this sense the medics' responsibility for wellbeing continues long after the events witnessed, and the accounts themselves take their place as one of the stages of recovery. Significantly, these texts do not cite any such reason for their voluntary efforts at communication. The urge to write seems to stem from a notion of responsibility in terms of witness testimony and showing it 'as it really happened'. Yet, while their own emphasis is on articulation rather than overcoming, there is an intrinsic dimension of therapy or healing involved, for themselves as well as for others. Discussions of witness testimonies and illness narratives often talk about the therapeutic and healing qualities of writing. Dori Laub explains:

> To undo this entrapment in a fate that cannot be known, cannot be told, but can only be repeated, a therapeutic process – a process of constructing a narrative, of reconstructing a history and essentially, of *re-externalizing the event* – has to be set in motion. This re-externalization of the event can occur and take effect only when one can articulate and *transmit* the story, literally transfer it to another outside oneself and then take it back again, inside.[55]

By externalising their experience these writers disentangle themselves from events, limiting the damage they perpetuate as unmediated trauma. This process resonates with Rathbone's earlier quote, 'give a feeling a form and it will cease to hurt', which we might interpret as the foundational principle of writing as therapy. The act of writing can be a therapeutic act, through the cathartic process of literally writing a feeling. There is perhaps also some therapeutic effect inherent in the process of constructing one's memoirs, or even in the bare fact of revisiting diaries and letters, and returning to details one may have forgotten. Dearden, for example, states in his introduction:

> Not a word has been changed, and not a phrase turned: and if at times there is more than a hint of a rawness that seems now deplorable, it serves, on a re-reading, merely to emphasise the effect on my mind of a narrative written by a stranger. Herein, indeed, lies its interest for me. It recalls much that would otherwise be as inaccessible as a previous incarnation; and if it should serve others of its

---

[55] Dori Laub, 'Bearing Witness, or the Vicissitudes of Listening', in *Testimony: Crisis of Witnessing*, 69 (italics in original).

readers in the same fashion I shall feel that it has, to that extent at least, justified its production.[56]

Dearden acknowledges that by rereading his writings, he is reminded of what he has forgotten, or repressed. While this example does not explicitly confirm the *act* of writing as therapeutic, it does support the idea that revisiting contemporary writings is an informing and recuperative process, for the writer and potentially for other readers.

The articulation of these experiences can become an opportunity for others not only to listen and share but also to recognise, and possibly learn from, the articulation of what is painful. Arthur Frank, in *The Wounded Storyteller* (1995), provides an illuminating discussion of Emmanuel Levinas's 'Useless Suffering', where Frank identifies the potential for suffering to become the basis for something 'new':

> Remaking begins when suffering becomes an opening to others. Emmanuel Levinas presents perhaps the darkest vision of suffering as what I have called monadic self-enclosure. Because pain 'isolates itself in consciousness, or absorbs the rest of consciousness,' suffering is, literally, a dead end: 'useless, "for nothing" . . . this basic sense-lessness.' Yet these very depths seem the precondition for a new impulse.[57]

In his discussion of Levinas, Frank demonstrates that the most destructive kind of suffering is that which is buried inside and closed off; where its antagonism to sense and value can only be consolidated. But if it is opened to others, then the opportunity arises for the necessary (medical) attention and care. In the instinctual desire to escape suffering, there is a temptation to bury pain, to just cover it with a bandage and ignore it. But the suffering experienced, like the wound inflicted, often requires the more radical attention of invasive surgery: the wound needs to be irrigated, the experience needs to be opened up and externalised, in order for long-term recovery to take place.

Remaking begins when we make suffering a useful, valuable resource in the sharing of experiences. These ideas link back to the earlier discussion of Benjamin, Scarry, and Bourke, which argued the need for new and evolving ways in which to talk about pain. Even silences can contribute to a 'pedagogy of suffering', and inform those uninvolved in the painful experience to develop sympathies with

---

[56] Dearden, *Duty*, 3.
[57] Frank, *Storyteller*, 176–7.

those who are suffering or have suffered. This impulse to share in order to inform, coming from the medic as witness, opens opportunities to consider how we express empathy, care, and understanding for another. Centrally, as Frank also notes:

> Listening and telling are phases of healing; the healer and the storyteller are one [...] The sufferer is made whole in hearing the other's story that is also hers, and in having her own story not just be listened to but heard as if it were the listener's own, which it is. The illusion of being lost is overcome.[58]

For Frank, healing resides in the communication and recognition of suffering. When we hear a tale of pain, something within it aligns with our own experiences of pain. More than being stated, it is shared, and so can contribute to a 'pedagogy of suffering'. Communication, like surgery, is 'an opening that heals', and can heal both speaker and listener.[59]

Following Frank's lead, I wish to foreground this idea of Levinas's 'half opening',[60] as the suggestion of an opportunity and 'a new impulse'. By acknowledging and speaking out about individual suffering, one participates in the voicing of pain: 'expressing pain [... can be] a necessary prelude to the collective task of diminishing pain'.[61] Suffering causes a tearing of the surface, and the only way in which to promote healing is to attend to the wound. The possible therapeutic qualities of writing come not from plugging the hole and filling in the space but from acknowledging and articulating the rupture. If we focus on the wound, if we give it the attention it needs, we can heal it.[62]

---

[58] Ibid., 183.
[59] Ibid., 185.
[60] Emmanuel Levinas, 'Useless Suffering', trans. Richard Cohen, in *The Provocation of Levinas: Rethinking the Other*, ed. Robert Bernasconi and David Wood (1988; London and New York: Routledge, 2002), 158.
[61] Scarry, *Body*, 9.
[62] This reading indeed privileges the role and power of narrative, but I am aware that this is not always possible. Angela Woods, in 'The Limits of Narrative: Provocations for the Medical Humanities', *BMJ Medical Humanities* 37 (2011): 73–8, prompts discussion of the limits of narrative, arguing that narrativity is not universal and not meaningful across all cultures and societies.

Revisiting and Revisioning

Autobiographical life writing contains a complex negotiation of multiple selves: a retrospective narrating self looking back to construct a narrated self. In the telling of their own stories narrators must occupy a position that itself contains multiple perspectives; not only do they draw on their own viewpoint across different temporal moments, they frequently revisit material written at different moments, often revising their narratives in response. The ways in which these writers craft their later representations in the light of self-reflection are revealed in significant differences between their immediate diaries and their revised memoirs or novels.

At stake in these retellings is the encounter between different selves: not only the intersection between multiple perspectives on the self but also the encounter between others and the self as observer of their experiences. In testifying to events, they are faced with the challenge of the self as subject and self as object: the participatory self and the outside, retrospective self. Their dual role comprises an experiential relation to the event, and a communicative relation to the reader. This division in their role as witness is further multiplied by their roles as witness of events, on their own behalf and on behalf of their patients.

We can identify this dynamic in the specific styling of La Motte's and Borden's works. Higonnet identifies a 'larger artistic strategy of splitting the nurse into two figures',[63] which they both employ to profound effect. As we have already recognised with regards to Borden's splitting and switching between perspectives ('She is dead already, just as I am – really dead, past resurrection'[64]), this serves to situate the nurse as an onlooker as well as involved in the action. While Borden achieves this through rapid alternation between first and third person, La Motte's style is different: she uses first person sparingly, and it is not until over halfway through the whole text that she begins to explicitly employ her personal perspective, when she declares, 'I must write you of what I have seen, the other side, the backwash.'[65] Dualities pervade these texts, so that the figure of

---

[63] Margaret R. Higonnet, 'Introduction', in *Nurses at the Front: Writing the Wounds of the Great War* (Boston: Northeastern University Press, 2001), xvii.
[64] Borden, 'Moonlight', in *Forbidden*, 43.
[65] La Motte, 'Women and Wives', in *Backwash*, 105.

the nurse becomes 'like a diptych'.[66] In the role of the nurse they are dissociated witnesses of events that are happening to other people, but at the same time they are wholly implicated in the somatic experience. Psychologically they may establish some kind of separation, but physically they are embedded. The power of La Motte's and Borden's writing resides in this diptych struggle, which implicates the reader as well. With an effect of bitter irony, both La Motte and Borden include apostrophic imperatives to an onlooker-reader, in the manner of a 'macabre tour guide':[67] 'Careful! Don't stand too close! He spits [. . .] Don't you see that his bed and the bed next are covered with rubber sheets?' 'Look! Look through the window. The old men are undoing the bundles inside this shed. Look, there's a face and there's an arm hanging down crooked.'[68] These reversions to the present tense implicate the reader as another witness, as if the reader too is compounded and immersed, and cannot look away.

La Motte and Borden provide especially overt, and shocking, examples of this situating rhetoric, but the same strategy is present in other narratives. Brittain too makes significant presentational choices, not only in the extensive descriptions of her hesitations and anxieties but also in her choice to title her memoir *Testament*. Richard Badenhausen argues that 'Brittain's title, *Testament* – deriving from *testor*, meaning witness – emphasizes her distance from the events she describes and her forced placement into the position of spectator.'[69] But this sense of 'placement into the position of spectator' oversimplifies the implications of Brittain's authorial voice. Rather, the form of testimony, and testimonial writing, creates and enforces a pluralised perspective, and thus multiple selves. One of these is indeed a 'spectator', but this is complicated by the meeting of past and present, as well as by the 'autobiographical gap' that is inherent in life writing. To emphasise only distance from the 'event' seems strange when we consider that witnessing implies closeness. Again we can see that the medic, in this case Brittain, occupies a dual role as witness: an experiential relation to the event, which is first-hand experience, as well as a communicative relation to the

[66] Higonnet, 'Introduction', xviii.
[67] Ariela Freedman, 'Mary Borden's *Forbidden Zone*: Women's Writing from No-Man's-Land', *Modernism/modernity* 9, no. 1 (2002): 115.
[68] La Motte, 'The Interval', in *Backwash*, 91; Borden, 'The City in the Desert', in *Forbidden*, 76.
[69] Richard Badenhausen, 'Mourning Through Memoir: Trauma, Testimony, and Community in Vera Brittain's "Testament of Youth"', *Twentieth Century Literature* 49, no. 4 (2003): 429.

reader. In articulating the experience, the medics' perspective necessarily multiplies – to communicate, they adopt a mediating position in relation to another, crafting their testimony as an author by using specific styles and literary devices.

The act of life writing demands plurality. Speaking in the context of narrative medicine, Rita Charon explains that 'writing the story of one's life allows past and present to coexist not only in the mind of the author but in the resultant text'.[70] The resultant text, then, brings together the past and the present self into one space, so that multiple selves reside within the narrative. The 'autobiographical gap', Charon tells us, provides self-reflection: 'this space between the narrator-who-writes and the protagonist-who-acts confers the very powerful distance of reflection, without which no one can consider his or her own actions, thoughts, or life'.[71] Life writing inhabits this reflective gap between present and past self, as well as, with reworked narratives, between present and past writing and reading. This model emphasises the changing perspectives of the individual across time, and implies that for life narratives to be most effective they must take account of the multiple perspectives and multifaceted position of the witness, often acknowledging the progression of a sequence of evolving perceptions.

We can explore the value of the 'reflective space', and the reconsideration both of events and of the associated writing, by looking at a specific example. A close comparative study of Rathbone's unpublished diary from 1918 and her later 1932 novelisation reveals some illuminating aspects of revisiting experiences and reworking the records of those experiences. Existing scholarly comments would lead one to expect Rathbone's unpublished diary to reveal graphic and alarming scenes that she chose to omit, alter, or dilute in her later novelisation. But while there is some evidence of her changing details (including marginalia showing her intent to shorten or omit), if anything the general trend is the other way around. Rathbone does not omit from the 'finished' novel; she omitted from the original.

Marcus, discussing Rathbone's work in relation to her real-life experiences, notes, 'Lynn Knight [...] suggests that the diaries recorded many unpleasant experiences which did not survive translation into fiction'[72] – but this is misleading. Rathbone's only available

---

[70] Rita Charon, *Narrative Medicine: Honoring the Stories of Illness* (New York: Oxford University Press, 2006), 20.
[71] Ibid., 70.
[72] Marcus, 'Afterword', 474.

diaries detail her time working at a YMCA rest camp in Boulogne in 1918. She does not omit harrowing wartime experiences from her novelisation; instead, she shortens passages detailing social events and concerts with soldiers and fellow camp staff, or petty jealousies of her female peers, for example. Marcus seems to misinterpret Knight's discussion, incorrectly inferring that Rathbone omitted much more of the traumatic side of her war experience; but the novelisation is not impacted by what is and is not translated from the first-hand diary of 1918. Her diary details her time at the rest camp, which was 'a wonderful change from hospital'.[73] The diary opens with a sense of jadedness – we might assume Rathbone needed respite from nursing – and the rest camp allowed her to continue participation, while physically distancing herself from the medical space (though this is not to suggest the work at the rest camp is any less demanding or valuable). Consequently, she actively and intentionally does not dwell on her nursing work, but remains in the present moment for the majority of her diary.

There are several layers of misrepresentation in the scholarly materials. While it is difficult to quantify revisions and omissions in written work, inspection of Rathbone's surviving material suggests that her later novelisation of events was not in fact a 'rewriting' of her experiences, edited to conceal or omit troubling memories, but instead an opportunity for writing the experience more fully. It is probable that she did not write a diary of her time nursing, and it is credible to suggest that she chose not to write, or could not find the words or form in which to do so at the time. The absence of an immediate record of her experience is addressed only in the space of her later novelisation.

We might surmise, then, that novelisation of the experiences provided a creative space in which to explore her memories and experiences. Perhaps the creative aspect itself allowed for a reflective distance, an autobiographical gap, enabling her to display more boldly the reality of her experience of wartime nursing, paradoxically allowing for more intimacy while holding readers at a distance by the veil of fiction. The novel fictionalises Rathbone herself as Joan Seddon, further distancing her from events by renouncing the personal 'I'. The novel, written in the early 1930s, also establishes a temporal distance, with intermediary consultation a further probable condition of its possibility. As Rathbone's example demonstrates, there may be layers in the articulation of experience, corresponding

---

[73] Rathbone, 'June 1918', in 'Unpublished diaries'.

with the multiple layers of witnessing. The layering of contemporary and retrospective voices parallels the juxtaposition of the retrospective and immediate viewpoints; and how perceptions and viewpoints change is often fundamental to the ways different narratives are articulated.

The reflective space is also a mediatory space, specifically evident in several examples from Brittain's work, such as this:

> No sudden gift of second sight showed me the future months in which I should not only contemplate and hold, but dress unaided and without emotion, the quivering stump of a newly amputated limb – than which a more pitiable spectacle hardly exists on this side of death.[74]

This passage is exemplary of Brittain's pervasive technique of bringing together differently tensed moments. It is a prolepsis, in which she prefigures a future event, when the flattened affect of her ability to work 'without emotion' will safeguard her ability to nurse. The whole, however, is retrospective narration, in which she positions herself emotionally in-between her initial inability to cope and her coping without emotion. This retrospective narrator's perspective mediates between these two remembered and experienced perspectives. There are thus three selves, one of which is the chronologically subsequent but emotionally intermediate, speaking self, who pointedly juxtaposes her multiple past selves.

Such plurality is also intensified in Brittain's work by the hybridity of voices. She explicitly acknowledges her use of older writings:

> I have also made as much use as possible of old letters and diaries, because it seemed to me that the contemporary opinions, however crude and ingenuous, of youth in the period under review were at least as important a part of its testament as retrospective reflections heavy with knowledge.[75]

Furthermore, her text is a montage of other voices, including letters, published and unpublished poems, and reported speech. Her chapters are preceded by poems: sometimes her own, sometimes those of her fiancé, Roland. She also includes extracts from his poetry left in manuscript after his death. Throughout, we receive glimpses of personal correspondence, especially with her brother, Edward. She includes many textual snippets and extracts: poetry by Rudyard

---

[74] Brittain, *Testament*, 216.
[75] Ibid., 12.

Kipling, George Eliot's *Daniel Deronda*, newspaper extracts, words to a hymn, and the lyrics and musical score for one of Roland's songs. The result is a communal assortment of voices, though in some ways filling authorial and narratorial gaps. It is a *bricolage* of intertextual references, which on the one hand aids her memory and her effort towards authenticity, but on the other hand may be interpreted as a form of distancing, keeping the reader at arm's length from her own words and consequently her own sentiments. However, it is more effective to think of it in terms of a layering of voices.

The layering of contemporary and retrospective voices also occurs in another striking example from Brittain:

> Only a short time ago, sitting in the elegant offices of the British Red Cross Society in Grosvenor Crescent [...] And there, in that secure, well-equipped room, the incongruous picture came back to me of myself standing alone in a newly created circle of hell during the 'emergency' of March 22nd, 1918, and gazing, half hypnotised, at the dishevelled beds, the stretchers on the floor, the scattered boots and piles of muddy khaki.[76]

Brittain details a sense of two places at once. The incongruity, which we explored in Chapter 2, is the effect of memory crossing space as well as time. Within this passage of her memoir she is detailing her time working in the hospital, but the description of the later moment in the offices intrudes on the representation, and all of it is framed within the even later narration of events. The narratorial-self steps out of the narrative into a later moment, and then back again, all within the further retrospective of the present narration. Again, the effect is that of three selves, three voices being conveyed. The emotion and intensity of nursing returns for her in the office, but this intensity is held at a distance – although she maintains an intermediary gap between the intense emotion and the retelling. With the present writing-self reporting on two past selves, we can see a form of figurative *mise-en-abyme* of selfhood. This is another example of layering: it nests witnessing for the other, which is imperative in medical care, *within* witnessing for the self. Rather than a subsequent distancing, there is a recursive relation between cumulative layers, between surfaces and depths.

Rathbone's contemporaneous diary makes even more explicit acknowledgement than Brittain of the evolution in perceptions, and the value of looking back. One of the characteristics of her 1918

[76] Ibid., 410.

diary is her persistent comparison between 1915 and 1918.[77] With this Rathbone presents a sense of an intermediary voice, or at least an awareness of changing and evolving attitudes across that short period. Her diary begins on 13 June 1918 when she arrives back in Boulogne, where she had holidayed three years previously and 'never thought to come back'.[78] Returning to the same spot seems to trigger her memory and awaken a need for storytelling, so that in looking back on her time in Boulogne at the start of the war from the perspective of her return, she states:

> I am 10 years older – nursing in military hospitals does not tend to preserve one's bubbling spirits, and there is a certain kind of youth which has died once and for all in the wards. That youth can never come back – the youth of keen inexperience and lightness of heart, but there is another kind, from I think out of the death of the first, which should last you all one's years, and help one to face up laughingly to every phase of life, and every high or hard adventure. I want to realise this thoroughly, or I may imagine that I shall slip back not only into the work, but into the outlook of 1915, and as this can never be, it would only result in dreariness and disappointment.[79]

We are instantly made aware of the difference in her character between these two visits to Boulogne. The excitement of the pre- and early war days is well and truly destroyed, and youthful innocence, the 'youth which has died', is replaced by experience working in military hospitals, and confronting the reality of war. However, to return to that previous attitude would be dangerous for her perseverance and survival, and she emphasises the gains of her toughened spirit. At another point in her diary she again draws out the contrast and change between 1915 and 1918, not just for herself but for the soldiers. As they marched off once again back to the front,

> some cheered as they went past – all smiled, but there was no light-hearted men [sic] and remembering the last men I had seen in any numbers marching away for the front, I saw that the new untried spirit of 1915 – the incredible exuberance, had died for even men know what the furnace is; you can see it on their faces, and in a way I felt less sorry for these men because they knew. It is enthusiasm combined with inexperience that is so infinitely pathetic. 1915 – the

---

[77] This is one of three significant aspects of the diary which Geneviève Brassard identifies. Brassard, 'From Private Story'.
[78] Rathbone, 'June 1918', in 'Unpublished diaries'.
[79] Ibid.

summer of hope – 1918 the summer of – almost – despair. Reflections on the war must be left in England. Out here in it all, they are out of place; but certain things knock at your heart. A courage worthy of the soldiers is the one thing to strive for just now.[80]

Rathbone draws out the psychological impact of first-hand experience of combat: the soldiers' naivety and innocence at first going to the front is now affected by cumulative knowledge and experience. Their 'untried spirit of 1915' has been broken, replaced by a profound resignation to the fact. This goes for all those witnessing and suffering first-hand. Though Rathbone foregrounds the soldiers' experience of this change, it is also her own, and it contributes to her qualification of sympathy: 'I felt less sorry for these men because they knew.' Their fate as victims is now slightly altered, because they *know* what is in store for them. When Rathbone poignantly parallels 1915 and 1918, 'the summer of hope' and 'the summer of [. . .] despair', it is her own perspective as well as the soldiers', and she goes on to articulate the resolve that her 'almost' still allows.

When we consider the relationship between concurrent and retrospective accounts, we have to be wary of conflating immediacy with authenticity. Hope Wolf's 'Mediating War: Hot Diaries, Liquid Letters and Vivid Remembrances' (2012) engages in a dialogue with previous comments on the value of immediacy in wartime accounts by Samuel Hynes in *A Soldier's Tale* (1997). Wolf observes that Hynes

> attaches the admiring term 'virtue' to 'immediacy'. 'Journals, diaries and letters' are said to 'have the virtues of immediacy and directness'; and 'memoirs', on the other hand, are deemed 'reflective, selective, more self-consciously constructed than the immediate reports'. His later twinning of 'direct' with 'undecorated' gives the impression that the value of texts in the first group is measured by what has not been done to them: virtue as a kind of innocence or purity.[81]

As Wolf argues, the attribution of 'virtue' to these texts is an unusual semantic choice, with its connotations of purity contrasted with the corruption of retrospective accounts. Immediacy might seem to offer greater 'authenticity', but it is also subject to risks like self-censorship and flattened affect. We must be careful when we talk about 'authenticity' and 'truth', recognising instead that the kind of 'truth' such

---

[80] Ibid.
[81] Hope Wolf, 'Mediating War: Hot Diaries, Liquid Letters and Vivid Remembrances', *Life Writing* 9, no. 3 (2012): 328.

texts offer is more importantly their manifestation of the emotional quality of the individual experience. An interesting example of the difference is offered in Baroness de T'Serclaes's memoir, *Flanders and Other Fields* (1964). In the description of an especially extreme and dangerous event she explains:

> When we started back to the ambulance the Germans peppered us with rifle-fire, then suddenly began to advance up the long main street with fixed bayonets, and we had to scoot for all we were worth. Mairi and I did not have time to climb in, and for what seemed an uncomfortably long time we were standing on the step clinging to the side, with bullets singing round us. Yet I wrote in my diary back at the Flandria Palace: 'It was a wonderful and grand day and I would not have missed it.'[82]

Here we have the inclusion of the immediate reaction as recorded in her diary. This immediate record seems entirely inadequate to the intensity of such a significant and potentially traumatising event; an occasion where they are literally holding on for dear life. In her act of self-reflection, T'Serclaes draws attention to an example of unconscious self-censorship, in the moment of record, where the diary maintains a *surface* or superficial view of events. The retrospective account that she offers both conveys the nerve-wracking experience of the event itself and draws our attention to how in the immediate aftermath she could only allow herself a muted acknowledgement of the exhilaration that it must have induced. This example shows us that immediate narration may be coherent and articulate while exhibiting flattened affect, just as retrospective narration may choose incoherent forms in an attempt to articulate the experience of trauma rather than contain it. Revisiting such experiences can offer greater insight and the possibility for a deeper 'truth' to be communicated.

There is great advantage in revisiting older writings, drawing on earlier perceptions and perhaps naiveties, to aid a revisioning of the overall experience. As Elizabeth Walker Black poignantly surmises in *Hospital Heroes* (1919), 'It is the telling about war work that makes it interesting. At the time it is tiresome and monotonous as any physical labor carried on day after day.'[83] Black alerts us to the fact that 'telling about' the experience unlocks more from the events than

---

[82] Baroness de T'Serclaes, *Flanders and Other Fields* (London: George G. Harrap, 1964), 45.

[83] Elizabeth Walker Black, *Hospital Heroes* (New York: Charles Scribner's Sons, 1919), 128.

might be accessible in the moment, when the medic may be overwhelmed, exhausted, and hungry. Experiencing war and describing war are very different. In the moment the individual's affect is flattened, and their level of awareness is reduced. It is through *revisiting* the experience that further insight can be found, and the retrospective act of writing the experience onto the page can often clarify what could not be articulated at the time. In the immediate moment the medic is performing a necessary role; only in retrospect are they able to step back and discern the greater meaning of their experience. Thus, we can see a tension between enactment and representation, one that is not an unequivocal antithesis but instead an entangled conflict. These accounts often reveal the difference between the performance and action of the moment and the articulation that involves the creative synthesis of hindsight and bearing witness.

It is through self-representation in the writing process, which is inherently creative and in which they are no longer performing or enacting a role, that these writers fully regain their agency. Life writing is a process of creating and articulating that can itself authenticate the experience; after all, 'it is now virtually in art alone that suffering can still find its voice'.[84] Whereas the demands of participation in medical war work produce a flattening of affect, so that the role of the medic exhibits symptoms of the traumatic nature of the experience, retrospective narration makes those aspects of the experience itself part of its subject matter. The crafted piece *re-enacts* the experience, and may seek to emphasise textual gaps and spaces. In such ways the writers can make deliberate rhetorical use of symptomatic form as a way of expressing the inexpressible nature of the experience. The text is a representational surface that allows writing to make the wound visible, and it is craft rather than raw symptom that articulates it.

---

[84] Theodor Adorno, 'Commitment', in *The Essential Frankfurt School Reader*, trans. Francis McDonagh, ed. Andrew Arato and Eike Gebhardt (New York: Urizen Books, 1978), 312.

Conclusion

The stretcher bearer who clears blood from the patient's eyes; the nurse who adds more gauze and pressure to a sudden haemorrhage; the surgeon who wipes his saw ready for another amputation, are all fully involved in the spaces of war. These are the medics who persist in providing care while under physical and psychological assault. It is not often in First World War literary discussions that attention centres on the medic, but it is the medic who first attempts to repair the damage of warfare: who cleans up, stitches back together, and does their best to heal the wounded soldiers.

The medic is deeply embedded in the war experience, presenting both continuity with and explicit difference from that of the combatant. Yet, the doctor, the nurse, the stretcher bearer, orderly, and ambulance driver are rarely central to the narrative: their voice is rarely heard, and, if it is, it is generally without consideration for their personal experience. Rarely do we see much of the detail of their actions, and, significantly, very little emphasis is given to their phenomenological, emotional, and psychological states, especially with regards to negotiating the stress of caregiving. However, the medic occupies a uniquely complex position in the military-medical context, with an unequalled experience of the distinct environment of the medical encounter. Such a role demands that we take notice. Throughout this book, I have sought to centralise the medical figure in the context of the First World War, applying a literary-critical approach to the role and writings of medical personnel in order to shed an important light on their perspectives, and establish the value of their own words as both testimonies and representations of experience.

The somatic, sensuous, and spatial geographies of military-medical care, and the experiences of the caregivers, are complex

Conclusion   219

and have far-reaching implications. A focus on such geographies requires an extensive spatial approach in order to reveal more about the medical experience and representations of those experiences and perceptions: liminality, especially as confined to the image of no man's land, is only part of the spatial story, and thus it has required a literal and figurative remapping in order to grasp the details of the medical experience. The multisensory and multi-spatial approach of this book contributes to both critical medical humanities and scholarship of First World War medicine, by opening up routes to explore and appreciate the lived experience of caregiving. The rich array of spatial concepts which inform and structure this book have demonstrated the importance of a more nuanced and extensive idea of space. I have developed such an approach through a focus on the medic's relation to the medical space; on literal and figurative dimensions of medical spaces; on the spaces of and in the body; on psychological and emotional spaces; and on textual spaces, drawing in each case on different yet theoretically complementary ideas of space and spatiality. It is important to consider 'space' and its different geographies in a number of ways: it is not enough to consider either the tangible or the psychological in isolation, as they are entirely linked. These complementary spatial approaches afford a more thorough understanding of the lived experience of caregiving.

Through a focus on the somatic and sensuous situation of the medic, Chapter 1 illustrated how bodies in war necessarily adapt to ongoing changing geographies, a need which is especially heightened at the intersection of military and medical spatial geographies. The military-medical landscape and the bodies of the medic and combatant are mutually implicated, navigation of the environment depending on an intimate physical continuity between body and landscape. The experience demands an intensely multisensory attention: haptic, auditory, and olfactory geographies become integral to the negotiation of space. The concept of 'corpography' provides a theoretical basis upon which to reconsider the somatic and phenomenological dimensions of the military-medical experience, in relation to the specific demands of this environment. The manifestations of corpography (processes of sensation, cognition, and affective response) involve continual negotiation between the somatic and spatial. This need is amplified for the medic, who must reconceptualise somatic and sensuous geographies in relation both to their own embodied experiences and to the wounded bodies in their care. These medics make sense of their spatial and medical environment by attending to the psychological and physical import of their bodily experience.

Part of the intention of this book has been to explore the span of medical spaces in the military-medical context. A focus on the medical encounters within different spaces has shown the complexities of their experiential and psychological qualities, and drawn out the need to consider physical spaces in terms of their figurative, cultural, and historical dimensions. In Chapter 2, I examined the figurative and emotional force of spatial identities in terms of the polytemporality of spaces. The literal medical space is a layered palimpsest of physical features, affective resonances, and figurative associations, juxtaposed and often conflicting, but all informing each other. This analysis is predicated on the foundational fact that these medical spaces are typically reappropriated sites, and thus repositories of the memories of previous forms, which emerge incongruously, in tension with the newly imposed identity. The tension between these various layers and conflicting characteristics acquires affective force as a manifestation of the fact that the world is irrevocably altered by the war, and will subsequently remain marked by reminders of it. War continues to rewrite and remap spatial identities.

Chapter 3 focused on the effort to make wounds visible and counter the silence surrounding acts of medical treatment. By looking at how bodily spaces are represented, and at the caregivers' relationships with the bodies of their patients, it opens up discussion of the emotions involved in applying care, and the struggle to reconcile the conflicting demands of the medical role. Once bodily boundaries are broken down, the interaction between medic and patient changes; I suggest this change manifests itself in this context as a tension between protrusion and intrusion. By adopting a self-conscious mode of expression, these medic-writers challenge the rhetoric of care by reflexively illustrating both the harm and violence that are felt to be part of the lived experience of their role. This representational mode becomes what I term a 'medical grotesque', a discourse serving to accommodate the conflicted nature of medical intervention, within which medical personnel can both represent and critique their roles as caregivers.

Chapters 4 and 5 provided a spatially reconceptualised focus on the manifestations of trauma in its expressive, representational form. Chapter 4 appeals to the concept of heterotopic counter-sites as mechanisms of coping, examining medics' representations of and reflections on how they coped in the immediate moment of caregiving and traumatic experience. The kind of coping these narratives depict relies on negotiation between different planes of consciousness and the psychological management of perspective by shifting towards a counter-site. By exploring the perception of psychological place, and especially the sense of moving between spaces within the narratives, we can gauge how these medical personnel experience the traumatic, and we can recognise the subsequent challenge of finding a way to express it. The psyche can alter its perspective and, by shifting between the real and imaginary, negotiate with experience by moving beyond its boundaries to counter-sites which are 'other' to the immediate situation. The narratives present the bodily experience of caregiving in parallel with the emotional and psychological experience of coping, offering a challenge to ways of seeing and to the politics of perception. In the triangulation of narrative angles, the caregivers' actions are juxtaposed with their navigations of the psychological terrain in the double vision of a 'radiographic' reading.

In Chapter 5, the representation of trauma is related to the idea of the text as a representational surface, affording the opportunity to explore textual spaces and representational gaps in both the narrative events and their articulation. By reading these texts as representational surfaces, we can explore how gaps in representation are themselves features of the representation. Communicative gaps suggest that insight can be born of silence, and of the articulation of those silences. With a reconsideration of symptomatic writing, as the negotiation of a conflict between the craft of narrative articulation and certain barriers to representation, it becomes clear that silences can be creative responses to the crisis of representation and the problems of communicating difficult experience, even as they exhibit the ruptures and absences in representation. Expression and representation are further challenged by the entanglement between their duty to be true to their own experience and their complex responsibility as witnesses to the suffering of their patients. The recurrent concern that their accounts may not be immediately recognisable is offset by an affirmation of the authenticity of their own personal experience; after all, 'one may only write what is true for oneself'.

This book contributes to the current trajectory in the critical medical humanities, establishing the need to critique the clinical encounter from a range of conceptual angles. Moving away from a binary discourse where the medical practitioner and medical institution is set against the patient, this book has instead reorientated the discussion to consider more deeply the position of the medic or practitioner and the environment of the medical encounter. The interdisciplinary, literary-critical approach, in particular, intervenes to centralise the voice of the caregiver, and encourages a sustained consideration for the lived experience of caregiving. Although I have focused on the specific context of the First World War, and by extension military medicine, the arguments of this work offer a framework that can be applied to further medical settings, ranging from high-pressure emergency contexts to quotidian routines of general practice or hospital specialisms.

Caregiving is a common yet inherently subjective experience. To care for another requires connection and openness, but comes at a potential cost to the individual. The medics providing wartime medical treatment put their own wellbeing at stake, offering care at considerable physical and psychological risk to themselves in roles that place conflicting, antithetical demands upon them. Writing on 25 July 1917, Julia Stimson addresses the conflict between the personal and the impersonal, inherent in caregiving but intensified by the scale and toll of war. The challenge of the responsibility itself is redoubled by that of expressing it:

> I do not know how to write about our doings of the past few days, for I cannot write numbers, and it is only numbers that would give you any idea at all of what we have been doing.
> [...]
> No one over here thinks in any numbers less than 50 or 100, and what can the serious condition of Private John Brown of something or other, Something Street, Birmingham, matter? One's mind is torn between the extremes of such feelings, for when a nurse takes the pulse of a wounded sleeping man and he wakes just enough to say 'Mother,' she goes to pieces in her heart, just as though he weren't only one of the hundreds of wounded men in just this one hospital.[1]

Giving the number of casualties, or the number of days of endless work, might quantify the momentousness of the event, but it betrays its human reality. Words offer more, foregrounding the intensity over the scale of the experience; there is no way to represent the state of mind of the medic, torn between detachment and empathy, through numbers and statistics alone. To be 'torn between the extremes of such feelings' is precisely to experience the gap between the impersonality of numbers and the personality of names. An interdisciplinary, literary-critical attention to these medics' writings can help us recognise the overlooked details of their experience, and give due weight to the voice of the witness-to-pain, and to the individual's experience of direct or vicarious suffering. Such a reading compels us to look at these experiences, see the bodies, and the hands patching

---

[1] Julia Stimson, *Finding Themselves* (New York: Macmillan, 1918), 78–81.

them together, but also extends beyond the visual, to a more encompassing sense of immersed spatial and sensuous experience. In doing so, we can attain a more thorough realisation and representation of the multiple and complex geographies of care.

How might we apply this framework to other contexts? We underestimate how much of a medical encounter relies on touch, for the practitioner to look the patient in the eyes, for the patient to sit or lie down for examination – to lay on those healing, knowing hands. How, in entering a medical space, bodily identity changes. We might not quite realise how much we rely on these things until they are no longer possible, then we miss them. Most of us take for granted that we will receive the healthcare we need when the time comes; that an ambulance will pick us up, we will be admitted for treatment, that our loved ones can visit us. But this is not universal, and nor is it guaranteed.

The COVID-19 crisis, which has not only damaged millions of lives worldwide but has strained healthcare services, brings the material of this book into sharp relief. Writing a book that argues for the centrality of caregivers' voices and lived experiences during crisis, during the global pandemic, has reinforced the need to privilege first-hand experiences and offers a stark reminder to readdress the authority of caregivers. The great casualties of healthcare workers, not just to the disease and complications but in the residual trauma that may not yet be apparent, will be felt for years and decades to come. The grief will not be processed in our lifetime. The images of temporarily erected field hospitals and overflow morgues, out of place, will be hard to forget, and should not be forgotten. Writing in *The Lancet* in July 2021, palliative care doctor Rachel Clarke describes how the pandemic has transformed medical spaces and the significance of caregiving for her and her colleagues:

> As a front-line COVID-19 palliative care doctor, I would hear staff describe their wards and intensive care units as 'warehouses', 'factories', 'laboratories', and 'war zones'. This is death by conveyer belt, stripped of touch, tenderness, love and humanity.[2]

That the spaces designed for care have come to be associated with war, industry, capitalism, experimentation, and depersonalisation is striking. It reminds us that physical and figurative aspects of medical environments play a crucial role in receiving and delivering care.

---

[2] Rachel Clarke, 'Sparks Through the Stubble: Dying in a Pandemic', *The Lancet* 398, no. 10294 (3 July 2021): 19.

Atmospheres matter. Healing cannot take place in a space that is equated with battle or conflict, or in which there are poor working conditions in the name of consumerism. If the language to describe a site of caring has so completely been 'stripped of' its ability to care, what does that tell us about the structures of welfare? When the 'capacities of those employed to provide care are severely diminished through ongoing exploitation, understaffing, poor pay, time constraints, inadequate or non-existent job security and a lack of training and support',[3] caregiving for others and the self breaks down. Already, the language of the pandemic is invoking the same images of war – and like wars and conflicts before, welfare for the caregivers is once again subordinated. Do we perpetuate this pattern? The spaces of medical care have transformed into 'war zones', into restricted spaces which, while necessary to stem contagion, separate the caregivers from the world. The caregivers have become emblems of heroism, distributing a discourse of sacrifice, which we consume all too easily. The invocation of war and military images is harmful in medicine, but it has also become weaponised by politics and media to excuse the loss of caregivers.

Yet, the pressure on services and caregivers is not confined to times of crisis, at least not in terms of war or epidemics. In her 2019 collection *Constellations*, reflecting on multiple health issues and hospital admissions, Sinéad Gleeson positions the need for care as dividing: 'This may not be war, but there are two sides. The well and the unwell; doctors and patients; staff and visitors.'[4] Patients are set in opposition to caregivers, speaking to the fact that the patient's experience is different to that of practitioners: they inhabit different worlds, and often oppose one another. While this binarism of the caregiver set against the caregiven is not new, Gleeson's comment speaks to the wider issues concerning the delivery and receipt of care, and demonstrates the perpetuation of experiencing care as conflict. Like Clarke in her attention to the hospital atmosphere, Gleeson, too, invokes the image of the 'warehouse': 'a warehouse sprawl of technology, temporarily housing people, but devoid of the familiarity of home'.[5] The panopticonism of the hospital as 'a place of necessary quarantine where control must be abdicated'[6] becomes

---

[3] The Care Collective, *The Care Manifesto: The Politics of Interdependence* (London: Verso, 2020), 15.
[4] Sinéad Gleeson, *Constellations* (London: Picador, 2019), 114.
[5] Ibid., 111.
[6] Ibid.

increasingly cold, depersonalised, invasive, violating, and ultimately, uncaring.

Arguably, more than ever it is vital that we listen to the testimonies of the caregivers in the thick of it. I do not offer a straightforward solution: there is none. But, I want to suggest that considering the spaces, environments, and atmospheres of care delivery, in literal and figurative senses, might help to develop a healthcare landscape that works for everyone. We need to be attentive to the medical space, and the potential impact of architectures, terrains, and landscapes, especially with regards to the affective force of objects, spaces, and atmospheres.

The role of caregivers and the weight of their words about it deserve greater attention, belated though it is. It is too late to offer retroactive support for the medics of the First World War, or indeed subsequent conflicts; but perhaps we can learn from these texts that the words of caregivers, and all those in pain, in all contexts, deserve to be heard properly. We can better grasp the complex demands of medical care by heeding the words of those who know first-hand how extreme the demands of caregiving can be. Otherwise, before long, we will have to dress the wounds of the wound dressers. And we must begin to take care of the caregiver.

Bibliography

Acton, Carol. 'Diverting the Gaze: The Unseen Text in Women's War Writing.' *College Literature* 31, no. 2 (2004): 53–79.

Acton, Carol and Jane Potter. '"These frightful sights would work havoc with one's brain": Subjective Experience, Trauma, and Resilience in First War Writings by Medical Personnel.' *Literature and Medicine* 30, no. 1 (2012): 61–85.

Acton, Carol and Jane Potter. *Working in a World of Hurt: Trauma and Resilience in the Narratives of Medical Personnel in Warzones*. Manchester: Manchester University Press, 2015.

Adorno, Theodor. 'Commitment.' In *The Essential Frankfurt School Reader*. Translated by Francis McDonagh. Edited by Andrew Arato and Eike Gebhardt. New York: Urizen Books, 1978. 75–89.

Ahmed, Sara. *The Cultural Politics of Emotion*. Edinburgh: Edinburgh University Press, 2014.

Albee, Fred. H. *A Surgeon's Fight to Rebuild Men*. New York: E. P. Dutton, 1943.

Albrinck, Meg. 'Borderline Women: Gender Confusion in Vera Brittan's and Evadne Price's War Narratives.' *Narrative* 6, no. 3 (1998): 271–91.

Alcoff, Linda. 'The Problem of Speaking for Others.' *Cultural Critique*, no. 20 (1991): 5–32.

Alcott, Louisa May. *Hospital Sketches*. Boston: James Redpath, 1863. Kindle.

Allitt, Marie. 'Somatic, Sensuous, and Spatial Geographies of First World War Medical Caregiving Narratives.' PhD Thesis, University of York, 2018.

Allitt, Marie. 'The Traumatised Body in First World War Combat Literature.' MSc by Research Dissertation, University of Edinburgh, 2014.

Antliff, Mark and Patricia Leighten. *Cubism and Culture*. London: Thames & Hudson, 2001.

Anzieu, Didier. *Psychic Envelopes*. London: Karnac Books, 1990.

Appleton, Edith. *A Nurse At the Front*. Edited by Ruth Cowen. London: Simon & Schuster, 2013.

Armstrong, David. *Political Anatomy of the Body: Medical Knowledge in*

Britain in the Twentieth Century. Cambridge: Cambridge University Press, 1983.

Armstrong, Tim. *Modernism, Technology and the Body*. Cambridge: Cambridge University Press, 1998.

Arya, Rina. 'Abjection Interrogated: Uncovering the Relation Between Abjection and Disgust.' *Journal of Extreme Anthropology* 1, no. 1 (2017): 48–61.

Bachelard, Gaston. *The Poetics of Space*. Translated by Maria Jolas. 1958; Boston: Beacon Press, 1994.

Badenhausen, Richard. 'Mourning Through Memoir: Trauma, Testimony, and Community in Vera Brittain's "Testament of Youth".' *Twentieth Century Literature* 49, no. 4 (2003): 421–48.

Bagnold, Enid. *A Diary Without Dates*. London: William Heinemann, 1918.

Bakhtin, Mikhail. *Rabelais and His World*. Translated by Hélène Iswolsky. 1964; Bloomington: Indiana University Press, 1984.

Barbusse, Henri. *Under Fire*. Translated by W. Fitzwater Wray. 1988; Floating Press, 2009.

Barthes, Roland. *Camera Lucida: reflections on photography*. Translated by Richard Howard. 1981; London: Vintage, 2000.

Bates, Victoria, Alan Bleakley, and Sam Goodman, eds. *Medicine, Health and the Arts: Approaches to the Medical Humanities*. London: Routledge, 2015.

Beauchamp, Pat. *Fanny Goes to War*. London: John Murray, 1919.

Bede. *The Old English Version of Bede's Ecclesiastical History of the English People*. Translated by Thomas Miller. Cambridge, ON: In Parentheses Publications, 1999.

Benjamin, Walter. *The Arcades Project*. Translated by Howard Eiland and Kevin McLaughlin. 1982; Cambridge and London: The Belknap Press of Harvard University Press, 2002.

Benjamin, Walter. 'The Storyteller: Reflections on the Works of Nikolai Leskov.' In *The Novel: An Anthology of Criticism and Theory 1900–2000*. Edited by Dorothy J. Hale. Malden, MA: Blackwell, 2006. 361–78.

Bergen, Leo van. *Before My Helpless Sight: Suffering, Dying and Military Medicine on the Western Front*. Translated by Liz Waters. Aldershot and Vermont: Ashgate, 2009.

Black, Elizabeth Walker. *Hospital Heroes*. New York: Charles Scribner's Sons, 1919.

Bleakley, Alan. 'Force and Presence in the World of Medicine.' *Healthcare* 5, no. 58 (2017): doi:10.3390/healthcare5030058.

Bonadeo, Alfred. *Mark of the Beast*. Lexington: University Press of Kentucky, 1989.

Booth, Allyson. *Postcards from the Trenches*. New York: Oxford University Press, 1996.

Bourke, Joanna. *Dismembering the Male*. 1996; London: Reaktion Books, 1999.
Bourke, Joanna. *The Story of Pain*. Oxford: Oxford University Press, 2014.
Borden, Mary. *The Forbidden Zone*. 1929; London: Hesperus Press, 2008.
Borden, Mary. *Journey Down a Blind Alley*. New York and London: Harper & Brothers, 1946.
Borden, Mary. *Poems of Love and War*. Edited by Paul O'Prey. London: Dare-Gale Press, 2015.
Botcharsky, Sophie and Florida Pier. *They Knew How to Die: Being a Narrative of the Personal Experiences of a Red Cross Sister on the Russian Front*. Edinburgh: Peter Davies, 1931.
Boyd, William. *With a Field Ambulance at Ypres*. Toronto: Musson, 1916.
Boylston, Helen Dore. *'Sister': The War Diary of a Nurse*. New York: Ives Washburn, 1927.
Braid, J. 'Unpublished diary.' The Liddle Collection. University of Leeds Special Collections. LIDDLE/WWI/GS/0185.
Brassard, Geneviève. 'From Private Story to Public History: Irene Rathbone Revises the War in the Thirties.' *NWSA Journal* 15, no. 3 (2003): 43–6.
Brighton Dome. 'History & Heritage.' Brighton & Hove. https://brightondome.org/about/history_heritage/.
Brighton Museums. 'Oscar Wilde in the Royal Pavilion, November 1884 Review.' Brighton & Hove. http://brightonmuseums.org.uk/discover/2011/11/21/oscar-wilde-in-the-royal-pavilion-november-1884-review/.
Brighton Museums. 'Royal Pavilion: History.' Brighton & Hove. https://brightonmuseums.org.uk/royalpavilion/history/.
British Pathé. 'History of British Pathé.' British Pathé. https://www.britishpathe.com/blog/history/.
Britnieva, Mary. *One Woman's Story*. London: Arthur Baker, 1934.
Brittain, Vera. *Chronicle of Youth: War Diary 1913–1917*. Edited by Alan Bishop and Terry Smart. 1981; Glasgow: Fontana/Collins, 1982.
Brittain, Vera. *Testament of Youth*. 1933; London: Penguin Books, 2005.
Brooks, Peter. *Enigmas of Identity*. Princeton, NJ: Princeton University Press, 2011.
Brophy, John, ed. *The Soldier's War: A Prose Anthology*. London: Dent, 1929.
Bryan, Julien H. *Ambulance 464: Encore des blessés*. New York: Macmillan, 1918.
Butler, Judith. *Precarious Life: The Powers of Mourning and Violence*. London: Verso, 2004.
Carden-Coyne, Ana. *The Politics of Wounds: Military Patients and Medical Power in the First World War*. Oxford: Oxford University Press, 2014.
Carden-Coyne, Ana. *Reconstructing the Body: Classicism, Modernism and the First World War*. Oxford: Oxford University Press, 2009.
The Care Collective. *The Care Manifesto: The Politics of Interdependence*. London: Verso, 2020.

Carel, Havi. *Phenomenology of Illness*. Oxford: Oxford University Press, 2016.
Cartwright, Lisa. *Screening the Body: Tracing Medicine's Visual Culture*. Minneapolis: University of Minnesota Press, 1995.
Caruth, Cathy. 'Recapturing the Past: Introduction.' In *Trauma: Explorations in Memory*. Baltimore: Johns Hopkins University Press, 1995. 151–7.
Caruth, Cathy. 'Trauma and Experience: Introduction.' In *Trauma: Explorations in Memory*. Baltimore: Johns Hopkins University Press, 1995. 3–12.
Caruth, Cathy. *Unclaimed Experience: Trauma, Narrative, and History*. Baltimore: Johns Hopkins University Press, 1996.
Casey, Edward. *Getting Back into Place: Toward a Renewed Understanding of the Place-World*. Bloomington: Indiana University Press, 1993.
Charon, Rita. *Narrative Medicine: Honoring the Stories of Illness*. New York: Oxford University Press, 2006.
Charon, Rita et al. *The Principles and Practice of Narrative Medicine*. New York: Oxford University Press, 2016.
Church, James Robb. *The Doctor's Part*. New York: D. Appleton, 1918.
Clarke, Rachel. 'Sparks Through the Stubble: Dying in a Pandemic.' *The Lancet* 398, no. 10294 (3 July 2021): 18–19.
Cobley, Evelyn. 'Violence and Sacrifice in Modern War Narratives.' *Substance* 23, no. 3 (1994): 75–99.
Cole, Sarah. *At the Violet Hour: Modernism and Violence in England and Ireland*. New York: Oxford University Press, 2012.
Connor, Steven. 'The Modern Auditory I.' In *Rewriting the Self: Histories from the Middle Ages to the Present*. Edited by Roy Porter. London: Routledge, 1997. 203–23.
Conway, Jane. *A Woman of Two Wars: The Life of Mary Borden*. N.p.: Munday Books, 2010.
Conway, Kathlyn. *Beyond Words: Illness and the Limits of Expression*. Albuquerque: University of New Mexico Press, 2013.
Coyle, Edward R. *Ambulancing on the French Front*. New York: Britton, 1918.
Danius, Sara. *The Senses of Modernism: Technology, Perception, and Aesthetics*. Ithaca, NY and London: Cornell University Press, 2002.
Das, Santanu. *Touch and Intimacy in First World War Literature*. 2005; Cambridge: Cambridge University Press, 2008.
Dearden, Harold. *Medicine and Duty*. 1928; Ilminster: Richard Dennis, 2014.
Delafield, Elizabeth M. 'Preface.' In *We That Were Young*, by Irene Rathbone. New York: Feminist Press, 1989. vii–viii.
Deleuze, Gilles and Félix Guattari. *A Thousand Plateaus*. Translated by Brian Massumi. 1987; London and New York: Bloomsbury Academic, 2016.

Dent, Olive. *A Volunteer Nurse on the Western Front*. 1917; London: Virgin Books, 2014.

Derrida, Jacques. *Of Grammatology*. Translated by Gayatri Chakravorty Spivak. Baltimore: Johns Hopkins University Press, 1976.

Dickinson, Emily. 'Pain – has an Element of Blank –.' In *Emily Dickinson: The Complete Poems*. Edited by Thomas H. Johnson. London: Faber and Faber, 1970. 323.

Didi-Huberman, Georges. 'Viscosities and Survivals.' In *Ephemeral Bodies: Wax Sculpture and the Human Figure*. Edited by Roberta Panzanelli. Los Angeles: Getty Research Institute, 2008. 154–69.

Diedrich, Lisa. *Treatments: Language, Politics, and the Culture of Illness*. Minneapolis: University of Minnesota Press, 2007.

Dodman, Trevor. '"Going all to pieces": "A Farewell to Arms" as Trauma Narrative.' *Twentieth Century Literature* 52, no. 3 (2006): 249–74.

Dollar, Mark Edwin. 'The Grotesque War: British Poetry of World War I.' Dissertation, Purdue University, 2000.

Donne, John. 'Hymne to God my God, in my sicknesse.' In *The Divine Poems*. Edited by Helen Gardner. 1952; Oxford: Clarendon Press, 1959.

Donner, Henriette. 'Under the Cross: Why V.A.D.s Performed the Filthiest Task in the Dirtiest War: Red Cross Woman Volunteers, 1914–1918.' *Journal of Social History* 30, no. 3 (1997): 687–704.

Duhamel, Georges. *The New Book of Martyrs*. Translated by Florence Simmonds. New York: George H. Doran, 1918.

Duhamel, Georges. *Vie des Martyrs*. Paris: Mercure de France, 1917.

Durnin, David. *The Irish Medical Profession and the First World War*. Cham: Palgrave Macmillan, 2019.

Dyer, Geoff. *The Missing of the Somme*. London: Hamish Hamilton, 1994.

Eakin, Paul John. *The Ethics of Life Writing*. Ithaca, NY and London: Cornell University Press, 2004.

Edgar, Andrew. 'The Art of Useless Suffering.' *Medicine, Health Care and Philosophy* 10 (2007): 395–405.

Edwards, Justin. *Grotesque*. London and New York: Routledge, 2013.

Egan, Susanna. *Mirror Talk: Genres of Crisis in Contemporary Autobiography*. Chapel Hill and London: University of North Carolina Press, 1999.

Einhaus, Ann-Marie. 'Modernism, Truth, and the Canon of First World War Literature.' *Modernist Cultures* 6, no. 2 (2011): 296–314.

Elden, Stuart. 'Secure the Volume: Vertical Geopolitics and the Depth of Power.' *Political Geography* 34 (2013): 35–51.

Ellman, Maud. 'Skinscapes in *Ulysses*.' In *The Nets of Modernism: Henry James, Virginia Woolf, James Joyce, and Sigmund Freud*. Cambridge: Cambridge University Press, 2010. 151–66.

Fell, Alison S. and Christine E. Hallett, eds. *First World War Nursing: New Perspectives*. New York: Routledge, 2013.

Felman, Shoshana. 'Education and Crisis, or the Vicissitudes of Teaching.'

In *Testimony: Crisis of Witnessing in Literature, Psychoanalysis, and History*, by Shoshana Felman and Dori Laub. New York and Abingdon: Routledge, 1992. 1–56.
Felman, Shoshana and Dori Laub. *Testimony: Crisis of Witnessing in Literature, Psychoanalysis, and History*. New York and Abingdon: Routledge, 1992.
Field, Frank. *British and French Writers of the First World War*. Cambridge: Cambridge University Press, 1991.
Fifield, Peter. *Modernism and Physical Illness: Sick Books*. Oxford: Oxford University Press, 2020.
Finzi, Kate. *Eighteen Months in the War Zone*. London, New York, Toronto and Melbourne: Cassell, 1916.
Foucault, Michel. *Discipline and Punish*. Translated by Alan Sheridan. London: Penguin Books, 1977.
Foucault, Michel. 'Of Other Spaces: Utopias and Heterotopias.' Translated by Jay Miskowiec. *Diacritics* 16, no. 1 (1986): 22–7.
Foucault, Michel. *The Birth of the Clinic*. Translated by A. M. Sheridan. 1963; Abingdon: Routledge, 2005.
Fox, E. C. 'An Officers' Hospital in France During the War.' In *Reminiscent Sketches*. London: John Bale, Sons and Danielsson, 1922. 61–4.
Frank, Arthur. *The Wounded Storyteller: Body, Illness, and Ethics*. 1995; Chicago: University of Chicago Press, 2013.
Frayn, Andrew. *Writing Disenchantment: British First World War Prose, 1914–30*. Manchester: Manchester University Press, 2015.
Freedman, Ariela. 'Mary Borden's *Forbidden Zone*: Women's Writing from No-Man's-Land.' *Modernism/modernity* 9, no. 1 (2002): 109–24.
Freud, Sigmund. 'Introduction to *Psycho-Analysis and the War Neuroses* (1919).' In *The Standard Edition of the Complete Psychological Works of Sigmund Freud: Volume XVII, An Infantile Neurosis and Other Works*. Translated by James Strachey. London: Hogarth Press, 1955. 207–15.
Freud, Sigmund. *The Uncanny*. Translated by David McLintock. 1919; London: Penguin Classics, 2003.
Fussell, Paul. *The Great War and Modern Memory*. New York: Oxford University Press, 1975.
Genette, Gérard. *Narrative Discourse: An Essay in Method*. Translated by Jane E. Lewin. 1972; Ithaca, NY: Cornell University Press, 1983.
Gennep, Arnold van. *The Rites of Passage*. 1909; Abingdon: Routledge, 2004.
Gilbert, Sandra M. '"Rats' Alley": The Great War, Modernism, and the (Anti)Pastoral Elegy.' *New Literary History* 30, no. 1 (1999): 179–201.
Gilmore, Leigh. *The Limits of Autobiography: Trauma and Testimony*. Ithaca, NY and London: Cornell University Press, 2001.
Girard, René. *Violence and Sacrifice*. Translated by Patrick Gregory. 1972; London: Johns Hopkins University Press, 1977.

Gleason, Arthur and Helen Hayes Gleason. *Golden Lads*. Toronto: McClelland, Goodchild & Stewart, 1916. Kindle.

Gleason, Sinéad. *Constellations*. London: Picador, 2019.

Goebel, Stefan. *The Great War and Medieval Memory: War, Remembrance and Medievalism in Britain and Germany, 1914–1940*. Cambridge: Cambridge University Press, 2007.

Gregory, Derek. 'Corpographies: Making Sense of Modern War.' *The Funambulist Papers* 58 (2014). https://thefunambulist.net/history/the-funambulist-papers-58-corpographies-making-sense-of-modern-war-by-derek-gregory.

Gregory, Derek. 'Gabriel's Map: Cartography and Corpography in Modern War.' In *Geographies of Knowledge and Power*. Edited by Peter Meusburger, Derek Gregory, and Laura Suarsana. Dordrecht: Springer, 2015. 89–121.

Gregory, Derek. 'Gabriel's Map: Cartography and Corpography in Modern War.' Social Theory Lecture, University of Kentucky, 25 January 2013.

Gregory, Derek. *Geographical Imaginations*. Blog. http://geographicalimaginations.com.

Gregory, Derek. 'The Natures of War.' *Antipode* 48, no. 1 (2016): 3–56.

Gristwood, A. D. *The Somme*. 1927; Columbia: University of South Carolina, 2006.

Gross, Elizabeth. 'The Body of Signification.' In *Abjection, Melancholia and Love*. Edited by John Fletcher and Andrew Benjamin. London and New York: Routledge, 1990. 80–103.

Hallett, Christine. *Containing Trauma: Nursing Work in the First World War*. Manchester: Manchester University Press, 2009.

Hallett, Christine. *Nurses of Passchendaele: Caring for the Wounded of the Ypres Campaigns 1914–1918*. Barnsley: Pen & Sword History, 2017.

Hallett, Christine. *Nurse Writers of the Great War*. Manchester: Manchester University Press, 2016.

Hallett, Christine. *Veiled Warriors: Allied Nurses of the First World War*. Oxford: Oxford University Press, 2014.

Hallett, Christine. '"A very valuable fusion of classes": British Professional and Volunteer Nurses of the First World War.' *Endeavour* 38, no. 2 (2014): 101–10.

Hanley, James. *The German Prisoner*. 1931; Ontario: Exile Editions, 2006.

Hansen, Arlen. *Gentleman Volunteers: The Story of the American Ambulance Drivers in the Great War, August 1914–September 1918*. New York: Arcade Publishing, 1996.

Hardy, Barbara. 'Introduction.' In Helen Zenna Smith, *Not So Quiet . . . Stepdaughters of War*. 1930; London: Virago, 1988. 7–13.

Harrison, Mark. *The Medical War: British Military Medicine in the First World War*. Oxford: Oxford University Press, 2010.

Haslam, Sara. *Fragmenting Modernism*. Manchester: Manchester University Press, 2002.

Haslam, Sara. '"The moaning of the world" and the "words that bring me peace": Modernism and the First World War.' In *The Edinburgh Companion to Twentieth-Century British and American War Literature*. Edited by Adam Piette and Mark Rawlinson. Edinburgh: Edinburgh University Press, 2012. 47–57.
Hawkins, Anne Hunsaker. *Reconstructing Illness: Studies in Pathography*. 1993; West Lafayette, IN: Purdue University Press, 1999.
Hemingway, Ernest. *A Farewell to Arms*. 1929; London: Arrow Books, 2004.
Herbert, A. P. *The Secret Battle*. 1919; Barnsley: Pen & Sword Books, 2009.
Higonnet, Margaret R. 'Authenticity and Art in Trauma Narratives of World War I.' *Modernism/modernity* 9, no. 1 (2002): 91–107.
Higonnet, Margaret R. 'Cubist Vision in Nursing Accounts.' In *First World War Nursing: New Perspectives*. Edited by Alison S. Fell and Christine E. Hallett. New York: Routledge, 2013. 156–72.
Higonnet, Margaret R. 'Introduction.' In *Nurses at the Front: Writing the Wounds of the Great War*. Boston: Northeastern University Press, 2001. x–xiv.
Higonnet, Margaret R., ed. *Lines of Fire: Women Writers of World War I*. New York: Penguin Plume, 1999.
Higonnet, Margaret R. 'Telling Trauma: Women and World War I.' In *Savoirs et littérature*. Edited by Jean Bessière. Paris: Presses Sorbonne Nouvelle, 2002. 123–36.
Higonnet, Margaret R. 'Women in the Forbidden Zone: War, Women, and Death.' In *Death and Representation*. Edited by Sarah Webster Goodwin and Elisabeth Bronfen. Baltimore: Johns Hopkins University Press, 1993. 190–209.
Higonnet, Margaret R., Jane Jenson, Sonya Michel, and Margaret Collins Weitz, eds. *Behind the Lines: Gender and the Two World Wars*. New Haven, CT: Yale University Press, 1987.
Hodges, Katherine (North). 'A Driver at the Front.' Private Papers of Miss K Hodges. Imperial War Museum Collections, Documents.1974.
Holder, V. L. 'From Handmaiden to Right Hand – World War I and Advancements in Medicine.' *AORN Journal* 80, no. 5 (2004): 911–23.
Horton, Charles H. *Stretcher Bearer!* Edited by Dale Le Vack. Oxford: Lion Books, 2013.
Hurley, Kelly. *The Gothic Body*. Cambridge: Cambridge University Press, 1996.
Hutchinson, Hazel. 'The Theater of Pain: Observing Mary Borden in *The Forbidden Zone*.' In *First World War Nursing: New Perspectives*. Edited by Alison S. Fell and Christine E. Hallett. New York: Routledge, 2013. 139–55.
Huyssen, Andreas. *Present Pasts: Urban Palimpsests and the Politics of Memory*. Stanford: Stanford University Press, 2003.

Hynes, Samuel. *The Soldier's Tale: Bearing Witness to Modern War.* 1997; London: Pimlico, 1998.
Hynes, Samuel. *A War Imagined: The First World War and English Culture.* London: Pimlico, 1992.
Hyson, Samuel and Alan Lester. '"British India on trial": Brighton Military Hospitals and the Politics of Empire in World War I.' *Journal of Historical Geography* 38 (2012): 18–34.
Imbrie, Robert Whitney. *Behind the Wheel of a War Ambulance.* New York: Robert M. McBride, 1918.
Iserson, Kenneth V. and John C. Moskop. 'Triage in Medicine, Part I: Concept, History, and Types.' *Annals of Emergency Medicine* 49, no. 3 (2007): 275–81.
Iserson, Kenneth V. and John C. Moskop. 'Triage in Medicine, Part II: Underlying Values and Principles.' *Annals of Emergency Medicine* 49, no. 3 (2007): 282–7.
Isherwood, Christopher. *Goodbye to Berlin.* 1939; New York: New Directions Books, 2012.
Isherwood, Ian. 'The British Publishing Industry and Commercial Memories of the First World War.' *War in History* 23, no. 3 (2016): 328–32.
Jensen, Kimberly. 'A Base Hospital is Not a Coney Island Dance Hall: American Woman Nurses, Hostile Work Environment, and Military Rank in the First World War.' *Frontiers: A Journal of Women Studies* 26, no. 2 (2005): 206–35.
Jones, Edgar and Simon Wessely. *Shell Shock to PTSD: Military Psychiatry from 1900 to the Gulf War.* Hove: Psychiatry Press, 2005.
Judd, James R. *With the American Ambulance in France.* Honolulu: Star Bulletin Press, 1919.
Jurecic, Ann. *Illness as Narrative.* Pittsburgh: University of Pittsburgh Press, 2012.
Jurecic, Ann and Daniel Marchalik. 'Breathing Lessons: Paul Kalanithi's *When Breath Becomes Air.*' *The Lancet* 388, no. 10062 (10 December 2016): 2859.
Kaplan, Ann, E. *Trauma Culture: The Politics of Terror and Loss in Media and Literature.* New Brunswick: Rutgers University Press, 2005.
Kayser, Wolfgang. *The Grotesque in Art and Literature.* Translated by Ulrich Weisstein. 1957; Bloomington: Indiana University Press, 1963.
Keegan, John. *The Face of Battle.* London: Penguin, 1978.
Kelly, Alice. *Commemorative Modernisms: Women Writers, Death and the First World War.* Edinburgh: Edinburgh University Press, 2020.
Klein, Holger. 'Introduction.' In *The First World War in Fiction.* London: Macmillan, 1976. 1–9.
Kleinman, Arthur. *Writing on the Margins.* Berkeley: University of California Press, 1995.
Kokanović, Renata and Meredith Stone. 'Listening to What Cannot Be Said: Broken Narratives and the Lived Body.' In 'Representing Trauma;

Honouring Broken Narratives.' Special medical humanities issue, *Arts and Humanities in Higher Education* 17, no. 1 (2018): 20–31.

Kolnai, Aurel. *On Disgust*. Edited by Barry Smith and Carolyn Korsmeyer. Chicago and La Salle: Open Court, 2004.

Kowaleski Wallace, Elizabeth. 'Recycling the Sacred: The Wax Votive Object and the Eighteenth-Century Wax Baby Doll.' In *The Afterlife of Used Things: Recycling in the Long Eighteenth Century*. Edited by Ariane Fennetaux. London: Routledge, 2014. 152–65.

Kristeva, Julia. *Powers of Horror*. Translated by Leon S. Roudiez. New York: Columbia University Press, 1982.

La Motte, Ellen N. *The Backwash of War*. 1916; London: Conway, 2014.

Larabee, Mark D. *Front Lines of Modernism: Remapping the Great War in British Fiction*. New York: Palgrave Macmillan, 2011.

Laub, Dori. 'Bearing Witness, or the Vicissitudes of Listening.' In *Testimony: Crisis of Witnessing in Literature, Psychoanalysis, and History*, by Shoshana Felman and Dori Laub. New York and Abingdon: Routledge, 1992. 57–74.

Lawrence, Sir Walter. Copies of extracts from censored Indian mails, Mar 1915 – Mar 1916. British Library. Mss Eur F143/83-91.

Lawrence, Sir Walter. Indian Military Hospital, Royal Pavilion, Brighton. *A Short History in English, Gurmukhi and Urdu of the Royal Pavilion, Brighton, and a Description of it as a Hospital for Indian Soldiers*. (1915). British Library. Mss Eur F143/94.

Lee, Janet. '"I wish my mother could see me now": The First Aid Yeomanry (FANY) and Negotiation of Gender and Class Relations, 1907–1918.' *NWSA Journal* 19, no. 2 (2007): 138–58.

Leed, Eric J. *No Man's Land: Combat and Identity in World War I*. Cambridge: Cambridge University Press, 1979.

Leese, Peter. *Shell Shock: Traumatic Neurosis and the British Soldiers of the First World War*. Basingstoke: Palgrave, 2002.

Lefebvre, Henri. *The Production of Space*. Translated by Donald Nicholson-Smith. 1974; Oxford: Blackwell, 1991.

Levinas, Emmanuel. 'Useless Suffering.' Translated by Richard Cohen. In *The Provocation of Levinas: Rethinking the Other*. Edited by Robert Bernasconi and David Wood. 1988; London and New York: Routledge, 2002. 156–67.

Leys, Ruth. *Trauma: A Genealogy*. Chicago: University of Chicago Press, 2000.

Liddle, Peter. *Britain and a Widening War, 1915–1916: Gallipoli, Mesopotamia and the Somme*. Barnsley: Pen & Sword Military, 2016.

Luard, Kate. *Unknown Warriors: Extracts from the Letters of K.E. Luard, RRC, Nursing Sister in France, 1914–1918*. London: Chatto and Windus, 1930.

Macallan, Derek. 'COVID-19: Why It's Time to Drop the Term "Frontline".' *Commentary*, Royal College of Physicians (March 2021): 16.

Macdonald, Lyn. *The Roses of No Man's Land*. 1980; London: Penguin Books, 2013.

MacDonald, Robert H. *The Language of Empire: Myths and Metaphors of Popular Imperialism, 1880–1918*. Manchester: Manchester University Press, 1994.

McLoughlin, Kate. *Authoring War: The Literary Representation of War from the Iliad to Iraq*. New York: Cambridge University Press, 2011.

McLoughlin, Kate, ed. *The Cambridge Companion to War Writing*. New York: Cambridge University Press, 2009.

Macnaughtan, Sarah. *A Woman's Diary of the War*. London: Thomas Nelson and Sons, 1916.

Manning, Frederic. *Her Privates We*. 1929; London: Serpent's Tail, 1999.

Marcus, Jane. 'Afterword: The Nurse's Text: Acting Out an Anaesthetic Aesthetic.' In *We That Were Young*, by Irene Rathbone. New York: Feminist Press, 1989. 467–98.

Marcus, Jane. 'Corpus/Corps/Corpse: Writing the Body in/at War.' In *Arms and the Woman: War, Gender, and Literary Representation*. Edited by Helen M. Cooper, Adrienne Auslander Munich, and Susan Merrill Squier. Chapel Hill and London: University of North Carolina Press, 1989. 124–67.

Marcus, Laura. *The Tenth Muse: Writing about Cinema in the Modernist Period*. Oxford: Oxford University Press, 2010.

Martin, Arthur A. *A Surgeon in Khaki*. London: Edward Arnold, 1915.

Martin, Ian. '"When needs must": The Acceptance of Volunteer Aids in British and Australian Military Hospitals in World War I.' *Health and History* 4, no. 1 (2002): 88–98.

Martin, Nancy. '"And all because it is war!": First World War Diaries, Authenticity and Combatant Identity.' *Textual Practice* 29, no. 7 (2015): 1245–63.

Mattingly, Cheryl and Linda C. Garro, eds. *Narrative and the Cultural Construction of Illness and Healing*. London and Los Angeles: University of California Press, 2000.

Mayhew, Emily. *A Heavy Reckoning: War, Medicine and Survival in Afghanistan and Beyond*. London: Profile Books in association with Wellcome Collection, 2018.

Mayhew, Emily. *Wounded: The Long Journey Home from the Great War*. London: Vintage, 2014.

Mazzei, Lisa A. 'Silent Nothings: Undisciplined Language.' In *Nothingness: Philosophical Insights into Psychology*. Edited by Ditte Winther-Lindqvist and Jytte Bang. New York: Routledge, 2016. 211–24.

Mégret, Frédéric. 'War and the Vanishing Battlefield.' *Loyola University Chicago International Law Review* 9, no. 1 (2011): 131–55.

Mellown, Muriel. 'One Woman's Way to Peace: The Development of Vera Brittain's Pacifism.' *Frontiers: A Journal of Women Studies* 8, no. 2 (1985): 1–6.

Mellown, Muriel. 'Reflections and Pacifism in the Novels of Vera Brittain.' *Tulsa Studies in Women's Literature* 2, no. 2 (1983): 215–28.
Meinig, D. W. *The Interpretation of Ordinary Landscapes*. Oxford: Oxford University Press, 1979.
Merleau-Ponty, Maurice. *Phenomenology of Perception*. Translated by Colin Smith. 1945; London and New York: Routledge Classics, 2005.
Meyer, Jessica. *An Equal Burden: The Men of the Royal Army Medical Corps in the First World War*. Oxford: Oxford University Press, 2019.
Meyer, Jessica. *Men of War: Masculinity and the First World War in Britain*. Basingstoke: Palgrave Macmillan, 2009.
Micale, Mark S. and Paul Lerner. *Traumatic Pasts: History, Psychiatry, and Trauma in the Modern Age, 1870–1930*. Cambridge: Cambridge University Press, 2001.
Miller, Nancy K. 'Facts, Pacts, Acts.' *Profession* (1992): 10–14.
Miller, Nancy K. and Jason Tougaw. *Extremities: Trauma, Testimony and Community*. Urbana and Chicago: University of Illinois Press, 2002.
Miller, William Ian. *The Anatomy of Disgust*. Cambridge, MA and London: Harvard University Press, 1997.
Mitin, Ivan. 'Mythogeography: Region as a Palimpsest of Identities.' In *Cross-Cultural Communication and Ethnic Identities*. Edited by L. Elenius and C. Karlsson. Luleå: Luleå University of Technology, 2007. 215–25.
Moncrieff, Alexia. *Expertise, Authority and Control: The Australian Army Medical Corps in the First World War*. Cambridge: Cambridge University Press, 2020.
Montgomery, Kathryn. *Doctors' Stories: The Narrative Structure of Medical Knowledge*. Princeton, NJ: Princeton University Press, 1991.
Montgomery, Kathryn. *How Doctors Think: Clinical Judgement and the Practice of Medicine*. New York and Oxford: Oxford University Press, 2006.
Moran, Dermot. *Introduction to Phenomenology*. New York: Routledge, 1999.
Mortimer, Maud. *A Green Tent in Flanders*. New York: Doubleday, Page, 1917.
Muir, Ward. *Observations of an Orderly: Some Glimpses of Life and Work in a English War Hospital*. London: Simpkin, Marshall, Hamilton, Kent, 1917. Kindle.
Mukherji, Subha. 'Introduction.' In *Thinking on Thresholds: The Poetics of Transitive Spaces*. London and New York: Anthem Press, 2011. xvii–xxviii.
Newton, J. H. *A Stretcher Bearer's Diary: Three Years in France with the 21st Division*. 1931; London: Arthur H. Stockwell, 2009. Kindle.
Ngai, Sianne. *Ugly Feelings*. Cambridge, MA: Harvard University Press, 2005.

North, Michael. *Camera Works: Photography and the Twentieth-Century Word.* New York and Oxford: Oxford University Press, 2005.
Nussbaum, Martha Craven. *Upheavals of Thought: The Intelligence of Emotions.* Cambridge: Cambridge University Press, 2001.
O'Flaherty, Liam. *Return of the Brute.* London: Mandrake Press, 1929.
Ollivant, Alfred. 'The Indian Hospital.' In *The Brown Mare, and Other Studies of England Under the Cloud.* London: George Allen & Unwin, 1916. Reprint, Leopold Classic Library. 83–101.
Orcutt, Philip Dana. *The White Road of Mystery.* New York: John Lane, 1918.
Panzanelli, Roberta. 'Compelling Presence: Wax Effigies in Renaissance Florence.' In *Ephemeral Bodies: Wax Sculpture and the Human Figure.* Edited by Roberta Panzanelli. Los Angeles: Getty Research Institute, 2008. 13–39.
Panzanelli, Roberta, ed. *Ephemeral Bodies: Wax Sculpture and the Human Figure.* Los Angeles: Getty Research Institute, 2008.
Parkins, Illya. 'Feminist Witnessing and Social Difference: The Trauma of Heterosexual Otherness in Vera Brittain's *Testament of Youth*.' *Women's Studies* 26, no. 2 (2007): 95–116.
Pheasant-Kelly, Frances. 'Towards a Structure of Feeling: Abjection and Allegories of Disease in Science Fiction "Mutation" Films.' *Medical Humanities* 42 (2016): 238–45.
Phillips, Terry. 'The Rules of War: Gothic Transgressions in First World War Fiction.' *Gothic Studies* 3 (2000): 232–44.
Phillips, Terry. 'A Study in Grotesques.' *Gothic Studies* 7 (2005): 41–53.
Pilar Blanco, Maria del and Esther Peeren, eds. *The Spectralities Reader: Ghosts and Haunting in Contemporary Cultural Theory.* New York: Bloomsbury Academic, 2013.
Poirier, Suzanne. *Doctors in the Making: Memoirs and Medical Education.* Iowa City: University of Iowa Press, 2009.
Porteous, J. Douglas. *Landscapes of the Mind: Worlds of Sense and Metaphor.* Toronto: University of Toronto Press, 1990.
Potter, Jane. *Boys in Khaki, Girls in Print.* 2005; Oxford: Oxford University Press, 2008.
Rathbone, Irene. 'Unpublished diaries.' The Private Papers of I B Rathbone. Imperial War Museum Collections, Documents.557.
Rathbone, Irene. *We That Were Young.* 1932; London: Virago, 1988.
Reid, Fiona. *Broken Men: Shell Shock, Treatment and Recovery in Britain, 1914–1930.* London: Continuum, 2010.
Reid, Fiona. *Medicine in First World War Europe: Soldiers, Medics, Pacifists.* London and New York: Bloomsbury, 2017.
Remarque, Erich Maria. *All Quiet on the Western Front.* Translated by Brian Murdoch. 1929; London: Vintage, 1996.
Reus, Teresa Gomez. 'Racing to the Front: Auto-mobility and Competing Narratives of Women in the First World War.' In *Women in Transit*

Through Literary Liminal Spaces. Edited by T. Gifford and Teresa Gomez Reus. Basingstoke: Palgrave Macmillan, 2013. 107–22.

Reznick, Jeffrey. *Healing the Nation: Soldiers and the Culture of Caregiving in Britain During the Great War*. Manchester: Manchester University Press, 2004.

Robinett, Jane. 'The Narrative Shape of Traumatic Experience.' *Literature and Medicine* 26, no. 2. (2007): 290–311.

Rodaway, Paul. *Sensuous Geographies: Body, Sense and Place*. London: Routledge, 1994.

Roper, Michael. *The Secret Battle: Emotional Survival in the Great War*. Manchester and New York: Manchester University Press, 2009.

Rothberg, Michael. *Multidirectional Memory: Remembering the Holocaust in the Age of Decolonization*. Stanford: Stanford University Press, 2009.

Rutherford, Andrew. *The Literature of War: Five Studies in Heroic Virtue*. London: Macmillan, 1978.

Rylance, Rick. 'The Theatre and the Granary: Observations on Nineteenth-Century Medical Narratives.' *Literature and Medicine* 25, no. 2 (2006): 255–76.

St. Clair, William. *The Road to St. Julien: The Letters of a Stretcher-Bearer from the Great War*. Edited by John St. Clair. Barnsley: Pen & Sword Books, 2004.

Salisbury, Laura and Andrew Shail, eds. *Neurology and Modernity: A Cultural History of Nervous Systems, 1800–1950*. Basingstoke: Palgrave Macmillan, 2010.

Sassoon, Siegfried. *Memoirs of an Infantry Officer*. 1930; London: Faber and Faber, 1997.

Scarry, Elaine. *The Body in Pain*. New York: Oxford University Press, 1985.

Scott, Bonnie Kime. 'We That Were Young by Irene Rathbone; Not So Quiet by Helen Zenna Smith.' *Tulsa Studies in Women's Literature* 9, no. 2 (1990): 339–42.

Sedgwick, Eve Kosofsky. *Between Men: English Literature and Male Homosocial Desire*. New York: Columbia University Press, 1985.

Shapiro, Johanna. '(Re)Examining the Clinical Gaze Through the Prism of Literature.' *Families, Systems & Health* 20, no. 2 (2002): 161–70.

Shelley, Mary. *Frankenstein*. 1818; London: Penguin Popular Classics, 1994.

'Shell Shock in Cows', *The Lancet* 191, no. 4927 (2 February 1918): 187–8.

Shepard, Ben. *A War of Nerves: Soldiers and Psychiatrists, 1914–1994*. Pimlico, 2002.

Sherry, Vincent, ed. *The Cambridge Companion to the Literature of the First World War*. Cambridge: Cambridge University Press, 2005.

Silverman, Max. *Palimpsestic Memory: The Holocaust and Colonialism in French and Francophone Fiction and Film*. New York: Berghahn Books, 2013.

Silverman, Max. 'Trips, Tropes and Traces: Reflections on Memory in French and Francophone Culture.' In *Anamnesia: Private and Public Memory in Modern French Culture.* Edited by Peter Collier, Anna Magdalena Elsner, and Olga Smith. Bern: Peter Lang, 2009. 17–28.

Smith, Angela K. *The Second Battlefield: Women, Modernism and the First World War.* Manchester and New York: Manchester University Press, 2000.

Smith, Helen Zenna. *Not So Quiet . . . Stepdaughters of War.* 1930; London: Virago, 1988.

Smith, Lesley. *Four Years Out of Life.* London: Philip Allan, 1931.

Sontag, Susan. *Illness as Metaphor & Aids and its Metaphors.* 1979; London: Penguin Classics, 2002.

Sontag, Susan. *Regarding the Pain of Others.* 2003; London: Penguin Books, 2004.

Sparks, David Rhodes. *Red Poppies.* Cambridge: Privately Printed, The Riverside Press, 1918.

Spenser, Edmund. *The Faerie Queene*, Book I, Canto XI, 35. In *The Faerie Queene Books I to III.* Edited by Douglas Brooks-Davies. 1609; London and Vermont: Everyman Classic, 1987. 148.

Spivak, Gayatri Chakravorty. 'Translator's Preface.' In *Of Grammatology*, by Jacques Derrida. Translated by Gayatri Chakravorty Spivak. Baltimore: Johns Hopkins University Press, 1976. ix–lxxxvii.

Stein, Gertrude. *Paris France.* New York: C. Scribner's Sons London, B. T. Batsford, 1940.

Stepansky, Paul E. *Easing Pain on the Western Front: American Nurses of the Great War and the Birth of Modern Nursing Practice.* Jefferson, NC: McFarland, 2020.

Stevenson, Randall. *Literature and the Great War.* Oxford: Oxford University Press, 2013.

Stewart, Victoria. *Women's Autobiography: War and Trauma.* Basingstoke and New York: Palgrave Macmillan, 2003.

Stimson, Julia. *Finding Themselves.* New York: Macmillan, 1918.

Tal, Kali. *Worlds of Hurt: Reading the Literatures of Trauma.* Cambridge: Cambridge University Press, 1996.

Tate, Trudi. *Modernism, History and the First World War.* Manchester: Manchester University Press, 1998.

Thurstan, Violetta. *A Text Book of War Nursing.* London and New York: G. P. Putnam's Sons, 1917.

Todman, Dan. *The Great War: Myth and Memory.* London: Hambledon Continuum, 2007.

Toland, Edward. *Aftermath of Battle: With the Red Cross in France.* New York: Macmillan, 1916.

Tompkins, Joanne. *Theatre's Heterotopias: Performance and the Cultural Politics of Space.* London: Palgrave Macmillan, 2014.

Tomson, Philip. *The Grotesque.* London: Methuen, 1972.

Trigg, Dylan. *The Memory of Place: A Phenomenology of the Uncanny*. Athens, OH: Ohio University Press, 2012.
Trigg, Dylan. 'The Place of Trauma: Memory, Hauntings, and the Temporality of Ruins.' *Memory Studies* 2, no. 87 (2009): 81–101.
Tromanhauser, Vicki. 'Inside the "Butcher's Shop": Women's Great War Writing and Surgical Meat.' In *Literature and Meat Since 1900*. Edited by Sean McCorry and John Miller. Cham: Palgrave Macmillan, 2019. 19–33.
Trotter, David. 'The British Novel and the War.' In *The Cambridge Companion to the Literature of the First World War*. Edited by Vincent Sherry. Cambridge: Cambridge University Press, 2005. 34–56.
T'Serclaes, Baroness de (Elsie Knocker). *Flanders and Other Fields*. London: George G. Harrap, 1964.
Tuan, Yi-Fu. *Space and Place: The Perspective of Experience*. 1977; Minneapolis: University of Minnesota Press, 2001.
Tylee, Claire M. *The Great War and Women's Consciousness*. London: Macmillan, 1990.
Vidler, Anthony. *Architectural Uncanny: Essays in the Modern Unhomely*. Cambridge, MA and London: MIT Press, 1992.
Virilio, Paul. *War and Cinema: The Logistics of Perception*. Translated by Patrick Camiller. 1984; London: Verso, 1989.
Walker, Adelaide L. 'Experiences at a Base Hospital in France, 1914–1915.' In *Reminiscent Sketches*. London: John Bale, Sons and Danielsson, 1922. 54–60.
Warnock, Mary. *The Philosophy of Sartre*. London: Hutchinson, 1965.
'War Shock in the Civilian', *The Lancet* 187, no. 4827 (4 March 1916): 522.
Watson, Janet S. K. *Fighting Different Wars*. Cambridge: Cambridge University Press, 2004.
Watson, Janet S. K. 'Khaki Girls, VADs, and Tommy's Sisters: Gender and Class in First World War Britain.' *The International History Review* 19, no. 1 (1997): 32–51.
Weir, Becca. '"Degrees in nothingness": Battlefield Topography in the First World War.' *Critical Quarterly* 49, no. 4 (2007): 40–55.
West, Rebecca. *War Nurse: The True Story of a Woman Who Lived, Loved and Suffered on the Western Front*. New York: Cosmopolitan Books, 1930.
Whitehead, Anne. 'Facial Injury, Masks and the Negotiation of Beauty in Contemporary Anglo-American Fictions of the First World War.' Guest Lecture. University of Edinburgh, Edinburgh, 15 November 2013.
Whitehead, Anne. *Medicine and Empathy in Contemporary British Fiction*. Edinburgh: Edinburgh University Press, 2017.
Whitehead, Anne and Angela Woods with Sarah Atkinson, Jane Macnaughton, and Jennifer Richards, eds. *The Edinburgh Companion*

to the *Critical Medical Humanities*. Edinburgh: Edinburgh University Press, 2016.

Whitehead, Anne. *Trauma Fiction*. Edinburgh: Edinburgh University Press, 2004.

Whitehead, Ian. *Doctors in the Great War*. 1999; Barnsley: Pen & Sword Books, 2013.

Wilson, Ross J. *Landscapes of the Western Front: Materiality During the Great War*. New York: Routledge, 2012.

Winter, Jay. *Sites of Memory, Sites of Mourning: The Great War in European Cultural History*. 1995; Cambridge: Cambridge University Press, 1998.

Wolf, Hope. 'Mediating War: Hot Diaries, Liquid Letters and Vivid Remembrances.' *Life Writing* 9, no. 3 (2012): 327–36.

Woods, Angela. 'The Limits of Narrative: Provocations for the Medical Humanities.' *BMJ Medical Humanities* 37 (2011): 73–8.

Woolf, Virginia. 'Modern Fiction.' In *The Essays of Virginia Woolf Volume 4: 1925–1928*. Edited by Andrew McNeillie. London: Hogarth Press, 1984. 157–65.

Yaeger, Patricia. 'Consuming Trauma; or, The Pleasures of Merely Circulating.' In *Extremities: Trauma, Testimony and Community*. Edited by Nancy K. Miller and Jason Tougaw. Urbana and Chicago: University of Illinois Press, 2002. 25–51.

Yates, Wilson. 'An Introduction to the Grotesque: Theoretical and Theological Considerations.' In *The Grotesque in Art and Literature: Theological Reflections*. Edited by James Luther Adams and Wilson Yates. Grand Rapids, MI: W. B. Eerdmans, 1997. 1–68.

Zakharova, Lidiia. 'Diary of a Red Cross Sister in the Front Lines.' In *Lines of Fire: Women Writers of World War I*. Translated by Cynthia Simmons. Edited by Margaret R. Higonnet. New York: Penguin Plume, 1999. 184–7.

Index

ABBA, 81n
Abbey, Aoife, 25
abjection, 27, 104–12, 122
abstraction (sensory), 61–4
Acton, Carol, 2–4, 7–8, 14, 167
Adorno, Theodor, 217
Advanced Dressing Station, 16
Afghanistan War, 3, 14
Ahmed, Sara, 108
Albee, Fred H., 75, 127, 141, 155
Alcott, Louisa May, 132
ambulance
   vehicle, 1–2, 12, 16, 38–9, 41–5, 48–9, 99–100, 200, 223
   see also driving
American Civil War, 132
amputation, 49–50, 97, 108, 111, 119, 212, 218
   amputated limbs, 108, 111, 116
   phantom limb, 97
antediluvian, 21; *see also* flood
Anzieu, Didier, 174–5
ape *see* monkey
apocalypse, 21, 94–5
auditory geographies, 10, 57–62, 219; *see also* sound

baccarat, 74–6; *see also* gambling
Bachelard, Gaston, 84, 173
bacteria, 59–61, 95–6
Badenhausen, Richard, 209
Bagnold, Enid, 102, 113, 115, 120, 126–7, 132–6, 155, 160, 197–8

Bakhtin, Mikhail, 107, 113–4, 121
Barbusse, Henri, 94–5
Barry, Elizabeth, 22
battlefield, 6, 30, 33–6, 45–6, 49–50, 157
Beckett, Samuel, 22
Bede, 115
Benjamin, Walter, 27, 67–9, 183–4, 206
Bergen, Leo van, 17
billiards, 75; *see also* gambling
Black, Elizabeth Walker, 23, 61, 87, 114, 153–5, 159–61, 164–6, 216
Blunden, Edmund, 21
Booth, Allyson, 22
Borden, Mary, 22–3, 33–4, 36, 45, 50–1, 55, 59–61, 63, 73–6, 80, 85–7, 89–95, 114, 121, 123–4, 131, 133–5, 139–40, 169–71, 175–80, 190, 192–8, 208–9
Botcharsky, Sophie, 103–4, 115–6
Bourke, Joanna, 184–5, 206
Boyd, William, 46–7, 114, 121
Boylston, Helen Dore, 55, 136, 178
Braid, James, 39–40
Bray-sur-Somme, 22, 91
Brighton Dome, 77, 80–1
Brighton Royal Pavilion, 77–81
British Pathè, 165
Brittain, Vera, 58, 72, 92, 98, 117, 167–8, 198–1, 209, 212–13

Brophy, John, 16
Bryan, Julien H., 200–1
Bulgakov, Mikhail, 24
burns, 52–3, 119

camera, 168–9
cannibalism, 123
Carden-Coyne, Ana, 43–4, 53, 84, 137–8
Care Collective, The, 224
Carel, Havi, 9–11, 14, 33, 39, 44
Carrel-Dakin method, 53, 126
cartography, 31–2, 38, 53, 55, 59
Caruth, Cathy, 147, 183
Casey, Edward, 147
casino, 66, 73–7, 80, 87, 99–100
Casualty Clearing Stations, 15–16, 20, 34
chandeliers, 27, 76–81
Charon, Rita, 5, 24–5, 210
Château de Compiègne, 96
Chekov, Anton, 24
Church, James Robb, 69–73, 77, 88–9, 96–7, 127, 138–9
Clarke, Rachel, 25, 223–4
clinical gaze, 27, 52, 129–35, 169, 189
combatant experiences, 4, 8, 30–9, 46, 56–7, 60–4, 86, 105–6, 110, 151, 218–19
combatant memoirs, 18, 21, 23, 56, 93–5, 105–6, 110, 117–18
Connor, Steven, 61
conscientious objector, 39
Conway, Kathlyn, 182
corpography, 14, 26, 30–3, 36, 35–9, 44, 54, 59, 64, 219
corpse *see* dead bodies
COVID-19, 6, 223
cows, 8
Coyle, Edward R., 37–8, 41–3, 53–4, 58, 157
Crimean War, 15, 95–6
cubism, 23, 149, 169–71, 177
Curie, Marie, 149

Das, Santanu, 8–9, 11, 14, 16, 31, 33, 54, 57–8, 60, 94
dead bodies, 46, 59–62, 105–11, 117, 119
Dearden, Harold, 115, 117, 121, 123, 133–4, 141, 185, 205–6
Delafield, Elizabeth M., 190
Deleuze, Gilles, 15, 32, 45–6, 52
Dent, Olive, 84, 121, 158–9, 193–5
Derrida, Jacques, 69, 99
desert, 45–7, 89–96
Dickinson, Emily, 181–2
disgust, 27, 104–12, 121–2, 124, 129, 191
doll, 117–19
Donne, John, 52
double ground, 27, 67–8, 100
DOVO-SEDEE, 96n
Doyle, Arthur Conan, 24
driving, 38–9, 41–4, 48
Duhamel, Georges, 75, 110, 114, 117, 119, 130–4, 137, 141–3, 201–4
Dunkirk, 76
Durnin, David, 18n

earth
  landscape, 26, 32, 36–7, 39, 91–3
  soil, 70, 95–6
Egan, Susanna, 149
Einhaus, Ann-Marie, 20–1, 23
Elden, Stuart, 35
Eurovision, 81n
evolution, 92–4

Felman, Shoshana, 182–3
field hospital, 11, 20, 34, 66, 89–92, 223
Fifield, Peter, 22
Figley, Charles, 3
film reel, 165–6
film set, 28, 166
flâneur, 67

Index

flood, 91–5; *see also* water
flying ambulances, 49–50
Foucault, Michel, 14, 28, 130, 134, 148, 151–2, 156–8
    clinical gaze, 130
    docile bodies, 134
    heterotopias, 28, 148, 151–2, 156–8, 161, 165, 175, 179
food, 120–4, 128, 195
    eating, 121, 123–4, 195
    wounds, 120–4, 128
Fox, E. C., 99–100
Frank, Arthur, 5, 24, 183, 204, 206–7
Frankenstein, 138–9
Freedman, Ariela, 94, 209
Freud, Sigmund, 69, 71, 77, 83, 86, 88, 117
    screen memory, 83, 86
    the uncanny *see* uncanny
Fussell, Paul, 18, 150–1, 163

gala, 74–5
gambling, 74–6
gangrene, 59, 61–3, 76, 82, 87, 95, 133, 136, 140–1, 160
Genesis, 92
Genette, Gérard, 150n
Gennep, Arnold van, 12
ghosts, 72, 96–8, 100
Gleason, Arthur, 43, 56–7
Gleason, Helen Hayes, 43, 56–7
Gleeson, Sinéad, 224
Graves, Robert, 21
Gregory, Derek, 14, 26, 30–2, 36, 38–9, 59
Gross, Elizabeth, 111
grotesque, 27, 86, 105–7, 112–16, 119–21, 124–5
    medical grotesque, 27, 105–7, 125–9, 139, 141, 143–4, 220
Guattari, Félix, 32, 45–6, 52

Hallett, Christine, 17, 137, 170
haptic geographies, 8, 10, 14, 30–3, 45–8, 58–60, 219; *see also* touch
Harrison, Mark, 17
haunting, 62, 69, 72, 96–7
Hawkins, Anne Hunsaker, 5, 24
hearing, 56–62
heimlich see uncanny
hell, 94–5, 176, 213
Herbert, A. P., 32
heterotopia, 148, 150–1 157–8, 179–80
Higonnet, Margaret R., 23, 149, 169, 171, 187, 208
Hodges, Katherine, 1–3, 38–9
Hollywood, 166
horse, 46–7, 49, 62
Horton, Charles H., 47
hospital barge, 16; *see also* medical evacuation
hospital train, 16; *see also* medical evacuation
hotel, 66, 73, 81–2, 99–100
Hutchinson, Hazel, 170
Hynes, Samuel, 215

illness narratives, 2, 5, 24, 183, 205
Imbrie, Robert Whitney, 44, 49, 54, 57, 60, 62
Indian soldiers, 77–81
infection, 53–4, 59, 61–3, 76, 82, 87, 95–6, 115–16, 133, 136, 140–1; *see also* gangrene
Iraq War, 3
Iron Harvest, 96
Isherwood, Christopher, 168–9
Isherwood, Ian, 18

Jurecic, Ann, 24

Kalanithi, Paul, 24
Keegan, John, 31
Kelly, Alice, 22, 170
Kew Gardens, 76, 87
Kipling, Rudyard, 89, 212–13
Kleinman, Arthur, 5, 133

Knocker, Elsie *see* T'serclaes, Baroness de
Kolnai, Aurel, 109, 129
Kristeva, Julia, 105, 109–11

La Motte, Ellen N., 22–3, 61, 111–12, 140–1, 169–70, 189–91, 208–9
The Lancet, 8, 223
landmarks, 45–9, 52–3, 60, 69–70, 83, 89
　smellmark, 49, 62
　soundmark, 61–2
Larrey, Baron Dominique-Jean, 49–50
Laub, Dori, 205
Lawrence, D. H., 21–2
Lee, Hermione, 22
Leed, Eric J., 12, 14
Lefebvre, Henri, 69, 71, 83, 88, 95
Leighton, Roland, 212–13
Levinas, Emmanuel, 206–7
Lewis, Wyndham, 23
life writing, 2, 4, 9, 25–6, 149, 208–10, 217
liminality, 12–14, 219
lockjaw, 115
Luard, Kate, 108, 118–19, 122

Macdonald, Lyn, 17
Mackintosh, E. A., 98
Macnaughtan, Sarah, 77, 104, 121
magic lantern slides, 79–80
Manning, Frederic, 21, 56, 105–6
maps, 32, 36, 45–9, 52–5
Marcus, Jane, 122, 163, 189–92, 210–11
marionette *see* puppets
Marsh, Henry, 25
Martin, Arthur A., 21, 50–1, 59, 61, 95–7, 189, 197–8, 204
Maude, Ulrika, 22
Mayhew, Emily, 18
meat, 122–3

medical evacuation, 16, 35, 43, 121
medical grotesque, 27, 105–7, 125–9, 139, 141, 143–4, 220
medical humanities, 4–5, 9–10, 19, 22, 219, 221
medical memoirs (contemporary), 25–6
Mégret, Frédéric, 34–5
memento mori, 47
Merleau-Ponty, Maurice, 14, 32, 38, 63
Meyer, Jessica, 17–18, 40–1
microbiology, 95
Miller, Nancy K., 149
modernism, 20–3
modernist, 20–3, 33, 177, 190
Moncreiff, Alexia, 18n
monkey, 113–14
Montgomery, Kathryn, 24, 25n
Mortimer, Maud, 23, 48, 139, 157–8, 168–72, 174–5
mountaineering, 31
mouths, 114–16, 120–1
　tetanic grin, 115
　orifice, 114–16
　wounds, 120–1
moving pictures, 160–1, 164–6

Napoleon, 49, 96–7
nerves, 54–7, 62, 188
neurasthenia, 57
Newton, J. H., 40–1, 110
Ngai, Sianne, 146
Noah, 92
no man's land, 12–14, 171, 219
Nussbaum, Martha Craven, 38

O'Flaherty, Liam, 93n
Ollivant, Alfred, 78–9
olfactory geographies, 10, 14, 49, 62, 219; *see also* smell
orange (fruit), 120–1
Orcutt, Philip Dana, 60
ordnance, 96

palimpsest, 26–7, 66–73, 88–9, 98, 145–6, 148, 166, 220
Paris, 23, 168
Pathé *see* British Pathé
phenomenology, 2, 9–11, 31–3, 36–9, 44, 57, 63–4
photography, 164–8; *see also* camera
placelessness, 147–8
play-script, 193–6
Poirier, Suzanne, 25
posttraumatic stress disorder, 7–8; *see also* vicarious trauma
Porteous, J. Douglas, 84
Potter, Jane, 2–4, 7–8, 14, 167
Price, Evadne *see* Smith, Helen Zenna
proprioception, 42
Proustian stumble, 67, 87, 100
puppets, 119–20

Quaker *see* conscientious objector

radiography, 148–9, 152, 175–9, 221
RAMC *see* Royal Army Medical Corps
Rathbone, Irene
  'Unpublished diaries', 18, 185–7, 194–6, 205, 210–11, 213–15
  We That Were Young, 16, 57, 108, 116–22, 126, 128, 132, 141, 160, 162–4, 173–4, 190–2, 211
reconstructive surgery, 138
Regimental Aid Post, 16, 34
regridding, 32, 45–9
Reid, Fiona, 15
remapping, 83, 86, 219
Remarque, Erich Maria, 23
Richardson, Dorothy, 22
rites of passage, 12
Rodaway, Paul, 10, 14, 54, 58–63
Romanian Front, 1
Rothberg, Michael, 49

Rousbrugge, 22, 170
Royal Army Medical Corps, 40–1
ruins, 16, 90–2, 153, 165
Rylance, Rick, 121

safety-curtain, 162–4, 167
St Clair, William, 110
Salisbury, Laura, 22
Sartre, Jean Paul, 93, 118
Sassoon, Siegfried, 21, 94, 117–18
Scarry, Elaine, 184, 193, 206–7
school, 73, 99
Scottish Women's Hospitals Transport Unit, 1
screen memory, 83, 86
séance, 97
secondary trauma *see* vicarious trauma
Second World War, 3, 20
Shapiro, Johanna, 130, 135
shell
  covering, 173–5
  weapons, 16, 26, 40–1, 47–8, 57–8, 60–1, 127, 155
shell-sense, 57–63
shell shock, 7–8, 57
Shelley, Mary, 138–9
shrapnel, 116, 120–1, 149
silence
  sound, 57–62, 118–19, 130
  rhetorical, 28, 181–4, 206–7, 221
  see also sound
Silverman, Max, 67–9, 72, 87–9
skin, 52–4, 59, 118, 132, 138–40, 173–5, 179
slime, 93, 108, 122
smell, 30, 49, 59, 62–3, 87
smellmark, 49, 62
smooth space, 14, 32, 45–60, 90
Smith, Angela K., 21, 34n, 194
Smith, Helen Zenna, 16, 48
Smith, Lesley, 23, 52, 58, 61–2, 108, 115–17, 119, 122, 126, 154, 156–7

snow, 48–9
soil, 70, 95–6
Somme, 22, 91
Sontag, Susan, 6, 185
sound, 30, 57–63
  soundmark, 61–2
sous rature, 99
Sparks, David Rhodes, 21, 42
spatial medical humanities, 9–15; *see also* medical humanities
spectrality, 72, 98; *see also* ghosts
Spenser, Edmund, 115
Spivak, Gayatri Chakravorty, 69, 99
stage, 28, 151, 153, 156–9, 163–7
Stein, Gertrude, 16, 23
Stepansky, Paul E., 18n
Stimson, Julia, 56–7, 84–5, 222
stretcher bearers, 2–3, 16–20, 26, 39–41, 47, 110, 218
striated space, 14, 32, 45–6, 52
Styx, 94–5; *see also* hell
surgery, 97, 103–4, 127, 130–2, 136–41, 149, 155, 194–5, 204, 218
symptomatic writing, 28, 187–97, 221
synaesthesia, 58–64

Tal, Kali, 29
Tate, Trudi, 20–1, 105, 109–10
tetanus, 15, 115–16
theatre
  operating theatre, 11, 75, 79, 136
  theatrical theatre, 150–1, 157–63
Toland, Edward, 120–2, 128, 140–1
Tommification, 86
Tompkins, Joanne, 158
topography, 26, 39–41, 44–6, 54, 60, 64
touch, 8–9, 30, 58–60, 62–3, 103–4, 124–5, 136, 142–3, 223

Treaty of Versailles, 82
trench, 14–16, 26, 31–5, 37, 39–42, 46, 55, 85–6, 110, 165
trench foot, 117
triage, 16, 26, 49–52, 60
Trianon Palace, 82
Trigg, Dylan, 90–3, 98–9
Tromanhauser, Vicki, 122–3
T'Serclaes, Baroness de, 39, 55, 75, 87, 116, 216
Turner, Victor, 12

uncanny, 12, 27, 70–1, 74–7, 83, 86–7, 90, 93, 97–100, 106–7, 117–20, 128, 140

Verdun, 49, 60, 62
Versailles, 82
verticality, 35
vicarious trauma, 2–4, 7, 16–17, 33, 64, 185, 204, 222
Vidler, Anthony, 71, 77, 83
Vietnam War, 2–3, 8
Virilio, Paul, 35
viscosity, 118

Walker, Adelaide, 81–2
Warnock, Mary, 93
waste, 27, 105, 108–12, 116
water, 51–2, 91–5, 124, 154, 171
Watson, Christie, 25
wax, 117–19
waxwork, 117–18
Weir, Becca, 45–6, 48
West, Rebecca, 126
Westaby, Stephen, 25
Williams, William Carlos, 24
Wilson, John, 50
Wilson, Ross J., 46, 49, 86
Winter, Jay, 21, 95
witnessing, 2–5, 11, 28, 103, 107, 110–11, 124–5, 144, 182–5, 188–9, 192–5, 201–17, 221–2

Wharton, Edith, 16
Whitehead, Anne, 4n, 9
Whitehead, Ian, 17
Wolf, Hope, 215
Woods, Angela, 4n, 9, 207n
Woolf, Virginia, 16, 21–2
  'Modern Fiction', 196–7

x-rays, 15, 148–9, 169, 172–3, 176–80

Yates, Wilson, 112
Young, Winifred Constance, 48

Zakharova, Lidiia, 188

EU representative:
Easy Access System Europe
Mustamäe tee 50, 10621 Tallinn, Estonia
Gpsr.requests@easproject.com

www.ingramcontent.com/pod-product-compliance
Lightning Source LLC
Chambersburg PA
CBHW070324240426
43671CB00013BA/2355